STATE, CAPITAL AND LABOUR

Also by Gill Ursell and Paul Blyton (with N. Nicholson)

THE DYNAMICS OF WHITE COLLAR UNIONISM

Also by Paul Blyton

CHANGES IN WORKING TIME: An International Review

MANAGERS IN FOCUS (*with M. Poole, R. Mansfield and P. Frost*)

Also published by Macmillan

Alan Bryman, Bill Bytheway, Patricia Allatt and Teresa Keil (*editors*)
RETHINKING THE LIFE CYCLE

Tony Dickson and David Judge (*editors*)
THE POLITICS OF INDUSTRIAL CLOSURE

Nicholas Dorn and Nigel South (*editors*)
A LAND FIT FOR HEROIN?

Patrick Kerans, Glenn Drover and David Williams
WELFARE AND WORKER PARTICIPATION

Sheila McLean and Noreen Burrows (*editors*)
THE LEGAL RELEVANCE OF GENDER

Dennis Smith
THE CHICAGO SCHOOL

State, Capital and Labour

Changing Patterns of Power and Dependence

Gill Ursell
Principal Lecturer in Communications and Media
Trinity and All Saints College

and

Paul Blyton
Senior Lecturer in Industrial Relations
Cardiff Business School, UWIST

MACMILLAN
PRESS

First published 1988

Published by
THE MACMILLAN PRESS LTD
Houndmills, Basingstoke, Hampshire RG21 2XS
and London
Companies and representatives
throughout the world

Typeset by Wessex Typesetters
(Division of The Eastern Press Ltd)
Frome, Somerset

Printed in Hong Kong

British Library Cataloguing in Publication Data
Ursell, Gill
State, capital and labour: changing
patterns of power and dependence.
1. Labour and labouring classes—Great
Britain—History
I. Title   II. Blyton, Paul
305.5'62'0941   HD8388
ISBN 0–333–40703–2
ISBN 0–333–40704–0 Pbk

Contents

List of Tables

Preface

If democracy means meaningful participation in political and economic decision-making then, by any account, British labouring people have enjoyed a zenith in their powers this century. Why this should be so, and for how long, prompts our intense and not disinterested attention. But in that regard this book represents our feelings of frustration, need and a sense of *fin de siècle*. Frustration arises because much of the current debate about the status of British labour in contemporary capitalism has been conducted within an ahistorical and narrowly conceived framework which is typically constructed around *either* a political *or* an economic base, implying an absolute rather than culturally contingent reality in the dichotomy of politics and economics. The sense of need occurs because one major consequence of this narrowness has been an over-production of essentially descriptive material at the expense of understanding. In British and American social research particularly insufficient energy has been given to exploring the causal relations between state, capital and labour as social formations. This brings us to the question of time. The pattern of relations between these three social formations is now evidently changing. The structural conditions underpinning traditional forms of labour power are undergoing long-term erosion (although in places giving rise to new forms). Why this is so can be fully appreciated only if the account embraces the fuller historical context: a history of one century of sporadic and uneven increases in labour's influence *vis-à-vis* capital and the state, itself predicated on several centuries in which these three parties emerged from the transition of feudalism to capitalism and an agriculturally-based economy was transformed into an industrial one.

To make the case of a basic reverse in these power relations, we cannot examine labour issues from any single academic pigeon-hole, such as political science, sociology or industrial relations. Rather what seems now to be necessary is a broader approach to a reality which is no respecter of academic lines of demarcation. Such is the complexity of this reality that to adopt single-discipline perspectives is to reduce markedly the chances of adequately interpreting the essential changes affecting labour's position in society. Of course, the disciplinary dissection of reality is at times necessary—indeed vital—to achieving a depth of understanding and a richness of detail relating to particular elements and influences. However, specialisation can go too far. It can only be successful if it goes hand in hand with a broader theoretical consideration of the elements and their relationships.

The present book may be summarised as attempting to analyse the pattern of relations between labour, capital and the state in terms of the relative *dependence* of each on the other—dependencies which are far from constant but rather shift from one era to another. In the coming chapters we examine how, at different times and for different reasons, the economic and political status of labour has changed, culminating in a degree of bargaining power which enabled the realisation of objectives such as wider enfranchisement, greater democratisation, independent trade unionism and the acceptance of collective bargaining; and further, how at different times—particularly remarkable during this last generation—different factors have come together to degrade the fortunes of labour and reduce its claim on democratic participation within the systems of capital and the state.

To understand the development and contemporary condition of relations between these three main actors on the stage of capitalism, it is appropriate first to examine theoretically the nature of each and their interrelations. This is particularly necessary given that many writers have reduced the status of the state to one simply of being a derivative of capital, a position which we argue is overly economistic. One consequence of this economism is to obscure, even deny, the general political will of self-advancement, of which economic enterprise is merely one means among many (albeit a remarkably powerful one). This is an argument we advance in chapter 1. A second consequence is to obscure how economic enterprise, as a means to power, interacts with other means to power—notably the monopolisation of the means to violence which has become the prerogative and distinguishing feature of the modern state. The state and capital are not, we contend, subsumable into a single entity. Moreover, labour's status is 'fixed' not solely by its relation to capital, nor solely by its relation to the state, but rather by the interaction and particular requirements of the two, and, of course, also by labour's skills and resources in negotiating these relations. This is the substance of chapter 2, which forms the theoretical base for what follows—a broadly chronological examination of the changing relations between the three parties from the pre-industrial period up to the present day. Thus, chapter 3 takes us from feudalism to early industrialisation, while chapter 4 considers the 19th century and the years immediately preceding the First World War. Chapter 5 takes us approximately to the end of the Second World War, while chapters 6 and 7 document and assess the postwar period and in particular the declining fortunes of labour over the past 20 years. The concluding chapter looks more closely at the international dimension of the factors working their way through the British political economy, reconsiders the main theoretical propositions and anticipates the prospects for labour's future.

It will be apparent from the above comments and from a reading of the next chapter that the scope of this account is ambitious. It is a scope necessitated by our interest in tracing the course of democratisation processes (and their antitheses) in British history. The scale of the project does mean, however, that the imperfections will be as numerous as the inadequacies. Hopefully though, what is offered, both theoretically and empirically, will be regarded as of sufficient substance to prompt further enquiry and reflection. If we achieve that we shall be satisfied.

Finally it remains only to acknowledge with thanks the work of our typists Kath Hollister and Marguerite Sobol, who accepted with great forebearance our many requests and alterations; also our publishers for taking our missed deadlines in such good spirit.

Gill Ursell
Paul Blyton

'Man's capacity for justice makes democracy possible; but man's inclination to injustice makes democracy necessary.'

Reinhold Niebuhr

1 The Argument Outlined

The 20th century has seen, perhaps for the first time in human history, the emergence of some of the world's common people into the arenas of economic and political decision-making. That is remarkable. The very designation 'common people' is enough to tell us that these are people without the political clout of economic ownership or high status. Yet they can be shown to have exercised considerable, if not complete, influence over the policies of both state and entrepreneur via electoral and party access to a parliament and by independent trade union organisation. Such achievements are often construed as evidence of enlightened attitudes, of civilised society, of the realisation of the superior political ideals of liberal democracy—the Whig view of human progress. We, however, take a less congratulatory view. While democratic ideals and enlightened attitudes have mattered historically, there is still to be explained the slowness and sometimes too the bloodiness of the processes whereby common people have secured these measures of legitimate authority over their own conditions of existence. Democratisation, which is what we take these processes to be, demands further explanation than a reference to ideals and attitudes if only to give us some basis for prognostication, the latter being particularly urgent given the intensifying political predicaments of the western world and what many writers herald as the collapse of democracy in the west (Miliband, 1982; Moss, 1975; Hain, 1986).

DEMOCRACY AND THE DISTRIBUTION OF DEPENDENCIES

From the broadest overview of human political history, are there any general propositions which can be drawn? Certainly, relations between and among humans reveal marked elements of both co-operation and opposition. This indicates that some dynamic is active which both bonds people together but simultaneously obliges them to stand apart. Arguably that dynamic is the drive of social beings for self-actualisation or, as some writers express it (for example, Anderson, 1980) 'agency'. Actual-

1

isation of the 'self' (be that 'self' the individual, a family, tribe
or society) requires the co-operation of an 'other' but this 'other'
must nonetheless remain always distinct, always different. What
then do we do to each other that allows us to take needed or
desired things from each other but which at the same time
prevents us becoming, or becoming intolerably compromised by,
each other? The answer would seem to be the human invention
of terms of discrimination, of discriminatory social relations.
Through these we build structures of determination which
delimit and sanction the exercises of voluntarism. Thus, for
example we discriminate man from woman, young from old,
white from black, rich from poor, and what is socially permissible
or realisable for one 'category' is often denied the other.

Where the creative input to these determining structures is
not equally the product of all social members and where the
experience of determination is likewise inordinately borne by
some, we can speak of hierarchy. It appears as the very antithesis
of what is normally understood as democracy. That is, democracy
would seem to be those political conditions in which the
distribution of determinancies and agencies across all sectors of
society is more, rather than less, equitable. This certainly is the
assumption at the back of what constitutes the orthodoxies which
have developed around democracy as an object of study and
discussion. These orthodoxies (for example, Michels, 1966)
typically posit an irreducible link between efficiency and hierarchical forms of organisation, and the essential incompatibility of
such characteristics with democratic practices of direct participation (and in some formulations even indirect participation).
Such orientations associate naturally with micro-level concerns
about the scale of particular organisations, their formal structures
and rules of procedures; the numbers of people encompassed;
the impact or lack of it of different officials; the existence of
elites, and so on. In short, these orthodoxies have been keen to
identify the processes making for an inequitable distribution of
determinancies and agencies, often in contradiction to professed
values. While the evidence indicates that hierarchy does typically
recur, under some circumstances, however, it is not experienced
as an 'anti-democratic' political problem in that it is seen as
necessary to the self-actualising of those being led. The leadership
is legitimate in other words: the democratic will is for hierarchy.
The clearest example of such a condition is the 'social contract'

notions underpinning much of western political philosophy. Here the legitimation of the superior powers and position of the state is held to reside in its responsibilities as defender of the lives and properties of citizens.

But what of those instances where hierarchy is not legitimated by the democratic will, where it must be imposed? What accounts for the success of its imposition, since those at the bottom end, whose possibilities for self-actualisation are frustrated by the terms of discrimination, have a clear interest in changing things? The answer to this second question would seem to be a distribution of resources which, once turned through political action or accident in favour of any particular agent (individual, family, nation and such like) then becomes the basis for the consolidation and development of further advantage. 'Resources' in the human context are a big and broad category—not merely the material substances of life but social relations, contacts, rhetoric, communication systems, weaponry, culture, and so on. Political struggle between the advantaged and disadvantaged can take place over all or any of these resources—or it may not take place at all, if the discrimination is experienced as legitimate even by those disadvantaged by it, or if the odds seem too strongly in favour of the privileged. How resources are commanded, and by whom, clearly is central to the realisation or frustration of the democratic ideal.

Contrary to the democratic profile of some 20th century western nations, human history shows a marked tendency to hierarchical social formations, sometimes of considerable inequality, in which the relative or absolute deprivation of the majority is a necessary and structured condition for the privilege of the few. The interest of these privileged few can under most conditions be taken to lie in the perpetuation of their advantage. To that end they disproportionately command resources and they exercise their command in ways which secure and augment those resources. For example, some types of resource will be substitutable for others—the same or an improved outcome being secured, at lower cost and/or greater ease, by the application of a different mix of resources. The classic example here would be the development of tools, of technologies, which enhance or displace human labour power. But to the same end of perpetuating their advantage, the privileged few also have no interest in encouraging the disadvantaged to recognise the inequities or to organise around a strategy of rebellion or revolution. And it may well be the case that, in their choice of a particular mix of resources, they create conditions which debilitate those who might otherwise resist and rebel. Their behaviour in these regards does not need to be self-consciously aiming to protect elite status to be equally effective. If, for example, technology is seen as the antidote to human qualities viewed as inefficient, then entrepreneurial concerns for efficient production, military concerns for efficient warfare, and state concerns for public quietude, will all lead to the same outcome, namely, the technological displacement, diminution or greater control of human effort. Those subjected to displacement or to the diminution of their contribution, or to more efficient controls, will consequently have fewer or weaker grounds on which to structure their demands and objections. The powerful need act neither as a homogenous, single entity nor as conspirators for the end result to be the same.

That end result of the structural debilitation of popular resistance consequent upon particular elite applications of resources can be construed, we would argue, as 'massification'. 'Massification' here implies—as it did for the mass society theorists of yesteryear—that the structural conditions framing the social production of goods (warfare, social order, and the like) are such as to weaken and fracture relations occurring 'horizontally' among subordinates, while enhancing those occurring 'vertically' between subordinates and their commanders. Unlike the mass society theorists of yesteryear, however, the argument here is not declaring any deterministic inevitability about the appearance of such 'massification'. The structures do not come incontestibly from heaven; they come from elite decisions about the application of resources. Only so long as elites are fully free to make and execute these decisions, and only in the sense that elite privilege is served by massification, can we say that such an outcome is determined.

Recognised as humanly created, such determination can be better resisted. But under what conditions can resistance be forceful, even successful? At the most general level, assuming relations of expedience (as distinct from morality) to be the least open to deflection, resistance can be successful where elites are especially dependent upon subordinate co-operation for the achievement of elite purposes. This dependency will be expressed as a greater elite responsiveness to subordinates' demands for status, equality and material welfare. In short, the subordinates have something to bargain with. But the link between such conditions and subordinate political action is not automatic. Before elites can respond to demands, they must be articulated. This requires that subordinates resent elite privilege, recognise elite vulnerabilities and organise themselves to exploit those vulnerabilities. Failure to resent, failure to recognise and failure to organise, taken singly or together, will debilitate subordinate political action. Where there is no such failure, one could say the subordinates emerge as a class, as self-conscious and acting in concert to improve their political and material status.

Successful class action will genuinely widen the popular base of political participation, but it does not automatically resolve the issue of democracy. This is because the self-acting class of subordinates owe their position to particular elite dependencies upon them: they have a leverage, something with which to bargain. But other subordinates may not enjoy such bargaining counters, or they may not have the wherewithall to organise so as to exploit them, or—more seriously—they may be deliberately excluded from bargaining and from organisation by the actions of their peers trying to monopolise (and thereby to exploit to the maximum) a particular elite dependency. In other words, the terms and practices of discrimination recur: they are not confined simply to the discrimination between elites and subordinates but occur also between and among the subordinate sections themselves. Here they may not even ostensibly address the elite-subordinate relationship but may rather address other primary areas of human experience and interface such as between the sexes, between old and young and between different ethnic or national groups. Highly complex systems of status stratification will in short confound any simple dichotomy of society into elites and masses, into ruling and working classes, and moreover will be worked on and exploited in the various struggles of different individuals, groups and classes for agency.

In these various struggles, however, those with superior command over resources inevitably have the advantage. So it makes sense, for the purposes of exploring what makes for and against the democratisation of society, to return to the question of what conditions cause elite dependencies on subordinates to intensify so that subordinate demands prove less resistible. One contributory factor will be inter-elite rivalries. As already said, elites owe their place to an enhanced ability to exploit, one way or another, resources. Where elites compete with one another, they compete for resources. Where these resources include the labouring, consumption and military potentialities of subordinates, those subordinates must be negotiated. 'Negotiation' could entail repression and slavery, but that is a dangerous tack where rival elites might intervene to forge alliances with those so repressed and enslaved. It is more secure and more efficient to enlist subordinate co-operation and consent. In terms of the nation-state, this is typically based upon 'social contract' notions; that is, the state's greater powers are legitimated by its responsibilities for defence of the realm of which subordinates are the primary constituents. Inter-elite rivalries are communicated as a threat to the interests of the subordinates, and may objectively be so. Depending upon the nature of the efforts required from subordinates in these inter-elite rivalries, such communication may yet be inadequate to secure co-operation. In this case, elites will be obliged to extend a degree of patronage, even incorporation, to their subordinate supporters.

As Colin Sumner (1979) argues, elites have three basic tactics of political control—ideology, coercion and bribery. Incorporation, that is, some degree of admission to the arenas of decision-making, is one form of bribery. It is not a threat to elite advantage so long as the 'degree of admission' can be carefully controlled. In other words, the notion of incorporation implies that elites practice social closure, that is, that the routes into their preserves are few in number and very well guarded, and that elite members discriminate in favour of each other to the exclusion, or detriment, of non-elite persons. Such practices may well persist at the informal or clandestine level even when formal rights to participate have been awarded to subordinates (one thinks of C. P. Snow's 1964 *Corridors of Power*, or Giddens' work, 1974, 1979, on who rules Britain, in this connection). That outcome (of the informal 'scuppering' of formal subordinate participation) is predictable where formal rights are not underwritten by thoroughgoing constitutional and ownership changes such that the elites no longer exist. Without such thoroughgoing changes the political status and incorporation of subordinates is essentially insecure, can be outmanoeuvred and—should it become possible for the elites to lessen their dependencies—can be dispensed with.

A second factor which may contribute to the creation of elite dependencies, one also to do with accessing and exploiting resources, is technology. If patronage and incorporation are social techniques functional to exploiting human resources not otherwise exploitable, then technology comprises the material techniques functional to exploiting material resources not otherwise exploitable. And since human labour power is not only a social entity but also takes material form, it is thus one of the material resources to which technology is applied. The proposition here is that new technology originates with inventors and their patrons among the elites who alike are seeking new ways to increase their fame and fortune. (Doubtless this proposition understates the development of technologies inspired by altruistic motives. But the contention here is that altruism is not the primary dynamo of human social relations.) Where elites are concerned, the purpose of new technology is a dual one, of the better exploitation and the better control of those people who constitute their economic, political and/or military resources. Particular applications of science and technology are involved deeply and doubly in these endeavours at exploitation and control.

This is an argument both for and against technological determination. Against determination stands the recognition that technology ultimately is about enhancing the range and scope of human agency and that, where either knowledge of its principles and/or ownership allow, technology is the product and the servant of human will. Conversely, ignorance and/or non-ownership preclude the exercise of human will and, for those whose relation to technology is thus, determination may follow. 'May' follow because the social dimensions of hierarchy, advantage and differential dependencies have yet to be built in. Elite privilege will be founded upon either ownership and/or knowledge of the particular technologies crucial to the maintenance of the life and well-being of others. Elite action will attempt deliberately to exclude others from both ownership and knowledge. Such action may be directed at whole nations, sections of society, particular ethnic groups or women, using or reworking the available terms of discrimination—the general point being that the 'technologically determined' condition of those so excluded is thus structured by the political will of whoever are the elite.

Other possible power relations attach to technology. It is, for example, possible that ignorant owners can be subordinated to the will of knowledgeable inventors or knowledgeable workers in a particular technological field. This is the theme pursued by writers such as Stonier (1983) and Bell (1960) who—gazing at the late 20th century—identify the emergence of a post-industrial, information-based society in which scientists, professionals and bureaucrats rule the day. In line with the works of Touraine (1974) Gouldner (1976) and Mackenzie and Wajcman (1985), we would dispute that that is what is in fact developing. While there may be particular instances of such 'specialist' domination, the limit to the subordination of owners will be set by the extent to which the knowledgeable remain dependent upon owners for their continued employment, for research funds, for social contacts and social status. Those intellectuals whose livelihoods depend upon employment can be just as readily dispossessed of the fruits of their labours as can manual workers. While there are undoubtedly changes occurring in the power structures of the modern world, these we would say have more to do with the growing ascendancy of multinational capital and with the consequent destabilisation of the polities of nation states, than with increases in the employment of more specialised labour.

Additionally, all technologies in their application (prior to this age of Artificial Intelligence) have necessitated the development of particular forms of human organisation, of social systems. It has not been the case historically that such forms of organisation have invariably followed a singular logic of technical application. As Gouldner expresses it (1976: 256), 'technicians usually have more than one way of accomplishing some objective: the one they select is chosen partly . . . in terms of political and other considerations.' Such a construction says that technology is both an apparatus and a battleground for political contests over authority and agency, over co-operation and conflict. To the present date, technology could not be applied 'in the raw': it has had to be accompanied and expressed by some social apparatus of organisation, a social division of labour in which authority and status differentials were deeply implicated. That social apparatus of organisation has expanded and elaborated the mechanisms of political contest and the terrain on which that contest is fought out.

THE MODERN WESTERN EXPERIENCE

Earlier we spoke of certain orthodoxies developing around democracy as an object of study. One of their primary limitations would seem to be that they make propositions which stand in a political and historical vacuum. A focus on the nuts, bolts and implications of different social arrangements for democracy may meet many purposes but not that of explaining how the ambition came to be formulated in the first place, nor how the particular arrangements demonstrate characteristics which are explicable only in terms of other social phenomena. What is missing is a sensitivity to the contextual factors underpinning and shaping the particularities of developments towards greater democratic participation. Indeed some writers (Dachler and Wilpert, 1978; Gowler and Legge, 1978) argue the pre-eminence of such contextual factors in setting the boundaries for participatory behaviour. The foregoing discussion about the differential distribution of dependencies across society, and about the political leverages which may or may not be developed around such dependencies, has been an attempt both to clarify the relational dynamics for and against democracy, and to identify in abstract terms some of the contextual factors which set the boundaries for these processes.

Can we then move on to a contextualised, a more historically located, account? Allusion has already been made to the literature on the general theme of the collapse of democracy in the western nations of the 20th century, the referent here being almost exclusively the party and parliamentary systems of representation. There is another body of literature, also focusing on the west, which deals with issues of industrial democracy, that is, of democratic participation by workers in their organisations of employment. In these two bodies of literature there is a strong overall tendency to treat the economic and political spheres as substantially discrete (Crouch, 1979, Crouch and Pizzorno, 1978, and Strinati, 1982 being notable exceptions). Theories of civil democracy and surveys of the west's current condition advance with only minimal reference to workers' rights *vis-à-vis* employers. Meanwhile many industrial democracy studies focus primarily on institutionalised relations between employers and workers, or their representative bodies. Where treated at all, the political relations of the wider society are taken as essentially 'external' or secondary factors. Such approaches can be regarded as insufficiently detached from the cultures on which they reflect. Consider for one moment the shift in meaning from the phrase 'industrial democracy' to that of 'the democratic rights of working people in industrial society'. While the latter is rich in its dimensions, the former conjures a much narrower image referring solely to the employment relation. That loss of richness is by no means fortuitous. It is the natural child of an incestuous marriage between *laissez-faire* economic philosophy and classic liberal political ideals. The marriage leads to social practices which—with differing intensities depending upon circumstances and participants—would have us regard the economic sphere as somehow politically neutral, and certainly better kept preserved from political interventions by the state. In such a culture it may be regrettable but it is hardly surprising that academic theorisations about the survival of western democracy on the one hand, and about industrial democracy on the other, can stop so easily on either side of the factory gate without ever meeting.

By comparison, recent studies in the historical development of labour law (for example Hepple (ed.), 1986) tend not to fall foul of this customary bourgeois separation of economic from political realms. By the nature of its empirical focus an historical explanation of labour law identifies not only the rights, duties and limitations set by the state on working people but shows also the economic and political forces at work on and within the state in different periods and places, which in turn explain state policies towards industry and public order. Thus, although not viewing it from the point of view of democracy, Hepple's book *The Making of Labour Law in Europe* (1986) can identify three discrete stages of western social development—from feudalism through mercantilism to capitalism—each characterised by a particular social order in which elites, utilising the apparatus of the state, clearly endeavoured to 'fix' the place of subordinates in ways most conducive to wealth-generation and obedience. That the changing mode of production and, related to that, the phenomenon of workers' collective organisation made a profound impact on state policies is also ably demonstrated.

It becomes possible then, in light of such work as Hepple's and in light of our earlier discussion about relational dynamics and contextual factors, to consider at the very broadest level what makes for the democratisation of a society. The answer suggested by the above arguments is an historical coincidence of inter-elite rivalries with technologies, or modes of production, in the theatres both of war and of production which not only are highly labour-intensive but which require degrees of commitment and/or specialist knowledge from subordinates such that subordinates are not readily dispensed with or substitutable. Viewed across history, those technologies would seem to be industrial and, moreover, geared to the production of mass, standardised units of output. If these suppositions are correct, it is thus possible to conclude that the historical moments of industrialised mass warfare and industrialised mass production yield at one and the same time the ripest structural or 'economic' possibilities for both 'mass society' and 'class society'. As contended before, however, 'mass society' and 'class society' are regarded as political rather than as economic phenomena: expressions of both may well co-exist. Should one come to prevail it will do so as a function either of the political skills and differential advantages of the competing social groups in exploiting their respective bargaining counters, and/or of externally-derived contingencies such as the imminent prospect of foreign invasion.

Should over time the technological forms and/or inter-elite rivalries shift in such a way as to alter in favour of the elites the balance of elite-subordinate dependencies, then the structural bases for subordinate political action become commensurately weaker. Since it must be assumed that elites will always attempt to initiate change in this direction, any failure of subordinates to seize the moment of their peak powers so as to effect constitutional and ownership changes can be predicted to facilitate a sharp diminution of their status and welfare in the changed conditions. These changed conditions can only be based on one or both of a cessation of inter-elite rivalries (usually expressed through the forging of new alliances and new hierarchies), and new technological forms which make redundant ever larger proportions of human labouring, consumption and fighting powers.

One possible theme to be extracted from the above is that modern forms of technology (genetic engineering; lasers; automation; microprocessors; microelectronics; telecommunications; nuclear energy), because of their labour displacement potentialities, could be construed as making for a radical break in human social development. Some writers have expressed this break as the beginning of the end of wage-labour (for example, Jenkins and Sherman, 1979; Kumar, 1978). Others have debated whether it means more (for example, Gallie, 1978; Blauner, 1964) or less (Hill, 1981; Braverman, 1974; Woodward, 1970) authority over the job for the individual workers. Our concern is at the broader political level. We have assumed that all human history reflects struggles to secure the conditions of uncontestable, or at least defendable, sovereignty. To that goal, political-military leaders have had to harness the energies of their subordinates both to trade and to warfare. Labour has been to date the active ingredient, the productive element, whether as soldiers or workers. The political and cultural integrity of the social unit has therefore been crucial. Leadership has had to be 'earned' in most, if not all, levels of that social unit. But how crucial does such integrity remain, and therefore what of leadership, if developments in technology potentially or really displace the need for people in industry and in warfare? Where fighting wars and making wealth can be undertaken by robots and computers, the question arises whether the relations of expedience binding leaders with led, which previously informed human social organisation, will disappear, leaving relations only of morality and appeal. Without an instrumental need for the goodwill and co-operation of the common people, only altruism can remain to prompt the kindly regard of the privileged.

In all of these three areas of speculation (the end of wage-labour; the impact on employee autonomy; the consequences for the mechanisms of political integration) there is, however, rather too much and too simple an economic or technological determinism apparent. The arguments hold good only if worked out in their pure forms, and very little in human history indicates that pure forms of logical explanation are appropriate. On the contrary, altruism and other moral considerations—so far ignored—can be expected to penetrate contests over the terms of discrimination and to meliorate some of the relations of subordination. There will also be miscalculations and mistakes made in assessing one's own and others' respective strengths and weaknesses. Contradictions or imbalances may well develop between the (diminishing) demands for labour power of particular technological applications, and the needs of entrepreneurs for ever richer and more numerous customers to complete the valorisation processes of economic exchange. Indeed some sectors of production, on the basis of the new technologies, may well develop greater rather than lesser dependencies on labour power, albeit of a more highly specialised nature and from a smaller number of workers. But these more highly skilled, less readily substitutable, workers could contribute to new, more persuasive, forms of worker collectives: they could, if better remunerated, contribute to new or enhanced relations of social support for those newly disadvantaged in, or displaced from, labour markets. Further, it is a matter of fine political calculation how great a degree of public discontent and disorder can be tolerated by a state before it feels the need to make job-creating interventions.

Related to this will be the changing relations of state to capital. The liberal constitutional defence of private property has always rendered the state's access to the wealth of capital problematic and an exercise in horse-trading. Under conditions of multinational enterprise formation, where capital can to a greater extent pick and choose between national territories, each individual state must offer ever more attractive deals to secure capital's co-operation. In the alternative, the state must attempt to alleviate these particular dependencies by developing capitalism as a state property. But the state's relation to capital does not exhaust the arena in which it must negotiate its status and powers: its citizens and other states comprise the other arenas, failure in either of which can prompt state disintegration. In this connection is revealed precisely the nature of the state's needs for wealth. At bare minimum the state must be able to afford the 'defence of the realm' in terms of which citizens and other states learn to respect it. This brings us to the issue of war-fighting capacities, and the impact of modern technologies on the state-civil relationship. Nuclear weapons systems might imply a highly capital-intensive war footing (that is, one that does not require a large army), but the lack of flexible response inherent in such systems must persuade states to develop other, perhaps more labour-intensive, war strategies. Indeed, the costs and complexities of modern warfare imply that the state can no longer return or resort to *laissez-faire* policies of non-intervention. Practically speaking, defence of the realm responsibilities nowadays require that the state intervenes at a very high level in the economic sphere: if that same state publicly adopts *laissez-faire* policies, these can only apply to its welfare, not to its warfare, functions—

a discrepancy between what is preached and what practiced that may fuel popular resentments.

Further political moderations of the application of new technology can be anticipated. For example, the hand of established practice can be expected to weigh heavy: institutions, their occupants, social contracts and norms develop around the more enduring and significant relations of negotiation and representation. These people and their associates are likely to take a very considered view as to how readily they respond to any changes in the structural underpinning of those relations. Their resistance to change might well slow the rate of technological innovation and/or compromise the manner of its application such that certain jobs and authorities remain. Alternatively the existing personnel and organisations of subordinate resistance may decide to alter their modes or arenas of articulation: where in one historical moment they focus their attention and energies in the bourgeois political sphere, in another moment they may shift their activities to the economic realm. Such decisions alter the range and type of alliances, and the range and type of ideologies, open to these subordinate organisations for their exploitation. Similarly, the personnel of capital face a choice in how best to control their domains. Do they opt for the more traditional 'ownership of the means of production'? Or do they have the possibility of moving towards the more recently developed 'monetary' forms of control? That is, a system in which ownership is limited to just one crucial element in a total production-exchange cycle, but control is exercised over all the elements in the cycle through their commercial and productive dependency on the crucial part.

In short, while technological innovation most certainly carries the potential to destabilise particular social orders and while most certainly elites in command of such innovation can be expected to pursue their own sectional, rather than general social, interests in its application, whether, at what rate and how these processes of change proceed remains very much a matter of political contingencies, skills and contests.

What follows is an attempt to give greater theoretical cogency and a particular empirical test to the propositions thus far enunciated. The argument we advance is that democracy—understood as in the west as popular participation in the decision-making of the political economy—is the politically negotiated product of a particular conflux of different interests at a particular stage in societal development. The interests can be broadly classified as those of 'state, capital and labour' (greater theoretical attention to which concepts we give in the next chapter). The stage of societal development we can characterise as reflecting three primary features: (1) forms of political and economic organisation establishing themselves on the basis of nationally demarcated authorities over resources; (2) national rather than an international division of labour; and (3) labour-intensive technologies of economic enterprise and of warfare. Under such conditions, we contend, the state and capital, whether constitutionally separate or not, have been mutually interdependent in their respective advancements, and both have been dependent upon labour. Put crudely, universal suffrage and the right to independent trade union organisation have been the deals struck jointly (and not without some internal disagreements) by state and capital with labour during that transient historical phase when labour enjoyed a high degree of bargaining power. That bargaining power, however, has been, in significant though not complete measure, rooted in technological applications susceptible to alteration by their commanders, and deals made can be unmade. Technological innovation, pursued according to particular rationales of efficiency, in the theatres of war and of economy are now relieving some state and capital dependencies upon human labour, although creating new ones. These same developments, facilitating and augmented by new forms of economic organisation, are simultaneously introducing incompatibilities into the relation of state with capital; the sovereignty of the former in many instances being substantially eroded by the burgeoning powers of the latter. One can anticipate and already witness the flight of employers abroad, away from certain labour forces now found to be too costly and/or not sufficiently tractible when measured against new alternatives. One can also already identify the authoritarian responses of so-called liberal states as existing methods for influencing domestic and international affairs lose their efficacy. It is apparent also that the fortunes of labour, whether measured by the political tenor of labourist political parties or the popular support for trades unionism, are if not in decline certainly undergoing traumatic change. At some future date an historian will perhaps reflect on the century to the 1970s and judge it 'the golden age of democracy', now passed.

But an argument about cultural specificities (that is, the significance of contextual factors) must be sensitive to just that. While postulating that the relations of state, capital and labour can *generally* be analysed in terms of their respective dependencies on one another, the particular arrangements giving expression to these relations can be expected to vary among nations from epoch to epoch. We therefore give empirical attention to Britain as the first industrial nation and still an ardent advocate of liberal democracy in its public statements. The account begins around the 16th century, the transition from a feudal social order through mercantilism to capitalism being then evident. In these early sections, attention is given in particular to the development of the rule of law and to the bourgeois division of economic from political spheres of organisation. These features are significant not only for explanations of subsequent government practice, and the relatively free hand of capital in British development, but also to the management and behaviour of labour. Although statutory interventions affecting employment and workers have never been insignificant, developments in labour law really attend the 20th century when western states have found capital's management of labour inadequate in the circumstances. Up to that point, however, and particularly evident in Britain, labour or industrial relations have developed in the economic sphere as the normative equivalent of legally regulated relations in the political sphere, although, of course, subject to somewhat different pressures and considerations. Indeed, in Britain, organised labour has shifted its primary energies from one sphere to another over time—from the political sphere in the early 19th century (for example, Chartism), to the economic sphere in the later 19th century (trade unions; collective bargaining; labour relations)—and in the 20th century has remained divided between the two. The contents of this book reflect that shift, its middle chapters covering more of labour's experiences in the economic than in the political spheres of representation. Likewise, changes in relations among state, capital and labour inherent in the internationalisation of capital and in the forging of super-power alliances among states—phenomena of this century and the foreseeable future—influence the discussion of later chapters. That is, it becomes impossible to consider the political and economic status of the British common people without invoking state and capital developments at the international level.

Firstly though we must give greater consideration to the theorisation of our primary actors, the state, capital and labour.

2 Capital, State and Labour

A very great deal has been written about the political and economic features of the epoch dubbed as 'capitalism'. Much of this writing has been heavily theorised: quite properly so, given that the best achievement is to understand and not merely to describe. Since the ambition of the present book is to trace and analyse the fortunes of the common people within British capitalism, it is necessary not only that we offer our own theorisation but that we do so sensitive to what others before us have said. That is the purpose of this present chapter. We are mindful that the concepts of 'state, capital and labour' are theoretical abstractions rather than homogeneous empirical agents, and we need therefore to elucidate our understanding of them and their interrelationships.

A first point to be made is that while such concepts have great heuristic utility, put to the test of historical specifics they can easily dissolve. What theoretically can be manipulated as if it were a homogeneous agent becomes, under empirical gaze, people—people making friends and enemies, money and mistakes, intrigues and sacrifices. It is both the assumption and the constitutive function of theory that such activity has patterns and regularities which, once discerned and causally analysed, will yield explanations, predictions and suggestions for the more rational application of human effort. It is this second dimension of theory—its constitutive function—which ensures that epistemologically its status is perpetually problematic. Where theory persuades humans of its verisimilitude, it also persuades them to particular courses of action in accord with its own propositions, and thus it may initiate, perpetuate or alter that which is empirically realised in human affairs. As Sumner (1979: 70) writes, this implies that 'social being and becoming . . . should be studied in union with social consciousness in its many different manifestations, as a real yet ideal (or "ideological") component of the historical process in general'. Accepting such an argument would imply, among other things, that a conceptual framework which is possibly appropriate to the analysis of one historical point in time may not be appropriate for the next. In the immediate context, this would be to say that concepts such as state, labour and capital have only a transient historical validity.

A further reflection which follows from the above argument is that, should a deterministic explanation of human affairs be offered, it can at most be accepted as valid only *pro tem*. Any suggestion or contention that a particular aspect of human life (for example, technology or economics) is the ultimate determinant of everything else can be accepted, if at all, as true only for a limited period. Thus, any imputed determining agent should be seen as contingently active, raising questions automatically as to the nature of the contingencies: for example, what invited or allowed the determining agent onto the stage of human affairs?

In the range of classical accounts offering to explain the emergence of capitalist society, where 'economics' or 'the mode of production' is held to be the determining agent, the answer to that question is often rather obscure. As Johnston (1986: 124) argues, the conceptual dichotomy found in classic Marxist accounts between determinism and autonomy, between objective structure and subjective human action, is a false one since each condition exists in relation to the other. Thus, it cannot be 'maintained that there are any essential agents, whether individuals or classes, through which necessary processes or forms of action are teleologically realized or realizable'.

CAPITAL

The Dichotomy of Economics and Politics

As an example of the obscurity referred to above, consider the argument of some authors of the significance of incorporation which, as the dominant characteristic of 20th century modern society, they claim, has rendered the division of 'politics' from 'economics' invalid. They identify empirically the expansion of the state into economic affairs, the expansion of capital into political affairs, and the partial absorption of labour into both—these processes being imputed to the imperatives of economic growth and/or the needs of capital (for example, Harris, 1983; Wallerstein, 1974a). Yet the 'severance of the economic from the political', as Giddens (1982: 178) identifies and affirms, has been seen in the Marxist critique of capitalism as 'the foundation of capitalist class domination' insofar as it has politically enshrined and legitimated the private ownership of the means of production. Any incorporation thesis therefore which implies a reduced significance to, or compromised operation of, privately owned capital, must also be taken to infer that it is no longer appropriate to regard modern western societies as capitalist in the pure Marxist sense. Yet it is clear that the authors have no such intention.

Whether or not one accepts the argument that the development of the western nations over the last two to three centuries demonstrates the primacy of capitalist economic power, it is apparent that the dichotomy (of economics from politics) was never *simply* a conceptual nicety emerging with Enlightenment rationality. It was that too, of course. In the developing scientific and technical rationalities of the Enlightenment, what more natural than to objectify as distinct and different certain types of human behaviour and, having objectified, to develop them as realms of discrete and specialised practice. But the potency of such a dichotomy lay not only in its rational appeal but in its ability to legitimise the realities of power in late medieaval/early modern times and—by prescribing a constitutional-legal divide and separate realms of authority for competing but intertwined leaders—to limit the potential for conflict between them. Further elaborated, the rationalisation of the balance of forces at the dawn of capitalism indeed went beyond discriminating economic from political realms to identify the cultural sphere as yet also discrete. The bourgeois domain could then advance by discriminating individuals, groups and classes according to who was or was not to be properly admitted to these separate realms of production: thus capitalists and labourers belonged to the economic; persons of high birth, wealth and/or military capabilities to the political; and carefully patronised artists and intellectuals to the cultural (the endeavours of the lower orders in this sphere being dismissed as 'low' or 'popular').

Questions of Determinism and Political Will

Classic Marxist accounts, however, have gone further than this. Identifying the economic-political divide, they have then looked for the 'laws' of history or motion which explain it. The answer they arrive at is 'the mode of production'. The idea of economic leadership thus becomes immensely more complex and is designated 'capital'; it is also far more potent—the mode of production actually becomes the motive force of human history. In the capitalist epoch, argues the Marxist account, the mode of production dictates the nature of political decision-making and relations, the latter being construed largely as the realm of the state. In the theoretical movement from 'economic leaders' to 'capital' and from 'political leaders' to 'the state', the Marxist account thus automatically problematises relations between state and capital, and between them and the 'led' (civil society; labour). It then seeks to clarify that problematic by declaring the primacy of economic, that is, capitalist, interests: these are seen to penetrate to the very heart of the state, to subordinate it and civil society, the whole being expressed as the political economy of capitalism.

Clearly, classic Marxist accounts have attempted to grapple at a theoretical level with the very real, praxiological, bourgeois division of political from economic institutions. It does seem, however, that in that theoretical effort they have reified the separation by adopting the bourgeois argument that economic behaviour *is* somehow profoundly different in kind from political behaviour. There is an assumption or uncritical presentation of capitalism as running on a logic and dynamic which is in some way non-political. This is shown most clearly in the various attempts to define capitalism—for example, Wallerstein (1974a: 398) talks of it as

> production for sale in a market in which the object is to realize maximum profit. In such a system production is constantly expanded as long as further production is profitable and men constantly innovate new ways of producing things that will expand the profit margin.

Such a purely economic rendition of capitalism, together with the argument that the mode of production is the dynamo of human history, ensures that an economic determinist perspective is at the heart of the Marxist account. This instantly problematises the notion and role of free will or agency, and it also raises the question as to what replaces the mode of production as the historical motor in non-capitalist times. As we have argued before, however, determinism and voluntarism should be seen as conditions existing in relation to each other and, moreover, as the outcome of political negotiations in which the relative advantage of one party secures greater agency at the expense of the other's greater determination. In short, we argue that the dynamo of human history is not something inhuman but rather is human will, pitted against conditions of existence which there is a desire to alter, exploit or obliterate. The difficulties raised by economic determinism in analyses are resolved if economics is construed as a particular discourse of politics. If politics is understood as competition and co-operation among people in the distribution, exploitation and development of resources, then to invoke the rationale of economics is to lay a claim as to how best that competition and co-operation should be conducted. It is a discourse prescribing on the grounds of superior efficiency and benefit the operation of exchange relations and markets; a discourse where human actions are rationalised and legitimated in terms of the primacy of an efficiency construed as the extraction of maximum output from each unit of input at minimum cost (costs and revenues being typically but not invariably limited to pecuniary calculations).

Some writers identify such prescriptions with capitalism but the prescriptions in themselves do not address the issue of private and individual, as distinct from public and collective, ownership of the means of production. Yet it can be shown by reference to 20th-century Japanese or USSR state activities, for instance, that the discourse of exchange relations, markets and productive efficiency is as readily operationalised by public and/or collective forms of ownership as by private.

Questions of Ownership

Can we dub these public and collective forms as equally 'capitalist' without losing sight of the specific historical association of capital with the political structures of the western nations? If we wish *á la Marx* to make the case that the economic rationality of the market has existed in some way separate from, but with a profound influence on, the fashioning of state and civil society, then the separation would logically imply its crystallisation in the form of private ownership. For the sake of argument we could then say that to dispense with private

ownership dispenses with capital, although it does not dispense
with the broader phenomenon of exchange relations and markets.
Given the unease felt in trying to reconcile this theoretical
argument (that is, that capital can only be private property)
with our sense that modern western reality is capitalist, it would
seem sensible not to limit capital to the private ownership of the
means of production but rather to stress that capitalism is a
particular set of practices, that these practices combine modes
of exploitation and appropriation and that they can be adopted
by whichever social group or individual has the means and will
to do so. Thus, capitalism can be a state activity, and capital a
state property, without it being any the less capitalistic. Its
significance rather remains—whether state or privately owned–
that, while 'Many sociologists have seen property as a set of
exclusionary rights of possession . . . only property as capital is
immediately relevant to class analysis, *since it confers the capacity
to organise and subordinate those who are without it*' (Giddens,
1982: 188; emphasis added).

In other words, capitalism is not only a mode of exploitation
but also a mode of appropriation. It succeeds where command
over the means to survival is concentrated in the hands of the
few, thereby rendering the remaining majority dependent upon
and subordinate to those commanders. Capitalism is remarkable
not so much for its economic rationality as for the particular
manner in which it creates power relations and an inequitous
but relatively stable social order. Understood as such it becomes
easier to regard capitalism as an historically contingent and
politically unique form of command over the resources of
territories held in competition against, or in negotiation with,
rival command structures.

Even this understanding leaves room for further discrimination, in that financial and service sectors of capitalism were
evidently quite at home under the command structures of the
mercantilist state. They, among all economic operations dubbed
as capital (and Robinson, 1987: 14, is one writer who queries
whether they should be regarded as capital), did not seem
historically to require the constitutional separation of political
and economic spheres before they could operate successfully.
Rather it was particularly the manufacturing or industrial sectors
of British capitalism which pressed for and achieved that
separation. This would indicate *either* the contingent rather than

essential contribution of a particular constitutional arrangement to the development of capital, *or* that such an arrangement reflects the (transient) ascendancy of one sector of capital as against other sectors. Whichever of these two implications is correct, it indicates the possibility of alliances being forged between particular sectors of capital and particular interests within the state in pursuit of particular modes of exploitation and appropriation, against the will or interests of other sections of state and capital. Some commentators indeed see this as the case for Britain in the 1980s. Johnson (1982), for example, sees finance capital and an authoritarian government colluding to limit the influence of a 'liberalising' manufacturing sector, and the demands of organised labour.

Capitalism and Liberty

But it is difficult to insist that there is any automatic or necessary link between any form of capitalism and liberty. It has been argued that capital, so as to secure the lowest possible price for labour, requires that units of labour compete with one another by being 'free' to contract employment, the development of civil liberties being the awarding of such 'freedom' in the political-legal sphere. But many other authors (for example, Marx, 1976; Burawoy, 1979) have pointed out that such freedom in fact means being deprived of any other means of survival save the sale of labour power for wages. Others (for example, Wallerstein, 1983) have pointed out that capitalism can and does make use of slaves and serfs. Indeed, according to economic rationality, it might seem that slavery is the purest form of capitalistic labour, in that the human source is denied absolutely, no recompense is made to that source, and labour power exists solely as the property of the capitalist. But there is a contradiction here in that capitalism also needs predictability, certainty, management and, since we can safely assume (following Braverman, 1974, or Giddens, 1982: 212) that 'wherever they can do so, human actors devise ways of avoiding being treated as . . . machines', we can also assume that capitalists will find it necessary to negotiate, to recognise the human features of those who constitute labour. To ensure managerial and thereby factor efficiency, capital cannot absolutely ignore the humanity of its labourers. Neither can it sanction their genuine liberty and equality. The different interests represented here will be organised and expressed on an ideological terrain for what Burawoy (1979) has called 'the manufacture of consent'; the detail of particular packages of consent being dependent on 'the specific balance of power between Capital and Labour (leading) to effective resistance here and capitulation there' (Burawoy, 1979: 285).

Control and Resistance

That balance of power will in large part reflect the wit of the parties devising ever new ways of control and resistance. For example, notable at the present moment in Britain is the managerial language of 'labour flexibility', offered ostensibly as a description of changing labour market conditions (for example, Institute of Manpower Studies Report, 1984; NEDO's 1986 *Changing Patterns of Work*) but better understood as prescription. For the employer, the appeal of labour flexibility is two-fold: (1) that greater numbers of workers can be hired and fired at will; (2) that those kept in permanent employ will be multi-skilled and job-mobile. The Department of Employment's recent *Employment Challenge to the Nation* (1985) indeed identifies the cause of unemployment as the lack of such flexibility and counsels deregulation. Should this argument succeed, it would facilitate the dismantling of most trade union restrictive practices, and would discourage workers from regarding their occupation as a private property (see chapter 7 for further examination of the flexibility issue).

A second direction in which the larger corporations of capital are attempting to move is that of developing themselves more as 'polities': the personnel practices of Japanese and some US corporations are growing in appeal to other capitalists as older methods of control fail. Strategic personnel practices involve granting the permanent employee rights to participate and to enjoy material and status privileges in direct proportion to his/her indispensability and loyalty to the corporation. The process is characterised by the efforts of the entrepreneur to concentrate powers more completely at the organisational centre (these days as much by accountancy methods as by direct ownership), with the relation to employees being deliberately individualised. In place of the worker collectivities represented in collective bargaining and trade unionism, there is a trend

evident (especially where the more skilled, less easily substitutable core worker is concerned) towards the negotiation of a
personalised contract. Sometimes this personalised contract is
not even constructed as an employment relation but rather
as subcontracting or a franchise. Certainly franchising and
subcontracting are consistent with capital's move towards control
through monetary or accountancy regulation rather than through
direct ownership. This new mode of control attaches to new
forms of enterprise organisation (namely, 'just in time' systems—
see chapter 7) which appear to be replacing or supplementing
the internationalisation of the division of labour as a means to
reduce production costs and uncertainties. If successful (from
management's point of view), the effect of these various changes
will be to bind the individual worker more tightly to the
employer/contractor while loosening his/her relations to fellow
workers and craft traditions. The response of labour so far,
through the unions, has been largely reactive—to develop better
international alliances and to make greater efforts to recruit the
casually- and under-employed. Union practices are still, however,
largely dependent on the wage-labour relation, and the continuing ubiquity of this relation is now clearly under threat. Unions
would, therefore, seem to need to devise new bases on which to
organise and amplify worker resistance.

The Political Appeal of Capitalism

If capitalism is construed as a specific and political discourse
in negotiation and potential competition with other political
discourses, is there still value in defining capital (and labour) in
purely economic terms? The answer must be two-fold: yes, so
far as that allows us to comprehend and predict the economically
calculated actions of capitalists (whether state or private): no, if
it leads us to ignore how and where they articulate with other
arenas and discourses of politics. Culling the literature on
capitalism yields a checklist of primarily economic features.
Roughly speaking, the literature identifies capitalism with the
production of things as commodities to render them exchangeable
for money in the open market, with a view to profit maximisation
for the producer, who organises waged labourers in a division of
labour so as best to extract from them surplus value in proportions
adequate to fund further innovation in productive relations.

Authors differ on which elements of the above catalogue are essential and which not to the existence of capital—waged labour and the money economy being the most disputed, since these can be shown to predate capitalism.

As a description of bourgeois economic rationality, this kind of account is fine but as an historically and sociologically adequate one much remains to be added. This is not to say that the effort has not been made. The literature investigating what is construed as the transition from feudalism to capitalism is no less copious than is that predicting the future to which capitalism will lead us. In these accounts recourse is sometimes made to the causal contribution of essentially political factors (for example, Poggi, 1978, identifies the role of the *Ständestaat* in late 12th to early 14th-century western Europe, and links this to a gradual shift in the terms of discrimination of superiors and subordinates). More often though, the driving force is still implicitly or explicitly economic—or narrower still, profit motivation. Harris (1983: 255), for example, talks of nation states being created by international capitalism 'to administer the territories of its empire'. In similar vein, Wallerstein (1983) concludes that the cost of political imperium has now risen to the extent of hampering further developments of capitalism, and that this explains the adoption of new political-economic solutions such as the European Economic Community. These arguments would be more acceptable if there were not in both a rather simple equation of capitalism with economic activity geared to the profit motive.

Such an equation makes it instantly unlikely that subject populations would co-operate except where they are fearful of doing otherwise, or where they are suffering a bad case of false consciousness. Undoubtedly sanctions and misapprehensions have played their part but, more significantly, capitalism has never been only about the profit motive. The ethos of capitalism has been historically compelling because it was associated with promises to realise (or at least create the opportunities for realising) the moral, economic and political agency of individuals: moral, by securing individuals in situations of choice; economic, by enshrining the propriety of private ownership; and political, by vesting ownership with political rights. Additionally, capitalism promised the enhancement of material well-being and social progress by creating the allegedly most appropriate milieu (namely, the free market) for maximising innovation, creativity and productivity. In such terms, way beyond profit maximisation, has capitalism been legitimated.

The misrepresentation conveyed in these claims to legitimation has been apparent at least since Marx's critique was published. The goal of competition, market or other, is finally to get rid of competition, and while power remains heavily vested in property ownership, there is no necessity for that ownership to be private, nor indeed for the nature of the property to be politically significant. Never has this been better revealed than now, when corporate and state structures absorb ever greater areas of significant 'economic' property, and the meaning of private ownership becomes non-state rather than personal. Likewise, the association of individualism with capitalism is tenuous, being more of an historical accident in that individualism was built into British law and predated capitalism, and indeed part-way conditioned capitalism's development in Britain. Abercrombie, Hill and Turner (1986) point out that individualism preceded capitalism as an out-turn of the egalitarianism and universalism of monotheistic Christianity; such individualism did not cause capitalism; rather it was a case of 'elective affinity'. The 'elective affinity' came about because individualism was an element of consensus available to be used in the political attack on royal absolutism. As this attack succeeded, it created the space in which unconditioned market relations could flourish. Abercrombie and colleagues go on to query whether in this age of multinationals and trade unions collectivist ideologies might not now be more fitting.

Summary

In summary, assuming an essentially political rather than economic understanding of capitalism, we can contend that it has involved two related phenomena: (1) an historically transient but substantial decentralisation of power, founded upon control of economic resources which it was beyond the elite structures of the day to reach and to manage; and (2) an upward shift in the political status of material development and exploitation. *Politically* constructed as *laissez-faire* economic behaviour and as private ownership of the means of production, capital had an appeal to the elites of the day both as an activity which they could adopt, and as a set of people whom they were better advised to embrace, since the chances of outmanoeuvring them were at the time slim. Subsequently, developments in transport, in communications and surveillance, in state administrative bureaucracies and techniques, and in the state remit, have brought this 'problem' under control in all areas save the international finance houses and the multinational corporations. The relative decentralisation of the early stages did, though, favour the more rapid application of the emergent sciences (backed with coercive measures wherever necessary) to the tasks of resource exploitation, management and development (including human labour as a resource). One consequence of this was to swing world power dramatically in favour of the capitalist nations. A second was the release of materially productive energies sufficient not merely to cater for swelling populations but, in general terms, to improve their standards of living. A third consequence was to oblige the would-be political leaders to find new ways to address those they wished to retain or to embrace as their subjects, most especially those whose economic energies they wished to harness to political goals.

THE STATE

Territorial Domination and Expansion

The above perspective infers that the shape of the emergent modern state has been fashioned not simply by capital but rather by the power plays of elites varying in type over time and geography, seeking to govern a specified territory in their own perceived best interests. Some of these will lay a claim to political status on the basis of inherited nobility or divine right; some on inherent moral or intellectual superiority; some on the basis of armed strength; and some on the ability, in a highly productive manner, to apply scientific and economic rationality to the tasks of material exploitation. Whatever the nature of their claims, the common goal will be conquest and rule of a territory or territories. In achieving this goal there will be practical questions of supply and communicative systems that must underlie the exercise of rule, and these will set its geographical limits. Alliances, though, forged with other able and willing parties will help defend and even extend these geographical limits. For the dominant group or alliance to monopolise the means of violence is self-evidently the best way to secure internal compliance, and also to develop the means to deter outsiders from invasion. But such monopolisation is expensive, requiring the co-operation directly or through taxation of those living in the territory, and therefore needing some degree of legitimation. This further implies that successful command of a territory necessitates the harmonisation or unification under one rule of all major forms of social power—ideological, economic, military, and political (Mann, 1986).

Feudalism was one such unified rule, with monarchy at its centre. Capitalism is another, the monarchy being replaced by or rather, as in the British case, absorbed into the state. But just as the unity of feudalism could never be taken for granted, and just as its alliances were continually renegotiated, so too the alliances of capitalism are continually renegotiated. The state constitutes the central arena for many (but not all) of these renegotiations by virtue of its monopolisation of the means of violence and its ideological place in the territory's power relations. The state exists as an apparatus to preserve territorial integrity, rule and sovereignty. It must perforce address and negotiate the competing interests represented within that territory, including capital.

Capitalism developed because bourgeois rationality declared economics a specialised and important realm of practice. In Britain the development was given impetus by the constitutional separation of the affairs of state from those of the economy. This constitutional division was as much the product of political expedience as of any genuine belief in the free market. But that politically expedient division did not preclude the highly profitable joint ventures of state and capital foraging abroad in the periods of informal and formal empire: the state providing the military back-up and capital providing the money and non-military forms of social control. Nor was this undertaken simply in the interests of capital. As Cecil Rhodes said in 1895 (echoing Palmerston some 70 years before),

> My cherished idea is a solution for the social problem, that is, in order to save the forty million inhabitants of the United Kingdom from a bloody civil war, we colonial statesmen must

acquire new lands to settle the surplus production, to provide new markets for the goods produced in the factories and mines. The Empire, as I have always said, is a bread and butter question. If you want to avoid civil war, you must become imperialists.

That domestic social order was seen as 'purchasable' by economic growth in turn associated with imperialism is the clear message of this statement. It is quoted in Lenin's *Imperialism: the highest stage of capitalism* (1966). With the benefit of more recent evidence, one can see that capital's highest stage is global (indeed, inter-planetary, if the human race gets that far!) and rather argue that imperialism is the highest stage in the development of the nation state.

Monopolisation of the Means of Violence

It is now apparent that the geographical definition of the nation state and the monopolisation of the means of violence by the state apparatus have led it along a different path of development from that of capital. Global and domestic capital still have an interest in peaceful trading conditions but global capital at least can now more easily select among states and repudiate their authority. Meanwhile the individual states' war-fighting capabilities demand access to ever greater sources of surplus value. There is an ineluctable link between the economic strength of a country and its ability to threaten and wage war on those who would disturb it. The link is not one-way but symbiotic: it runs into trouble when the costs of warfare escalate beyond the capacity of the economic base to give support. There is a further ineluctable and also symbiotic link between the country's economic strength and its domestic political stability—instability being a sure path to economic regression and regression being a less sure predictor of instability. Desiring social peace, the state is obliged to oversee, cajole and trade with its citizens *qua* citizens. Desiring wealth, it must oversee, cajole and trade with the same people as labourers and entrepreneurs. Desiring to raid and trade abroad, and to resist those 'foreigners' who would act similarly, the state must deal with rival states and foreign entrepreneurs. But to sustain an adequate war footing and war-fighting capability in the face of other nations doing just the same predicts two developments: (1) that the state will penetrate and seek to administer ever more comprehensively the economic, social and political processes of the national territories (whatever its protestations of preference for *laissez-faire* government); and (2) a continual international arms race.

In the 20th century industrialisation and technical knowledge have speeded up that race to unparalleled proportions and costs. The unmanageability of this modern arms race has persuaded some nations to drop out, to accept a subordinate position in the world balance of power, or alternatively to strike up new political alliances where not only military resources are shared but where there is also a significant degree of economic co-operation. The permanent war economy is what in this century has come to characterise these new 'power blocs' of allied nations, compelling the individual states to balance ever more precariously the twin demands of welfare and warfare (see Harris, 1983, in particular, for a compelling description of the dilemma). This pattern also ensures the state's most thorough-going invasion into every economically and politically significant area of civil society. Trotsky argued that war is the locomotive of history: that argument is acceptable so long as 'war' is broadened to include preparation for war plus defensive postures, and so long as the symptom (war) is not taken for the cause (political will to self-determination, that is, agency). The will to agency of states has led in the 20th century away from consti-tutional liberalism to the creation of command structures which re-unify in real, if not yet declared, terms the economic, military, political and ideological sources of social power (McNeill, 1983). Modern command structures differ, however, from their ancestors not only in the scale and complexity of the military and economic power they muster, but also in the scale and complexity of their relations. The typical command structure of the feudal epoch assumed economic and military powers under one political line, one hierarchy—instability coming from rival-ries both within and between lines whenever the centrist grip seemed to loosen. Nowadays these lines, arguably, comprise power blocs of allied nations, centrist grip being exercised by the strongest in the pack but the clarity of their internal and external relations being confounded by a number of features: (1) that the weaker states within one bloc may yet have significant powers and autonomy in relation to individual member states of other power blocs; (2) that the current stalemate of war-fighting technologies puts a premium on diplomacy and on economic and other forms of competition, in which activities the 'weaker' states can play a major part; and (3) that moving in relative freedom between the blocs and thereby linking them are those sections of capital which have evolved beyond the reach of the single nation state. The overall picture is one of enormously complex interdependencies but little or no stability.

Moreover it is not completed by considerations of relations between state and capital. Following Weber (1927: 1964) and Mann (1986), it can be demonstrated that there exists a close relationship between war-fighting forms and the form of domestic political organisation. Armed forces that do not comprise mercenaries and in which the life of one man rests on the skills and loyalties of his fellows are forces making for egalitarianism (at least among fighting males). Where the war-fighting mode requires a *mass*, conscript army (Andrewski, 1954) and the general economic and social participation of an entire population (Marwick, 1981), it also associates strongly with development towards a democratic culture and with the extension of civil rights: the price paid, as it were, by the state for popular support in its military activities. Let it be clear that, in this kind of analysis, democracy is seen as the product of particular state needs deriving from inter-state rivalries and specific war-fighting technologies: it is not credited at all to the requirements of capital. The extension of civil rights encapsulated in the welfare state is seen to exist as the purchase price for the modern warfare state [and in these developments, state leaders in one nation have had much to learn (see Hepple, 1986) from the experiments and practices of other nations]. Or at least this was so prior to the development of the very latest war-fighting technologies. And, under conditions in which the wealthiest sections of capital have become international, it is a point of considerable interest how the state will balance its dual and related commitments to welfare and warfare.

The transition towards a fully 'technicised' war footing and war-fighting capacity was predicted by the escalating industrialisation of combat modes in the First and Second World Wars. In the first, the mass-oriented and cumbersome nature of the extant forms of industrial production expressed itself as a dependency upon millions of men swarming ant-like across the earth to throw destruction at each other. They were limited, however, by human needs for food, rest, recovery and transportation. By the Second World War these human limitations on military efficiency had been substantially overcome by a greater application of machine and electrical technologies. These technologies not only dispensed with the need for a mass army but they also redistributed more thoroughly the 'burden of suffering' towards the civilian population, in that land-based armies could now be overflown so as to strike deep into the domestic heartlands. This democratisation of the burden of suffering made more crucial the quality of the political relations between the state and all of its citizens: it generated new psychological demands which the people had to make on government, in addition to their longer-standing economic and social demands. Subsequently the shift towards nuclear and high-technology fighting modes has further built upon yet changed the psychological dimension of the state-citizen relationship. The novelty of the new modes is their combination of very low labour needs with very high kill efficiencies. Unlike previous, more manual, less destructive, war technologies, the new modes deny the fighter much of his previous justification in terms of defence of the homeland; relief in the prospect of his own and other's eventual recovery; and legitimation in terms of some greater evil being quelled. In short, the new war technologies admit of less honour and less hope in battle: their primary legitimation resides in deterrence. This, as a condition of stalemate, is for the state also a condition of some impotence—to be obscured by sabre-rattling and overcome by the urgent search for more usable weapons systems. Yet it is presently in terms of this sole legitimating element of deterrence that the state must negotiate its civic relations. *The modern state dependency is less on the physical presence and co-operation of citizens in military activities, and more on their wealth-generating, taxable capacities plus their preparedness to accept state definitions of the 'national interest'.* The 'national interest', heavily informed by military and security considerations, becomes the ideological terrain on which the state increasingly chooses to attack those whose 'disorder' threatens wealth-generation, and to justify its own actions. Among these actions is state secrecy—the refusal to inform the public and/or their elected representatives of certain matters. Such secrecy taken together with the highly specialised character of modern war technologies adds up to a gulf of incomprehension ever-deepening between those in command and the general population. This popular incomprehension in the face of the enormity of the nuclear threat constitutes an almost classic psychological condition for the widespread development of fatalism, apathy, hedonism and defensiveness. Together with the escalation of state secrecy and domestic surveillance, it implies the repudiation of democracy. Under such conditions the assertions of labour as a class are inevitably downgraded, but so also perhaps are the assertions of elected governments.

Parliamentarism

Government in the liberal democracies comprises the elected representatives of the people and is that part of the state apparatus to which the people have been enjoined to direct their political energies. The extent to which this kind of participation represents a genuine input to the decision-making of the state is debatable. Miliband (1982: 1) expresses the gist of the debate thus:

> ... the people in power may find themselves out of it as a result of a shift of opinion as expressed in a general election. This may be of much smaller consequence for the actual structure of power than is alleged or believed, but it may also have substantial policy implications and cannot be dismissed as of no consequence.

Whether the intention behind the invention of parliamentarism was ever specifically the frustration of the democratic will, it remains true that many sections of the state are not democratically accountable (especially those relating to national security), and that parliamentary control can often be negated (see, for example, Dangerfield's 1970 discussion of the emasculation of the Liberal government of 1910–14). Moreover, the pressure of electoral politics impels political parties towards marketing attractive images rather than elaborating complex political philosophies ... making for what one present Member of Parliament, Austin Mitchell (1987), has ascerbically termed 'government as a political version of the Consumer Association'.

The Rule of Law

Whatever the indications as to its real powers, parliamentarism can be seen as one mechanism of social control, absorbing popular sentiments and grievances and ideologically conditioning their generation and expression. In the same manner law can be regarded as a mechanism of social control. It has been held that historically the relation between the modern state and the people has been mediated substantially by law. Poggi (1978), for example, argues the near identity of law and the modern state, and Trotsky (1972: 39) sees the rule of law in liberal democracies as rendering all society's members legally equal as citizens and 'legislators'. These claims need to be qualified: first, the state has means other than law through which to mediate its relations to the populace, for example, its 20th-century expansion in welfare provisioning; and second, the constitutional realisation of people as citizens and 'legislators' has been contingent on the extension of the franchise and this, in many locations, has involved a lengthy and arduous popular struggle. Nonetheless, the law has been and continues to be a significant arena generating the definitions and terms of discrimination between, among other parties, capital and labour. Marx's arguments here seem essentially correct: in brief, that the legal relation of exchange specifies individuals as juridical subjects and makes them separable from the products of their labours. As such, it creates juridically free-acting agents, equal in the sense that the commodities exchanged are assumed to be of equivalence. Such juridical assumptions are appropriate, that is, they express objective social relations, where the market economy is structured simply around the exchange of commodities. Where, however, capitalist expropriation of the means of production creates a pool of dependent labourers, the commodities to be exchanged cease to be of equivalence. The contractual exchange of labour power for wages becomes a theft hidden by the legal assumptions of freedom and equivalence. The theft occurs in that the full value of labour power is not conveyed to the worker in wages but rather an element is retained by the capitalist. This he (the capitalist) then seeks to valorise via the market. But in the market it is the worker who, free of any means of production and therefore a dependent consumer, underwrites the valorisation process by the spending of wages. It is, argues Marx, in this occlusion of objective social relations of non-equivalence, that the law becomes an instrument of class or bourgeois domination.

While the Marxist argument is acceptable, it should not be read to imply that the law must, for the purpose of class domination, obscure the non-equivalence of the parties to the labour contract. In the English case, to the contrary, for the greater part of the epoch of classical capitalism (later 18th and 19th centuries), the law where it touched on the capital-labour relationship did so with overtones of feudalism. Under the Master & Servant Act, it construed capital as 'Master' and labour as 'Servant', the latter's unpropertied status rendering him/her legally liable to labour at the former's behest and determination (Kahn-Freund, 1977). Further, the law does not have to be active at all for the exchange between capital and labour to take place: one thinks of capital's exploitation of slave and serf labour in this connection, where no or very disadvantageous legal provisions pertain to the workers. Indeed, historical peculiarities may mean that it is either difficult or unneccessary for the state to mediate in the legal form (Fine, 1985). It may seek other or additional forms of mediation, or may elect for non-involvement. The extent and manner of state intervention in affairs construed as 'economic' has been a matter of debate since the dawn of capitalism: government decisions taken varying considerably over time and country, and with considerable import for the respective fortunes of the interested parties. The peculiarities of English law, where the absence (until the 20th century) of any clearly articulated contract of employment is substantially to be explained by the cultural-legal paramountcy of private property rights, is a case in point (Macfarlane, 1979; Denman, 1978; see also next chapter).

A more general point to be drawn from Marx's arguments is that the prescriptions and assumptions conveyed in law may or may not have a basis in objective social relations. That is an empirical question. So also is the extent to which the state tries to utilise the legal form to mediate the capital-labour relationship, and the extent to which particular representatives of capital and labour are, in their attitudes and behaviour, conditioned by legalities. In general terms, the legal form can be a declaration either of what the legal subject cannot do without fear of punitive sanction (prohibitions); or a declaration that in certain affairs the law will not intervene (immunities); or a declaration that it will uphold and defend specific acts of legal subjects (rights). Britain's particular liberal constitution comprises laws which specify rights to property ownership and rights to protection from injury or damage, but no more general rights. The bulk of English law has constituted prohibitions and in the case of economic affairs, until recent decades, immunities. Freedom from the law (immunities) does not lead to the same result as freedoms specified by the law. In the latter instance lawyers are obliged to define the legal subject to which the freedoms attach. In the former lawyers take no part in such definition. The history of the British trade unions, which from the second half of the 19th century began to enjoy legal immunities, is one of self-definition in negotiation with employers. British law, although constraining employers somewhat through protective employment legislation and although punitively sanctioning individual workers for disobedience, did not participate in the emergence of collective forms of representation and bargaining until the 20th century. Employers and unions thus developed their own forms of regulation and practice, dubbed industrial relations systems. In that sense we can understand British industrial relations as the quasi-legal structures developing in an economic sphere of relations from which the state, by the logic of its own liberal constitution, had virtually excluded itself.

The State-Capital Relationship

The British example of the state's relative and transient non-interference makes more clear than some instances that the objective reality of power relations in capitalism is essentially established in modes of appropriation and exploitation which effectively create capital (private or state) and labour. The moves to separate an individual's personal productive capacities directly from what he or she could consume (as, for example, with the enclosure of the common land), were long ago recognised by those with most to lose, and were resisted. The resistance ensured that such changes had to be enforced. The development of capitalism was thus politically contingent. It was so in a double sense, not only of enforcement but also of seduction. Many of the people hitherto bound together by the structures of a feudal political economy, elite and serf, saw the allure of capitalism in terms already discussed—as the road to fortune, status, power and freedom. Capitalism was not historically the first invention of expropriation and accumulation; rather it was a relatively novel and notionally more liberal form of these political processes.

This account of the state is somewhat at odds with the classic Marxist account both in its strong version ('the state is a derivative function of capital', for example, Harris, 1983) and in its weak version ('the state has a degree of autonomy but nonetheless is ultimately constituted and bounded by the operations of capital,' for example, Esping-Anderson *et al.*, 1976; Poulantzas, 1975). [Indeed the 'relative autonomy' school of thought has been dismissed by Hindess (1983) as mere 'gestural evasion' of what is finally an economic determinist perspective. Certainly it is a weak argument set against the recognition that all social beings, whether individually or collectively, exist in a state of relative autonomy.]

The view that the state is a legitimating agent acting on behalf of capital understates the extent to which capital is capable of making its own legitimating deals—at the grand level by invoking the philosophy of individualism and competition, at more local levels by participating in collective bargaining and industrial relations arrangements (see, for example, the work of Salaman and Thompson, 1980). Similarly, by construing the state as servant of capital, the extent to and manner in which the state makes use of and controls capital is obscured. This could be important to the development of capital since differential state attention will tend to favour and stimulate some sectors of capital more than others. The British state's very early recognition of the advantages of efficient credit and financial mechanisms (initially to fund privateering expeditions on behalf of the Crown: see McNeill, 1983), manifested in the establishment of the Bank of England in 1694, and its subsequent scrupulous attention to the demands of the City of London (ibid.; Harris, 1983) is a case in point. This raises the matter of cultural/historical specificities in the state-capital relationship. Both France and Britain, for example, stand as capitalist societies but the French have shown a repeated preference for subjecting capital to the political will of the Republic, whereas in Britain the state has, on balance and over time, more often adopted the politics of capital. Even here in the United Kingdom, however, the state in the 20th century has—as definer, provisioner and protector of the 'public good'—

moved into a position where, to a very high degree, it can impose terms on access to domestic markets, materials, labour power, investment capital, and so on. To do business in the UK, capital must accept such terms or find ways to circumvent or change them. Offe's (1984) argument, for example, of a capital-dependent welfare state also identifies the corresponding reliance of capital on state provision of public goods and contracts. The relationship is essentially one of 'brokerage', to use Boissevain's (1974) arguments, and one can suggest that it always has been. Elsewhere in the world the state has commandeered economic enterprise more or less *in toto*.

The State as a Polity

These various points raise what seems to be the most serious omission in the classic Marxist account. That is, the failure to accord much significance to political goals which are uniquely those of the state rather than direct or indirect expressions of the will of capital. Indeed there seems nowadays to be a consensus emerging that the state does have distinct interests, and that these lie in domestic order and international relations (see review by Pierson, 1984). Poulantzas (1978), for example, regards domestic political struggle so significant as to construe the very structuring of the state as 'constituted-divided' by domestic political tensions. This interpretation is related to the Marxist contention that, to develop, the capitalist order must have separated out the economic and political spheres of action, an argument we have already attempted to dismantle. It is often taken as a claim that the general population have always figured politically in the history of the modern state. In the sense of exercising negative control rather than proactive power, to invoke Olson (1965), that claim is credible. But it must be qualified by two observations: (1) that elite advantage succeeds precisely by excluding people from the political process; and (2) that exclusionary tactics can be maintained at informal levels where political management indicates they best be moderated at the formal. It is then a matter of empirical inquiry whether the history of particular modern states is a history of the extent to which the elite's exclusionary powers are genuinely eroded by popular pressure and leverage.

That 20th-century electoral politics have made a significant impact on state action is nowadays commonly acknowledged but variously interpreted (Skocpol, 1979; Miliband, 1982). Some writers (for example Djilas, 1957; Devine, 1985) identify 'state managers' as 'a class for themselves', constantly seeking to balance the demands of capital against those of the enfranchised working class. Other writers, such as Bornstein *et al.* (1984) instead highlight the significance of international political tensions to the shaping of the modern state; and Urry (1981: 82), stressing this aspect, argues that 'there is no single capitalist state, merely a multiplicity of conflicting nation-states.' Certainly, the 'relative autonomy' of the multinational sections of capital is helping to destabilise established political systems and therefore is provoking the political will to seek new modes of stabilisation. The new modes seem to be developing in two distinct arenas; one held by the nation states, the other by multinational capital. Taking the latter first, as already discussed, there are indications that the discrete organisations of multinational capital are developing as 'polities'.

The second arena of political change is that held by the nation states. Here it is reflected both at domestic and international levels. Domestically there are developments discernible which are similar to those evidenced within the multinational corporations. Via legislative and administrative interventions, the state is recentralising substantial areas of public expenditure decision-making (Robinson, 1978), is seeking to curb the scope and powers of trade union action, is displacing collective bargaining in favour of state fiat, is reducing the powers of local authorities, and is generally intensifying its ideological work. By these legislative and administrative interventions, the individual citizen is increasingly obliged to regard his/her rights and responsibilities as being in relation to central government rather than to intermediary bodies or non-state public organisations. The gradual demise of the intermediary and non-state public organisations reduces the scope for citizen-to-citizen ties and collaborative endeavours which might resist central government; thus, there is an erosion of the public sphere both in its meaningfulness and in its mechanisms. Should these trends persist, they would imply, albeit as a caricature, a society fashioned along mass lines: that is, a securely placed and more or less unified elite addressing a mass of individuals structurally and ideologically held in atomistic relation to one another.

The combination of these political developments among the elites of state and capital has produced what one commentator has described as 'the overworld', an international bourgeoisie (Levinson, 1978), although the epithet perhaps overstates the degree of unity of purpose among these people. At the international level, for example, the effort at economic and military co-operation among modern states has implied the construction of political systems potentially capable of containing the more independent sections of capital. Thus, just as the individual state developed partially in relation to home-based capital, now inter-state alliances are developing partly in relation to internationally-based capital. This is not to argue economic determinism, except in the very loose sense that prevailing capacities to generate wealth and its distribution will be of acute concern to those determined to rule. Nor is it to argue the capital-derivative version of the state. Political power remains as always an exercise in raid and trade, albeit disguised by legitimating ideological arguments. To the extent that raiding and trading could be conducted independently of the state, the state has perforce been obliged to negotiate with traders and raiders. Successful enterprise in these spheres, however, has augmented the powers of the state, allowing it gradually to subsume ever larger sections of economic and punitive capacities under its authority; a contradiction of capitalism perhaps that by its own successes in delivering the goods, capital strengthens the political machinery which eventually subordinates it.

Or rather, carries the potential to subordinate it. For there are limits to the process of subordination, and these lie in two directions. One is as already indicated: in relation to international and corporate capital the state may yet lack the ability to dominate and direct. For the other, in relation to those sections of capital which are potentially constrainable by the political machinery, the limits are more complexly determined, being very much a matter of calculation and belief about the political and economic costs of subordination. Political leaders, for example, may well be persuaded that further state control (to date usually manifested in the form of large-scale administrative bureaucracies) will damage productivity and innovation in important areas of enterprise. Additionally, they may regard the operations of the market as generating forms of social control and discipline which are expedient to state interests. Similarly, they may be persuaded that certain degrees of freedom must be allowed to the civilian population if the state is to remain legitimate. Why they should be so persuaded will in turn be largely contingent on the character, processes and directions of domestic political relations. One of the parties active in this scenario is 'the people'. To these our attention is now turned.

LABOUR

Dependency, Discrimination and Status

If capitalist interests dominated modern western societies in the two centuries from 1780, it is because other politically active elements were sufficiently persuaded, or cowed, to go along with them. Why might they be persuaded? How might they be cowed? Taking the latter first, we find no reason to differ from Marx's judgement (1976: 875) that the history of 'expropriation is written in the annals of mankind in letters of blood and fire'. As will be evident from the significance attached to the state's monopoly of the means of violence, discussed above, a clear connection is seen between rule and the capacity to coerce. But it is not the persuasive qualities of brutality and deprivation, or their threat, which is of interest. This is not a callous remark; merely that from an analytical point of view, these sanctioning operations are too simple to merit much investigation. What is of greater interest are those situations where the choice not to co-operate is still reasonable but constraints yet operate to favour co-operation. How in the abstract can we conceptualise the nature of these constraints? Here we concur with Giddens (1982: 199) that 'power relations in social systems can be regarded as relations of autonomy and dependence . . .' The earlier discussion of the brokerage relation between state and capital is a case in point. But are there similar brokerage relations between state and citizen, capital and labour?

Dependency relations can be/are substantially struc-tured—sometimes wittingly, sometimes fortuitously, but always with a political articulation and reflecting not simply the discrimi-nation between those who command resources and those who do not, but also the terms in which that discrimination is conducted and legitimised, the latter being central to the stability of the relation. Jean Genet once commented that power lies in the ability to impose definitions. That is not the full story, of course, since the ability to impose definitions is inevitably skewed in favour of those commanding resources. But to continue Giddens' point (ibid.: 200), 'actors in subordinate positions are never wholly dependent, and are often very adept at converting whatever resources they possess into some degree of control over the conditions of reproduction of the system'. How under capitalism is this degree of control achieved? From our previous arguments it will be evident that we do not accept the view of the state as a derivative function of capital. But it is the case that we so construe labour. Labour, that is, is created by the processes or modes of appropriation and exploitation which distinguish capitalism. The political input of capitalism is the creation of dependencies via the removal from the masses of people of any means to survival other than the exchange of their labour power. This is rationalised as an economic exchange, but the objective reality is that of a power relationship of considerable inequality. As such, the general interests of capital and state in securing rule through subordination are exactly matched. Nonetheless, differences in state policies can make a significant difference to the strengths of organised labour. Thus Huxley *et al.* (1986) report that the recent downturn in the fortunes of American trade unions cannot be explained by such things as the changing composition of the labour force, since the same trends are even more adverse in Canada where union membership continues to grow. The difference, they say, lies in Canada's collectivist and statist traditions of public policy as compared to America's individualist liberalism. (At the same time it needs to be noted that Canadian law, like US law, specifies which grades of worker may or may not unionise. Managerial workers tend to be legally debarred from unionising, a fact which persuades US employers to class unusually high proportions of workers as managerial.)

In a liberal arena the strong have the advantage. The people in command of the means of production are also in a position to dictate the basic terms on which other people enter (or are excluded from) the division of labour (Sabel, 1985; Reushemeyer, 1986). It is in the interests of such commanders that those seeking entry should do so in competition with one another. Such competition has not merely economic consequences for the price and availability of labour, it also has political consequences. These follow because, to create and maximise advantage in the labour markets, particular workers must organise to exclude others from entry to their trade. By operating restrictive practices, most especially around those points in the capital-labour relationship where employers have greatest need for specialised labour, workers can advance their interests, albeit sectionally. Thus workers of their own volition, in pursuit of immediate interests, will utilise the available terms of discrimination against other would-be workers. The terms of discrimination, whatever their particularities, will legitimate the greater rights and privileges of some by stressing the weaknesses, incapacities or unworthiness of others. Where the embracing polity is a nation state committed to defence of its sovereignty, the dominant culture will be both nationalistic and militaristic. The imperial and patriarchal impulses of the ruling elites will be duly conveyed in the practices of worker organisation such that women, children and non-nationals will be the prime candidates for exclusion from, or second-class status within, labour markets. The history of western trade unions shows that they succeed best where they are in a position to practice white, male chauvinism (Cockburn, 1983; Barker and Allen, 1976; Green, 1979). For working class political movements, of course, this is a serious failing in that it fragments rather than unifies popular resistance.

Under bourgeois arrangements, debates and decisions about the terms of discrimination have been held to belong most properly (although by no means exclusively) to the political arena, that is, to the constitutional mechanisms which relate citizens to state. But the state is by no means a disinterested party. It wants social peace, economic strength and an effective war-fighting capacity. The people, its citizens, are important in all these respects. *Only if they co-operate as law-abiding citizens, as workers and as soldiers, can the state's requirements be met. The people thus have a basic leverage.*

The dimension of citizenship is highly important to the manner in which capital addresses its workers. As has been pointed out before by Wallerstein (1983), in some countries capital makes use of slave and serf labour; his explanation is that such labour is so readily substitutable as not to warrant humane treatment from its owners, particularly when the labourers are not also the intended consumers. As he says, labour remains a commodity but the terms of its 'purchase' can differ widely from one situation to the next. One of the factors to delimit the situation will be the relation of the political authorities to the labourers. The beauty to the state of slaves and serfs is that they have no claim to political status, and therefore no claim to state provisioning or consideration. So long as their political potency can be kept enfeebled (by malnutrition, intimidation, prejudice or isolation) and so long as the state has *no direct need* of them, slaves and serfs cannot reasonably look to the state to save them. The battle for freeman status in medieval England was won gradually only as political authorities came to recognise that they stood to lose more than they might gain by resisting the changing social relations carried along by emergent capitalism. Even then, under Blackstone's influence (Kahn-Freund, 1977), notions of serfdom continued to colour English legal interpretations of the employment relationship until well into the 19th century.

The Phenomenon of Waged Labour

If the existence of waged labour cannot automatically be predicted by capitalist operations, then by logical extension the definition of capitalism cannot be grounded in the existence of waged labour or, related, of labour markets. For very many workers in capitalist society, there never was nor will be a clear, unmediated relation to the employer, such as is implied in the narrow economic construction of labour as a commodity sold for a price under conditions of market competition. Just as slavery and serfdom denote a political status *vis-à-vis* the exploiting elites, so apprenticeships, guilds, closed shops, family work, outwork, and so on, constitute the social and political conditioning of market relations between worker and employer. Children working at home to fulfil the terms of a subcontract secured by their parent from a local wool merchant are no less a part of capital's division of labour than is the factoryhand—although their experiencing of the relation may be substantially and significantly different. Similarly, the idea of competitive labour markets cannot be held to the point of ruling out recognition of labour immobility, often politically enforced for reasons of social order and administration, and inadequate market information. Labour immobility and ignorance of alternatives may sometimes work to capital's advantage, sometimes not, depending on circumstances.

In the industrialised western nations, labour typically is waged, so it is appropriate to ask under what circumstances such a phenomenon arises. The answer finally must be an empirical one but likely factors can be indicated theoretically as a four-fold configuration of the needs of employers for particular kinds of labour, not cheaply or readily substitutable; the needs of producers for workers who are also consumers with disposable incomes; the location of the labour force within a state polity which requires the support of workers as citizens, taxpayers and soldiers; and the political acumen and mobilising strength of the workers, that is, their ability to organise and negotiate around the perceived dependencies of political and economic leaders.

Labour and Class

In relation to this last point, some accounts of the impact of capitalism on labour seem over-determined. Melossi and Pavarini (1981), for example, argue that the external applications of discipline and the relations of direct dependence which character-ised feudal social rule fragment with the movement to market relations of indirect dependence, and prompt a reworking of social order mechanisms towards the internationalisation of discipline and towards systems of particular authorities rather than a general authority. The internationalisation of discipline, they say, following Foucault (1977), is part and parcel of the redefinition of the individual as 'worker', 'whose body can be habituated to determinate movements, to repetition and regularity' (1981: 91) so as to render it a machine or an appendage of a machine. While accepting that the impulses so to construct the worker are active in industrialised society, it remains true that many individuals remain able to identify and resist them—if for no other reason than that the disciplined worker so beloved alike of state and capital must be encouraged to self-indulgence as a consumer. It is also the case that disciplined workers, accustomed to co-operative organisation and direction in the workplace, can carry these learnt capacities into acts of resistance. Statesmen, capitalists, labour leaders and theorists alike have long since recognised the formidable threat which this potentiality poses to the political and economic order.

It is in this configuration that the phenomenon of 'class' should perhaps be located. 'Class' addresses the issue of relation to the means of production. These relations are expressed and mediated politically. Arguably, 'working class' should be taken not as embracing all those dispossessed of the means of production but more narrowly and particularly as referring to those whose relation to the capitalist political order is both determined *and* determining. Their dependent status would be otherwise if it were not for the elite commandeering of the means of production, but some bargaining power nonetheless accrues to them as a result of elite dependencies upon them. These dependencies can be manipulated and intensified by successful working class control of the labour supply and, in the period of enfranchisement, by working class action at the ballot box. Rioting and disorder can similarly be utilised to propel the elites into a dilemma of choice—either repression at the risk of alienating the people whose co-operation remains essential, or indulgence at the risk of increasing popular expectations. The usual choice is a bit of both, applied discriminately so as to divide and rule. But the general point stands, that the leaders of the political economy of the modern world cannot totally resist the claims of those who comprise the 'working class', and must therefore develop strategies and tactics of management. The repertoire of management techniques will be various according to the field of application (for example, workplace, parliamentary, welfare and so on), and will penetrate different dimensions of state-capital-labour relations according to calculations of the material and political costs of failure to do so. It can be theoretically anticipated that *where state and/or capital dependencies are acute, the repertoire will afford the working class many rights to participate in decision-making and to enjoy material comfort and security.*

Instability in the Relations of State, Capital and Labour

But, of course, there remain material inequalities among the parties and these—given the persistence of a political will to challenge or reassert them—ensure instability in the relations. Particularly the material inequalities are manifested and exacerbated by differential command over different areas of technological application. The mode of production and the mode of warfare figure on the human landscape not in the sense of being technological determinants but in the sense that, through these, inventors and elites alike seek their fame and fortune. Through their application, the political will of the few exerts constraining and determining influences on the many. But the pursuit of further advantage, or to dispel disadvantage, ensures that the political will is constantly being reformulated. For example, the level of state demand for soldiers is a function of the intensity of inter-state rivalries *and* the prevailing military technology. As military technology shifts away from the foot soldier to the machine, state demand for soldiers diminishes while its demands for a wealth-generating, tax-paying economy increase. Similarly, capital's demand for labour decreases where machine technology replaces human effort but rationalising that investment intensifies capital's demand for ever richer and more voracious consumers.

A series of paradoxes becomes evident. Where conscription into a mass army or into mass production cease to be major life-experiences for the majority, the internalised discipline of these experiences dissipates. Social order becomes increasingly contingent upon other citizenship and market relations. However, market relations—which may or may not still require discipline in employment from the individual as worker—more and more require self-indulgence from the same person as consumer. Similarly, the discourse of citizenship invites popular demand for the extension of political rights to include welfare rights. But the awarding of these then structures a greater popular dependency on the state and a substantial claim on state-commandeered resources. To the extent that the demands are met, they entail an expansion in the state's administrative mechanisms which simultaneously affords the state new or enhanced means of surveillance and control. In turn, the popular experience of this relation as repressive and debilitating can help foment popular unrest and disloyalty. But so also can state action which neglects the popular demand for welfare provisioning.

In short, so long as wealth-generating, tax-paying and consumption propensities attach to the mass of the population, both state and capital have irreducible dependencies on these people. They are in consequence caught up in a series of political tensions and paradoxes. One comes then to the conclusion that there exists an incentive to both state and capital to seek ways to locate wealth-generation, tax-payment and consumption elsewhere than in the masses, that is, rights can be withdrawn and claims ignored as dependencies can be made to diminish. Should it prove possible to be fully independent of the masses, then the rights and provisioning of those people could be withdrawn absolutely, relegating large sections of the working class to the ranks of the dispossessed or, conversely, blocking the entry of the dispossessed to the ranks of the working class. It could be argued that this last condition is already well-demonstrated in some countries, for example Brazil, Peru and Colombia, where the political economy has developed more in relation to world than to domestic conditions. Here, on average, 60 per cent of the population is calculated to exist in a 'black' or informal sphere, beyond the ambit of state and capital and not really significant to either. It could further be argued that the above logic is evident in western European nations as an historical process, that is, that there was a high point of working class rights developing from 1850 to 1950, contingent on extensive capital development, on the demands of mass warfare, and on a highly organised and strident labour movement. That configuration, it can be argued, has now largely passed: the ranks of the dispossessed are swelling, civil and employments rights are shrinking, the welfare state is 'withering away'.

There are, however, significant cultural differences between Third World and western experience, largely because capitalism grew from within the western nations rather than being an invader from abroad. A first and obvious point is that, in the west, neither state nor capital is yet able to dispense with the services of the vast majority of people. The working class is still around and still numerous. Moreover, its presence is politically embedded in the very fabric of the nation. The institutions which came into being with labour's rise to power, or were substantially penetrated by labour, cannot now be attacked without disturbing and provoking their incumbents and those whose interests they serve. Two of the parties who have seen their interests served by these institutions have been the state and capital. Both the state and capital have made their respective bids for legitimacy in part by demonstrating a preparedness to create and respond to labour through one or more of these institutions. At the same time, the institutions have been viewed expediently by capital and the state as tools of popular management and mediation. Now to disturb the institutions means disturbing the basis of claims to legitimacy: it also creates a need to design new means of management and mediation. These considerations make for conservation of the status quo. What makes for change would seem to be the changes of fortune among states, capitalists and labour forces springing from their political efforts at structuring new alliances and, related, their differential command and application of the new electronic and other technologies. It is apparent that while there may be overall a single, remarkable direction of social change, the rate at which it occurs and the particular expression it takes will be contingent on the historical specificities of the country, conglomerate or alliance concerned. It is therefore appropriate to turn attention now to one such historical case—Britain.

3 From Feudalism to Industrial Capital

LABOUR IN THE TRANSITIONAL PERIOD

Capitalism, said Marx, constitutes a radical change in the relations of interdependence. What he had in mind was, in one respect, the creation of landless labourers reliant on wages for survival and, in another, the political ascendance of those in command of productive, wealth-generating capacities. Speaking generally of the impact of capitalism on labouring people, Marx understood it as a process away from the personalised relations of subordination which characterised feudalism towards the alienation of labour power from its human source, and its commodification for sale on the market. Under the ethos of capitalist market relations, the seller of labour should logically be free both to contract (that is, to select and negotiate with the purchaser on equal terms) and to associate (so as to improve the commodity's price by controlling its supply). According to this logic the transition from feudalism to capitalism should be a transition in constitutional-legal terms from status to contract relations.

If one then asks the question, when did British labourers pass through this process, the answer in a strict sense is that they did not. In the operations of English law, no contract of employment began to emerge until well into the second half of the 19th century, and even now it is not fully realised. Under English contract law British workers have still to secure full legal equality: their condition remains essentially that of subordination to an employer accorded superior legal rights by virtue of his being the property owner (Hepple, 1986; Kahn-Freund, 1977). In other words, in the narrow sense of contract law the position of British workers is still that of status.

But there are, of course, real differences in the position of labourers this century which are traceable to developments in the past. While the law stands as a relatively clear expression of elite preferences and concerns, it does not automatically penetrate all forms of social relations and may be at some considerable remove from objective social practices. This has certainly been the case in British history. Further, contract law is not the only legal instrument impinging on the employment relationship. In Britain the contract of employment is, as it were, surrounded on the one hand by the English common law, and on the other, by statutory interventions. Under the operations of the common law, judges have a good deal of autonomy in implying the terms and conditions of a particular contract where these are not explicit. This has naturally allowed for a substantial judicial input to certain, legally tested, employment relations. In addition and enjoying supremacy, statutory interventions have conveyed (or rather, attempted to convey) Cabinet and parliamentary concerns into these relations.

But, as said earlier, the contract of employment did not begin to develop in Britain until late in the 19th century (with the repeal of the Master & Servant Act, 1875). Up to that point it was the operations of the common law (that is, judge-made law) and statutes which expressed elite concerns. Even then the law was often ten paces behind social developments.

What were these developments? The ideal-typical position for labourers under feudalism was serfdom, that is, servility to a seigneurial or monastic landowner. The serf as a 'natural' inferior had a duty to labour and pay rent on the estates of his/her 'natural' superior. But that superior was in return supposed to honour obligations to the inferiors in the sense of protecting them in their weaknesses, maintaining the peace between them, and not encroaching on the minimum access to land, foraging and grazing rights deemed necessary to self-sufficiency. Thus at one and the same time, the feudal hierarchy was explicitly economic and political. The problem with ideal-typical formulations, however, is that they capture the flavour of history but at the expense of its 'deviations'. It cannot be said that in Britain there was just one type of serf. In the 12th century the Saxon social order of Mercia and Wessex, and the Danelaw communities of the north and east, were overlaid by the occupying forces of a Norman warrior-caste. Out of that cultural mixture emerged by the late 14th century what Dobson (1983: 1) describes as 'an extraordinary complexity of social relationships . . .' At elite levels, the aristocrats and religious leaders had been supplemented by a new 'middle layer' of lawyers and judges, shire gentryfolk, the representatives of finance and merchant capital, and the representatives of urban administration. At subordinate levels the complexity comprised a mixture of rural workers (some still held serf-like on feudal estates, some holding new contractual tenancies), artisans operating in the towns and the countryside, town workers (sometimes contracted, sometimes not) and petty traders.

There is much dispute as to when the wage-labour form became common in England, the evidence being fragmentary. Duby (in Cipolla, 1972: 188) says that by the 11th century at least one-third of the English peasant population worked for a wage, this being the preference of many of the great landlords. It is consistent with other evidence indicating that the money economy was well-established by the 11th century, that is, within feudalism. But Brown (1982) argues to the contrary that even by the late 14th century, although spreading rapidly, the wage-labour form was not typical of work relations. Bridbury (1986), critically surveying the evidence and the arguments, is prepared only to conclude that there were more wage-earners in 1524 than in 1334, and that the majority of these were located in the countryside rather than in the growing towns. Nonetheless, the 1381 Peasant Revolt yielded much evidence of dissatisfaction with serf status, as working people sought the freedom both to take over land and work vacated by plague victims, and to access the royal law courts which by this time for freemen constrained the arbitrary rule of the seigneurial courts. This desire for freedom was typically expressed as a preference for the money-wage relation (Dobson, 1983).

In that they broke the older feudal notions of personal obligation upwards and downwards in a hierarchy, money-wage relations prompted the creation of new mechanisms of social order. These new mechanisms can be characterised as mercantilism: still an explicit unity of political and economic leadership and still a closed society structured on the servility of the propertyless. The closure was secured substantially by the creation of monopolies and oligarchies around the significant sectors of wealth-generation—namely, agriculture, commerce and artisan production—which in turn were regulated by public and crown-state authorities. In agriculture workers were either still locked into feudal structures or became wage-workers but with no gains in freedom under the law. Indeed the reverse is true. The crown-state of the 14th to 16th centuries saw agriculture as so crucial that it attempted via statutory interventions to direct labour to it, and to wage-fix within it. In the Statute of Labourers 1351 the crown-state (disturbed by the threat to its war finances of the acute labour shortages caused by the Black Death) fixed wages for what was then a predominantly agricultural economy at 1346 levels, required artisans and craftsmen not to raise their charges, and compelled all the able-bodied to work. At the same time attempts were made to limit labour mobility so that people could escape neither public administration nor low earnings, a theme picked up again in the 1376 Petition against Vagrants (Dobson, 1983). The Statute of Labourers legally enshrined the inequality of the parties—that is, the labourer was construed as servile and having a duty to labour on whatever terms a master might decree. The Petition against Vagrants imputed weakness and untrustworthiness to the status of vagrant, and began the process of discriminating deserving from undeserving poor. In 1563 the Statute of Artificers similarly attempted to wage-fix, to limit labour mobility, and to direct the flow of workers between agriculture and the emergent industrial occupations; while another Elizabethan statute which prohibited cottage-building to all who could not access a minimum of four acres constituted a direct attack on the non self-sufficient. By the 16th century notions of the right to work were widespread as an attribute of Protestantism but were understood as the right of the crown-state to assign work, premised on the universal obligation of the propertyless to labour. Throughout the mercantilist period such beliefs were instrumental in elite efforts to curb vagrancy, to regulate the poor and to ensure an adequate supply of labour to agriculture.

Any early hopes which British labouring people may have had in the freedom of the wage-labour form were dashed as the evidence mounted of the extent to which the politically dominant sections were prepared to use work and the law as agents of social control and exploitation. Moreover, the elites had additional means available for the extraction of wealth from labouring people, for example, fines, rents, fees for the use of monopolised essential services, dispossession of land and produce, and so on. Historically it is possible that these other means were more important than the use of the law to control wages and labour mobility. That would be the case if the law and objective social practices were sufficiently unsynchronised as to afford labouring people some relief, and there are some grounds for believing this to be so. The Domesday Book of William the Conqueror in the 12th century was the first systematic, official effort to gather information about the population, but that exercise was not repeated on the same scale until the late 17th century. (In both instances the official information was concerned to identify the forms and amount of income of different people and the degree of access which the state could secure to it. In the 17th century collation people were categorised into 'classes', each 'class' denoting tax-ability—George, 1953.) The evidence is thus inadequate, and we cannot be sure that wages were the predominant form of earnings in the late 14th century. Even where wages were earned it was often in conjunction with some other form of support for self and family. For example, a rural family might cultivate the common fields, take in washing, knit stockings, and do summer work on the estates. Only the last-named occupation might be waged. Nonetheless, the Black Death—having killed between one-third and one-half of a population of four million— did diminish sharply the supply of labour to the predominantly agricultural occupations. And although under the Statute of Labourers, between 1351 and 1377, some 9000 prosecutions were brought (Churchill, 1956), there is also evidence of farm workers combining to bargain for improved terms and conditions, and of local landowners and local justices colluding to meet their demands. The need for labour power seems to have been, in some places, a stronger force than that of the law, and indeed no prosecutions can be found to have followed in the wake of the 1563 Statute of Artificers. Just as the Tudor abolition of serfdom was irrelevant in the sense that the practice had almost died out, so the repeal (in 1813–14) of the wage-fixing provisions of the Elizabethan and Jacobean labour laws was similarly irrelevant, the legal maximum being often converted by local deals into a minimum.

In large part the inapplicability of the law related to the stringency with which local justices interpreted it—for many of them an occupation not specified was an occupation not legally bound. By the late 16th century the number of occupations not legally bound, although not yet large, was growing. This seems to have been the result of an elite-led consumer boom setting the multiplier effect into motion, and propelling the country out of feudalism into industrialisation. It is indicated by the 1688 survey (King, 1953) that 50 per cent of the five and a half million people in England and Wales were existing below subsistence. Consumer demand was certainly not coming from them. The recovery of population numbers over the period 1500 to 1630 seems to have kept real wages low and put pressure on land-working systems of support. But the techniques of farming and animal husbandry did improve across the 16th and 17th centuries, slowly but surely generating agricultural surpluses which could then be taken to the market towns and the cities.

It is estimated that the number of market towns in England and Wales during Tudor and Stuart reigns grew to around 800 (Brown, 1982). The development of these towns was another remarkable feature of the mercantile period which saw, as a further mechanism for maintaining a closed society, the swallowing up of many artisan trades by guild organisation. At their strongest from the 12th to the early 16th century, the guilds constituted oligarchic structures of commercial and organisational regulation. By dictating standards of work, they could also enforce apprenticeships as the mode of entry to the trade and thus regulate the numbers operating within it. Since entry was thus restricted, the guild masters could also dictate the terms and conditions of subordinates, which they did in all spheres of subordinate conduct, moral and domestic as well as craftsmanship. Thus was hierarchy and status secured. Guild masters were well represented in the political structures of local administration and, since these related to central government structures, mastership constituted an important route whereby politicians of the day could influence the labour markets. There was indeed much accommodation between political and economic interests. As Hepple (1986) reports, right into the early 19th century private entrepreneurs conceded the political need for some degree of limitation on the full freedom of the worker to contract and to associate. Commensurately the political construction of the guild trades and other forms of commercial enterprise was as a private property whose owners could not by definition therefore be servile. In 1604 a committee of the then House of Commons expressed it (as quoted in R. Moss, 1975: 119) thus:

All free subjects are born inheritable as to their land so also

to the free exercise of their industry, in those trades whereto
they apply themselves and whereby they are to live.

Nonetheless the slow and uneven growth of consumer demand
which had originally contributed to the growth of the guilds,
over time and in places, accelerated sufficiently to provoke their
break-up. Growing consumer demand prompted journeymen to
abandon their masters and to seek an end to servility and low
earnings in independent organisation. In many instances the
restrictive practices of the guilds drove new entrepreneurs to
establish industry in new locations—thus, for example, wool
came to Bradford in West Yorkshire. Whereas the guilds had
been the traditional form of artisan labour organisation from the
Middle Ages, securing legal recognition and sometimes a Royal
Charter to operate a monopoly in their trade, by the 18th
century their ability to impose restrictive practices was declining
substantially. Their appeals to the state to reassert their legal
rights fell increasingly on deaf ears. In these appeals the construal
of a trade as 'property' persisted. Well into the 19th century
the London artificers were speaking against the repeal of the
apprenticeship clauses thus:

> The apprenticed artisans have collectively and individually
> an unquestionable right to expect the most extended protection
> from the Legislature, in the quiet and exclusive use and
> employment of their several arts and trades, which the law
> has already conferred upon them as a property. (Quoted in
> Bythell, 1969: 99)

Their appeal was lost, however, and in 1814 the apprenticeship
clauses were repealed, thus finally and legally confirming the
limits of a guild master's authority, and making more meaningful
the notion of a worker's freedom to contract.

Throughout the mercantile period changes were evident
towards a more specialised division of labour, towards the
separation of what one had the possibility to consume from what
one personally produced, and towards the increasing role of
merchant, finance and agricultural capital. By the second half
of the 18th century, with a population whose growth was
beginning to escalate dramatically, these developments had
progressed to the point that serfdom was truly a thing of the

past, and the number and range of wage-paying jobs had proliferated and become a norm. Growing numbers and growing diversity implied yet again substantial disturbance to older political structures. In many respects the labourer was now in a worse position. No longer subject to feudal or guild domination, he or she was also no longer embraced by 'noblesse oblige' or patriarchal responsibility. Within the new relations of the labour markets, employers were under no obligation to attend to the human frailties of those under their command, nor of those who, for whatever reason, were unemployed.

Until the law sanctioned freedom of association, workers were exposed as individuals to the power of employers. New social problems began to be recognised, often prompted by popular protest, of employer abuse, of work injuries, of unemployment or of poverty and none but the state and public authorities accepted any responsibility for their amelioration. The modes of intervention, however, tended to be repressive rather than helpful—protective social legislation being essentially a phenomenon of the 19th and 20th centuries. Indeed, from the 1750s the actions of the state and public authorities demonstrate a clear, new and growing preference to protect the interests of all employers—whether aristocratic, industrial or commercial—against those of workers. Whereas in the previous half century, Parliament (primarily of landowners) had supported artisans and workers against budding industrialists, and had on appeal through local justices fixed wages in line with local price levels, by the end of the century the state was legally and punitively upholding the right of all employers to fix freely the terms and conditions of employment. For the period 1715 to 1800 Dobson (1980) has recorded 386 'trade union' type disputes. Often these disputes were a form of 'bargaining by riot'—perhaps not surprising since there was no formal recognition of labour organisation or labour representation. The governments of the day treated these occurrences on a par with crime and sedition. In the earlier part of the 18th century this was especially where they challenged the state as employer; by the second half of the century it was also where they challenged employers in the private sector. Across the century there were some 40 statutes against combination and strikes culminating in the Combination Acts of 1799 and 1800. In addition, following the arson attacks attending the Nottingham miners' strike in 1767, the Malicious

Injuries to Property Act was passed; and in 1794 the Friendly Societies Act distinguished between trade unions and friendly societies, declaring the former illegal. This they remained until 1825.

The year 1780 roughly speaking marks the opening of the first industrial revolution—of cotton and textiles, of iron, railways, steam power and mechanisation. It also marks the beginning of dramatic changes in political attitudes towards state involvement in the economy and civil society. Formal, 'bureaucratised', organisation of employment was clearly not the norm for British economic enterprise in the 18th century. The only area of economic activity structured on the basis of rationalised organisation was in textiles, notably cotton. In the last quarter of the 18th century the cotton industry was still tiny, probably responsible for no more than one per cent of Gross National Product (GNP), although growing faster than any other sector save iron. But it was here that the vision of systematic, factory-organised production, structured around a new industrial technology, was stirring the political imagination. So well, in fact, did it stir that imagination that entire public policies were proposed in its terms. In the first quarter of the 18th century wage-labour had been the main focus of elite domestic action, and economic theories had stressed the relevance of wage levels to the balance of trade. By the last quarter, Adam Smith, population growth and the seductive prospects of the application of science to people and machines came together to change all that.

Between 1780 and 1841 Britain's population doubled to around 20 million. Proving the limits of the old medieval technology and the as yet inadequate spread of industrialised occupations, poverty both on the land and in the towns accelerated. The loss of the American colonies in 1783 had disturbed both business and military confidence, and these confidences were not recovered by subsequent success against Bonaparte. The engagement with France had brought acute labour shortages in agriculture and provoked inflation. With the close of hostilities, one-quarter of a million men were suddenly released onto the labour markets just as corn prices fell. The result was severe wage reductions and increasing numbers seeking poor relief. Since poor relief was a charge on property rates—even though it involved means testing and a compulsion to work if able—the increase in relief expenditures provoked calls for its abolition. The proposals were heard by politicians informed by the arguments of influential theorists such as Smith (1976), Bentham (1938–43), Defoe (1728) and Locke (1696, 1964, 1975), and of judges such as Blackstone (1765). Locke and Blackstone were together in arguing the right to property as 'natural' (that is, inalienable), Locke proposing that 'government has no end but the preservation of property' (1975). Smith, probably the most influential, was at the same time arguing that self-interest, freed to express itself economically, would lead to a balance of the economy and to consumer sovereignty. This became the rationale of *laissez-faire* economics, a rationale for aggressive, socially irresponsible capitalism. In such a perspective the government's role was to be limited to the maintenance of a legal and social framework within which economic enterprise could be left to its own dynamic. But this was never interpreted to mean that politicians were redundant: there was still the important business of ensuring territorial integrity and sovereignty. In terms of domestic affairs, the interpretation of that continuing political responsibility evolved as one of facilitating self-help. The duty of the state was to construct the conditions that would enable and encourage people to be fully responsible for themselves (exceptions being seen as women and children, who were to the contrary construed as the responsibility of a male head of household or of the public authorities).

Such encouragement extended to cultural and other interventions. Thus, in the wake of the wars with France, the Million Act of 1818 committed one million pounds of public expenditure to the building of churches in the growing urban-industrial centres. This is one reflection of elite concerns with popular motivations, older beliefs on the matter being challenged by the social and political writers of the day. Smith's theories, for example, for the first time concentrated theoretical attention on the significance of consumption, and on the possibility/likelihood that use-values of commodities need not be reflected in market values. In this theoretical shift, the imbalanced view of wage-levels being relevant only to production costs was implicitly challenged, but so also were notions of what might motivate labourers to work. Bentham, for his part, addressed specifically the issue of poor law relief. His solution was predicated on the more common belief that poverty made for industriousness, obedience and lower wage demands: legislative intervention was not to disturb but rather to support that motivational link to capital accumulation. To that end he proposed, for the poor and labouring peoples, the provision of workhouses, schools, prisons and relief systems which would both inculcate attitudes of obedience and create systems of administrative control (Annette, 1979). The goal was the individualised internalisation of discipline; for Bentham, the means was the PANOPTICON, a central tower pierced with windows from which unseen warders could survey the occupants of a surrounding cell-like building. A more thoroughly oppressive and repressive administrative structure is difficult to imagine but in this form the first clear proposal for the systematic control of the British labouring and poor peoples was laid before Parliament.

It is perhaps fortunate that Bentham's ideas for 'social engineering' proved too radical and were rejected. So also was regarded the proposal to abolish poor relief—the Amendment Act of 1834 instead continued its basic provisions, although making significant changes in the mode of administration (see chapter 4). Some authors have pondered whether this implies a resurgence of paternalist and/or religious conscience in government policy-making (Brown 1982: 71; Dunkley, 1979). Possibly; but if so, a thoroughgoing paternalism best expressed in Blackstone's judicial treatment of labour relations. His contribution to British labour law, effective from 1776 until well into the 19th century and building upon the presuppositions of the Statutes of Labourers and Artificers, was to locate the labour relationship in the Law of Persons, that is, in family law. The worker, legally treated as 'servant', was construed as a responsibility and subordinate of the patriarchal 'master', just as were the wife and children (Kahn-Freund, 1977). That the world outside the heads and life-experiences of the judges was a different place did not matter. By such legal interpretations any British development of a clear, coherent, usable contract of employment was delayed until the second half of the 19th century.

The 18th century closed with the process of industrialisation well underway in the north of the country, with new employers joining the older ones in enjoying political privilege and legal rights, and with the British labouring classes, however diversified in their work experiences, still heavily subordinated by elite mechanisms of control and exploitation. But, albeit as yet undeveloped, the popular experiences, resentments and most importantly the groundwork for collective organisation and resistance were also in place, gathering momentum for the 19th century.

THE ROOTS OF THE TRANSITION

The above has sought to demonstrate changes in work relations and authority structures for British labouring people in the period from feudalism to early industrialisation. These changes are associated typically with what has been characterised as the emergence of capitalism, and Britain has been the nation accredited with its first showings. It is appropriate, therefore, to consider what were the conditions in Britain which fed these developments. On that point a large number of theses are already available. Some writers emphasise the pressure of general population growth on resources: in the earlier period of the 14th century this is seen to have been abruptly exacerbated by dramatic labour shortages caused by the Black Death (Postan, 1972); in the later period of the 18th century it is attributed to the availability of cheap food generated by the Agricultural Revolution (Mathias, 1969: 15). Some indicate the significance of merchant capital's accumulation of profit in the Middle East subsequently seeking European investment outlets (Sweezy, 1954). Poggi (1978) by comparison identifies the political role of semi-autonomous European towns around the 14th century, and within them the ascendance of an urban middle class able to practice and proselytise new impersonal and contractual modes of civil conduct. Duby (1974) for his part points more simply to the desire of the great landlords to increase their wealth through technical innovation: Hilton (1978) talks of elite efforts to outmanoeuvre peasants increasingly rebellious as a consequence of excessive taxation; and Wallerstein (1974a) argues for Britain to be seen as a subunit of an emergent world economy in which all economic activities including the division of labour are internationalised.

Some empirical evidence can be offered to support any one of these arguments, only Wallerstein's rejecting a contingent account in favour of a systemic one. Even supposing Wallerstein's arguments to be fitting, they still leave open the empirical question of the precise articulation of capital (the dynamo of his emergent world economy) with Britain's extant ruling interests. In that regard, we would argue strongly for inclusion, indeed dominance, on the list of contingencies, of elite concerns to establish and preserve a territorially-demarcated sovereignty and social order. In this we coincide with the arguments of Veblen (1964, 1970) and Schumpeter (1934, 1961).

Territorial command necessitates both an internal and an external focus of attention and energies, and the apparatus to effect policies in both directions. The apparatus will have to be paid for, which further necessitates would-be commanders to attend to wealth-extraction. Thus, power and wealth will be sought not only for the pleasure but also for the more instrumental reason that without them rivals and insurgents cannot be quelled. More precisely, this means that wherever a set of people attempt to command a specific territory, they must have the means to make war on outsiders, to impose law and order on insiders and to extract wealth from sources at home and beyond. Can these imperatives of command be turned to the explanation of the emergence of capital (and thus of labour as its derivative)? If the answer to that question is yes, then we move from a contingent and empirically-constrained account to a more systemic and general one. Such an answer is what we attempt below. In brief we look firstly at the consequences for economic developments of elite political and military competition; and secondly at the consequences for the domestic population of elite concerns for subordinate obedience and productivity.

Economic Consequences of Elite Competition

For our purposes, the first territory to be settled was Britain: a land subjected for centuries to invading armies and not until the close of the Anglo-French dynastic wars in 1453, and the resolution of the War of the Roses in 1485, more or less secure. Even then the tensions around a Catholic versus a Protestant monarchy kept political stability at bay until the 1688 Settlement. As Straka puts it, 'politically speaking, the Middle Ages in England do not end in 1485 but in 1688' (1973: ix). Those Middle Ages are characterised by a feudal social order evolving into mercantilism.

As already argued in chapter 2, strong associations exist between the social organisation of war-fighting capacities and the political structure. These are especially clear under feudalism. As Young (1981: 47) describes it, 'social organisation in the early middle ages was based on war, at least in most of western Europe'. Under attack from barbarian migrations, the old centralised institutions of the state in western Europe had crumbled, and the wealth of the Mediterranean countries and beyond had ceased to be accessible. The only way to pay soldiers was perforce to give them land. 'As a result, a new way of raising a new kind of fighting force developed . . . the system . . . came to be known as feudalism' (ibid.: 47).

This reward system was, however, also the seed of its own demise: by giving away rights to land, the central power was dissipated (Anderson, 1974: 223). Monarchist absolutism (although always weak in Britain) and mercantilism were the result of endeavours to re-establish it. These changes were reflected in, among other things, the forms of organisation and control of armies along lines more readily associated nowadays with capitalism; that is, they were 'rationalised' and centralised. From the 14th century in England the professional soldiers of the King's Army were centralised in the sense of being paid for by the Exchequer, but they were not state-organised and directed until Cromwell's creation of the New Model Army in the 17th century. The 1688 Settlement subsequently included in its Bill of Rights the abolition of standing armies, other than those organised and controlled by the state. Thus was taken the major step towards state monopolisation of the means of violence. (Up to that point in history the English 'trained bands' were still essentially organised and directed by the warrior-lords of the feudal order.) From Richard II (1377–99) onwards soldiers were paid wages. This was much to do with securing the motivation of the ordinary foot-soldier, in that as a feudal hangover only the nobility were construed as able to achieve honour in battle. Only for the nobility was this a Christian duty. Thus, according to negotiated terms and 'going rates' the mercenary was hired for a fixed period of service at a fixed rate of pay, plus provision for bonus payments if ransomable enemy prisoners were taken. Although not legally construed as a contract of employment, the outlines of such an instrument are clearly visible in this early military practice. (Under Italian *Condottierre* arrangements, the contracts even ran to pension and insurance schemes.) While ransom debts could be enforced by a court of law, no such sanction was available for non-payment of fees to the campaigning soldiery, however, and pillage was seen as an acceptable and normal way by which hard pressed soldiers might support themselves.

Similarly features of the market attach to late mediaeval arms production. Weapons systems were by modern standards undeveloped but cannons and handguns were increasingly in use. The technology for their production was, however, pre-industrial, that is, small batch and handcrafted. Producing sufficient numbers of sufficient quality meant, firstly, standardisation (the Brown Bess musket was the standard issue for the British Army for 150 years from 1690), and secondly, arms manufacture in the hands of private rather than state entrepreneurs. Only by allowing arms manufacturers to face an open market could the fluctuations in demand from individual states be counteracted, and production kept up at a steady pace. The combination of irregular but high-level demand plus the limits of an artisanal technology persuaded the western European states not only to leave arms production in private hands but to stimulate its growth there.

Indeed European monarchs generally demonstrated an early business acumen. For example, 16th-century sea power was essentially private, that is mercenary, but it was utilised by all European monarchs including Elizabeth I, regular navies not developing until the 17th century; Henry VIII's stimulation of a King's Navy was a 16th-century exception prompted by Britain's island geography. These naval 'privateering' ventures followed fairly closely the logic of the market—they were proposed and had to attract investment funds in terms of their projected returns. Elizabeth I not only enriched the nation by these raid and trade activities but also substantially increased her own personal fortunes by assiduous investment in particular foraging ventures—Drake and subsequently Raleigh being only two of those honoured for their ability to line the royal pocket. George I, a later example, was adept at property investment, again for his own purposes.

More importantly for the development both of British capitalism and the growth of British military power, the general dependency of all European monarchs by the 16th century on the international money and credit market for war finance was reduced, in the British case, by the 1694 creations of the Bank of England (as a private institution) and the National Debt. The initial purpose of this was to provide for the government an efficient, centralised credit mechanism for financing war (McNeill, 1983: 178). It not only did that but subsequently became a mechanism whereby governments of the day could make major monetary interventions into the British and other economies. The Bank of England did not displace the City of London as an international capital market but it did introduce a new state-associated institution into it. Service or finance capital became increasingly crucial to the running of the National Debt and, since any mistaken judgement on their part threatened national bankruptcy and thus loss of power, the finance capitalists secured increasing political power (Cain and Hopkins, 1986). Thus the 'great bourgeois financiers and merchants' were able to seek and secure 'office, title and favour within absolutist courts and their growing state apparatus' (Robinson, 1987).

From 1688 to the mid-1850s in Britain the aristocracy were the essential members of the state, and their continuing commitment to territorial security and aggrandisement meant the development of a strong alliance of landed interests with finance capital. This alliance lubricated the shift to agricultural capitalism and held strong until the 1850s, when provincial manufacturers were gaining in profitability and therefore in commercial interest relative to agriculture. But long before this, the emergent fields of commerce and industry had been seen as offering profitable opportunities to many different quarters. One of these was the landed aristocrats for whom feudal forms of exploitation and power were losing their potency from the 13th century onwards. By redeploying their land-derived fortunes into the new industries of wool, iron, coal and agriculture, many of these aristocrats not only survived but prospered (Starkey, 1986; Beckett, 1986). The de Vere's family of Suffolk, for example, arriving in England with William the Conqueror and dying out in 1703 after 20 generations, by their wool-merchandising activities in Tudor times propelled Lavenham into the top ten of rich towns. As Earls of Oxford the family provided Henry VII with his closest advisers. Similarly, the Ashburnhams, whose family spanned the period from 1183 to 1953, and which provided bosom friendship to Charles I, capitalised their agricultural holdings and developed iron works providing cannon shot and cathedral bells. They were also actively involved, via the establishment of the Bank of England in 1694, in the Crown's fiscal operations, Lord Ashburnham being a major financier at the time. By 1795 the Earl of Ashburnham was moving in to exploit the Welsh coalfields. The two businessmen with whom he was operating, however, eventually fleeced him and brought the family down.

Other aristocrats more successfully joined their pedigrees to the new business classes, usually by marrying the inheriting offspring. The list of examples is extensive, the general point being that England's nobility showed from an early date a strong commercial instinct, expressing itself both in their becoming capitalists and in their willingness to trade with other, non-noble, sections of emergent capital. They did so, however, while largely retaining a sense of their own essential superiority as nobility and as familiars of the Crown. This leads to the image of early modern England not as comprising an embattled aristocracy yielding political power to an emergent, thrusting capitalist class, but rather of an emergent industrial class having to deal with an aristocracy which could often outmatch them in capitalist terms and which, moreover, could claim all sorts of symbolic and material privileges on the basis of inherited nobility and relation to the Crown. By marriage, family inheritance, gentlemen's clubs, educational privilege and patronage these entrepreneurial aristocrats could exercise high degrees of social closure over the commanding heights of the polity and economy. Entry to status was largely on their terms, and the aspiring *nouveau riche* responded accordingly. Far from there being a clear transition from feudalism to capitalism, the former persisted in vigorous fashion to create and condition much of the latter.

Profitable enterprise was not confined to the domestic sphere though. The New World was plundered from the 16th century on, generating funds that could then be turned to domestic investment. Such plundering, however, should not be seen narrowly as economically motivated: rather it should be seen in the context of the foreign policy of a mercantilist state. As Crowson (1973) discusses, the great aim of Tudor foreign policy was defence against invasion. But defence costs were generally low for the Tudor monarchs. Their attention could thus be given to two supplementary objectives. The first of these was the quelling of 'anarchy' by the creation and imposition of a unified administrative and ideological order. The second and lesser objective was the pursuit of economic advantage. 'Tudor governments realised more and more that "this island, which hath been but as the suburbs of the old world, hath become the bridge to the new". . . . From 1540 onwards, the surplus energies of nation and government were increasingly committed to transoceanic exploration, colonisation and aggression' (Crowson, 1973: 5). By the 18th century the pursuit of economic advantage had, however, become a primary rather than a subordinate element of foreign policy. This was because the feedback patterns between colonial exploitation, domestic order and military prowess were not only highly developed but also were officially recognised as critical to national sovereignty. Economic advantage was sought, but for political reasons. Thus, in the context of other European nations doing likewise, Britain's defence of its realm became increasingly contingent upon the ability to commit ever larger quantities of economic resources to the tasks of political competition—which in turn meant foreign plunder and domestic economic growth. It is estimated, for example, that between 1757 and 1815 Britain took from India some '£1,000 million compared with a national income for 1770 of no more than £125 million' (Hayter, 1981). Similarly, Mandel (1968) calculates that 'between 1760 and 1780, profits taken from the West Indies and India roughly doubled the amount of capital available for investment in the industrial revolution of the United Kingdom'.

Perhaps needless to say, the same elite efforts at creating a unified administrative and ideological order at home extended into the new territories. British explorers, traders, settlers and missionaries went into the West Indies, the Indian subcontinent and Africa certain of their moral, cultural and even biological superiority to the peoples they found there. As Cairns (1965: xii) comments, the 19th century British literature on Africa reveals that the white man was seen 'In moral, spiritual and technological matters . . . as a giant among pygmies . . . As objects of salvation, obstacles to rapid travel, or as faithful followers, [Africans] are relegated to a secondary position.'

The creation of the Bank of England for war-financing; Henry VIII's encouragement of shipbuilding and the Royal Navy; the new forms of hierarchical, disciplined, centrally controlled, and armed land-fighting units which sprang out of Cromwell's New Model Army; and Britain's seaboard position, had combined in the 16th to 18th centuries to give Britain startling advantage in the exploitation of America, Africa and the Indian Ocean. As McNeill (1983: 143) observes, it was not a case of bread *or* guns: both could be had with relative ease, relatively cheaply and with maximum return. The feedback patterns whereby 'naval power and expenditure reinforced commercial expansion while commercial expansion simultaneously made naval expenditures easier to bear' (ibid.: 184) held good to the last quarter of the 18th century. Such opportunities made foreign policy and overseas trade the primary concerns of government. Success in these areas meant both that domestic stability could be bought and that a competitive edge could be maintained in relation to other states.

At the same time the expansion of frontiers and the persistence of interstate rivalries ensured continual attention to military efficiency. In terms of naval power, the mechanism of Bank of England funding meant that ships no longer foraged according to privateer calculations of profit but rather were directed by political and military considerations. In other words, the Royal Navy's operations ceased to be directly influenced by the market.

Where the Army was concerned, efficiency implied improvements in communication and command systems, maps, payment to troops, promotion criteria, motivation, and so on. One major point of resistance to change was the erosion of old ideas of honour in battle—man to man as equals—and the insertion of a new principle, namely, maximum fatality to the enemy at minimum risk to self (McNeill, 1983: 175). To secure troop obedience to this new principle, pay was regularised and improved, bright uniforms were issued, hospital and disability provisions improved, regimental identities stressed and drill, endless drill, demanded. The Army was thus 'rationalised'. It awaited only Cort's iron-puddling innovations of 1783 (stimulated by state sponsorship and custom for military purposes) for the industrialisation of warfare to take off. Increasing state attention to the welfare of the troops was part and parcel of that transition. And throughout the 18th century increasing state attention was given also to the specification of weaponry which designers had then to realise. This relationship of state-led innovation in defence-relevant production was to become the norm in subsequent centuries, particularly where new and expensive technical developments were concerned for which otherwise no financial backing would have been forthcoming.

Elite Concerns for Subordinate Order and Productivity

McNeill, in his discussion of *The Pursuit of Power* (to which we are indebted), concludes that 'war and the heavy cost of waging it accelerated the entire process of the market penetration of European society' (1983: 114). While that is true, it is also the case that war and the heavy cost of waging it simultaneously accelerated the state's administrative penetration of the economy and civil society. Feudal aristocrats may have sneered at commercialism, 'shopocracy' and manufacturing as ignoble, but their needs for such services were irresistible, especially in wartime. The distinctiveness of the commercial contribution to national security and material well-being was so well-recognised that, as early as the 12th century, monarchs were officially sanctioning the mercantile rationale in the form of Royal Charters which granted particular towns relative autonomy in the running of their affairs. Richard I seems to have regarded his kingdom solely as a source of revenue for his crusades and is reputed to have said: 'I would have sold London itself if I could have found a rich enough buyer' (Delderfield, 1970, 2nd ed.: 45). The urban merchants, administrators and professionals rapidly learnt the lesson that financial assistance to the war effort could lead to the royal underwriting of their exercises in local government. But such a devolution of power was never without a commensurate absorption of the new public authorities into the administrative structures of central government.

However, while the awarding of political status secured the co-operation of some, there was for the state still the problem of gaining general acquiescence to various forms of domestic taxation. Prior to 1688 the Crown was able to raise war funds (although rarely adequate) by selling off tax-collecting rights. With the 1688 Bill of Rights fiscal policy passed into parliamentary authority. But this was a Parliament dominated by the landed and aristocratic interests. Such interests were strongly disinclined to impose land-based taxation, much preferring purchase tax. By the later 18th century, government and defence expenditures were the fastest growing sectors of the economy (Cain and Hopkins, 1986). Taxation went up accordingly but, to meet with landed interests, was heavily skewed towards customs duties. This had two major consequences: (1) it focused government attention on the need to stimulate overseas trade while nonetheless contradicting the principles of free trade by the imposition of custom duties; and (2) it pushed up prices to British consumers. This latter contributed to recurrent popular protests and crises of public order throughout the 1760s and 1790s—Wilkes and Wyvill being just two to campaign against 'old corruption' and lack of accountability in government. Thus, just as the Peasants Revolt of 1381 can be partly attributed to excessive war taxation (Dobson, 1983), so can be the popular protests of the late 18th century. And just as the popular pressures of 1910–14 were to be quelled by the advent of the First World War, so the popular pressures of the 1790s were quelled by the opening of hostilities with Bonaparte.

The British state's war with Bonaparte was not, of course, prompted primarily, or at all, by a desire to unite the populace in patriotic fervour. Bonaparte's ambitions were threat enough, and were made worse by the republican sentiments and the *levée en masse* insurrectionary example of the French people. Fear of similar developments among British workers exacerbated elite concerns about worker combinations, and stimulated state resort to legal attacks upon them.

The law indeed had been long developed as a major instrument for securing domestic stability. Henry II (1154–1189) had deliberately built upon the English common law so as to undermine the powers of his Norman barons while simultaneously securing the allegiance of the conquered Anglo-Saxons (Churchill, 1956). His Crown courts upheld notions of truth and justice publicly established according to criteria of rational inquiry and impartiality, a precursor of the scientific rationality which was later to become ubiquitous. At the same time, the law reflected political tensions and competitions within England's social structure. Thus the barons with the Magna Carta (1216) forced the monarch to abide by the rule of laws made scientifically rather than according to the monarch's 'divine' inspiration. This both inhibited the development in Britain of monarchic absolutism and proclaimed the legal sanctity of private property.

The propensity for political alliances of all those in England who were propertied is remarkable. Indeed, property ownership rather than notions of individualism or participatory democracy seems to provide the basis for civil rights in England and its territories. It is the case that England, from the 13th century onwards, was unique in giving property owners extensive rights (Macfarlane, 1979; Dobson, 1983). It is perhaps the tax-grabbing history of the Crown, its 'absentee landlord' status throughout much of the Middle Ages, and its continued presence in British government, which has ensured a political philosophy which identifies liberty not with democratic rights but with the private ownership of properties which the state is not allowed to access. Certainly English lawyers (in part to aid their personal acquisition of manors and estates being vacated by impoverished aristocrats) developed unique legal means of rendering property ownership a private affair, not for public or state knowledge (Denman, 1978).

Even in plebian sections, sentiments seem to have been much the same. When peasants in the 1380s protested for freeman status, they did so because they wanted thereby to be able to acquire land and to access the royal law courts which would protect such acquisitions from seigneurial intervention. Similarly the arguments of the Levellers and Diggers in the 17th century linked civil with land-utilisation rights. The egalitarianism of these movements was certainly there—not least because of active support from Cromwell's Ironsides, many of whose officers were, at Cromwell's determination, 'common men, and even poor and of mean parentage' (Earl of Manchester, quoted in Young, 1981: 95). But the egalitarianism never developed into a full-blooded republicanism as it was to do in France. This was perhaps because, from late Tudor times, the British monarchy was developing a strong line in populist rhetoric which stressed the 'national interest' and the virtue of patriotism, and which mobilised symbols such as 'God's Elect Nation', 'Britannia' and 'John Bull' to declare British superiority. It may also have to do with the spiritual malaise and susceptibilities of a people who, in the course of a few generations, had witnessed acute religious conflicts, the beheading of a king, a civil war, a foreign war, a plague and the Fire of London. These events were typically taken as signs of God's displeasure, an interpretation which propelled people towards the religious atonement offered in Puritanism and the influence of the priesthood, who bridged most effectively the gap between Crown and populace (O'Day and Heal, 1981; Little, 1978; Knappen, 1965).

The political philosophy, developing as classic liberalism, which proposed private property as the protector of individual freedom against the state had two most important corollaries: (1) it did not enshrine equality but rather rationalised the reverse: (2) it supported the elite construal of propertylessness as *the* social problem, the source of demands on *their* wealth and of threats to *their* order. And it was in terms of such attitudes that elite policies towards labouring people were formulated.

The Marxist argument about contract law's presumption of the equivalence of the exchanged commodities may be correct but, right into the 20th century, British labour laws were not about exchange. They were about order. Labouring people were seen by the elites to be obliged to sell themselves for cash and therefore to be contemptible. They were regarded as inclined to idleness, to moral turpitude and insubordination. Worse, they were inclined to poverty which was a drain on the 'wealth of the kingdom' (Gregory King, 1953). These feudal prejudices were carried forward into history by the warrior-lords' descendants whose position had been consolidated not only in the Glorious Revolution of 1688 but also in the market; and by the newcomers of capitalist commerce, finance and industry, who readily invoked the rhetoric so as to improve their own profits, security and status. Masterless men and women were seen as a threat to the social order and to the nation's wealth. The solution was seen to lie with emergent commerce and industry in the form of new occupations into which men and women could be driven by the law, there to be 'mastered'. In these occupations, as also in the older ones on the estates, they were to be kept as poor as possible—both as an incentive to work, and as a means to keep production costs low. Poverty in families was to be overcome by putting the wife and children to work (John Locke, 1696; Daniel Defoe, 1728) and/or by holding more than one occupation. Thus was capitalism to contribute to the pace of economic development and social peace.

But the new occupations meant new urban centres of population and new possibilities for worker organisation. The industrialising towns were not readily subjected to the older authority systems of the nobility, church and justices of the peace. At the same time, pre-industrial technologies were pressed to their limits by demand and across most of the 18th century further expansion of output could only come from additional applications of labour to the old methods. The result was, despite steady population growth, to raise money wages, especially in the non-agricultural sectors. This provided at least some labourers with the conditions to break loose from poverty and servility, and provoked governments to concede defeat in wage-fixing but to make instead new efforts to curb labour organisation. Such curbs were doubly recommended as far as the ruling sections were concerned because, as Cain and Hopkins (1986: 508) express it: 'Industrialists were the shock troops of capitalism, and the hostility which they generated by the late eighteenth century onward undermined some of the authority which wealth would otherwise have given them'.

Organisation does indeed seem to be a key feature of the 17th and 18th centuries—the first applications of scientific rationality to the management of people and materials—in the armed forces, in the new cotton factories and in the government of society. In the beginnings of organisation of labour by labourers, it flowed from entirely different principles of solidarity. People who were done-to rather than doers reacted as best they could by clinging together for mutual support and comfort, by protesting and by attempting to exploit such leverage as they had. For this they were often severely punished. But the oppressive hand of the state was about to be eased somewhat. As the 1800s proceeded, the alliance of landed interests and finance capital grew sensitive to the escalating imbalance of government expenditures at home and abroad set against the diminishing returns from the same. Social peace and economic growth had to be the goals but at lower cost. To that end, the politicians initiated policies of cheap government including public expenditure cuts from 1815, and tariff reductions from the 1820s. With the 1832 Reform Act, which brought the professionals of finance capital and the provincial industrialists into political participation, the scene was set for the next move to a fully *laissez-faire* political economy.

In summary then, a combination of high spending and demand set against the limits of extant technologies and of available labour constituted an irresistible pressure to innovate new modes of exploitation. In the economic transition of feudal England to industrial Britain, the competitive behaviour of political elites was crucial since it was this very largely which set the levels and directions of investment and demand. It was this competition which prompted the innovation in modes of wealth creation and appropriation, the innovation being at once technical, organisational and institutional. 'War is but an extension of politics', to paraphrase Clausewitz. We would add, 'and so can be economic relations'. Without doubt it was the industrial mode of production which changed labour relations, but the Industrial Revolution 'emerged out of an already highly successful capitalist system, and it took place without any fundamental transformation of property ownership' (Cain and Hopkins, 1986: 509). It took place also without any fundamental transformation in the subordinate status of labour.

4 The Century of Industrialisation

This chapter indicates the inappropriateness of imparting too much homogeneity to the three interest groups of state, capital and labour. During much of the period under discussion, labour is clearly divisible into those scarce skilled trades on which unionism was founded, and the mass of unskilled labour, a substantial proportion of whom were impoverished by the social experience, if not the economic rewards, deriving from industrialisation. Indeed, during the early period of industrial growth the upper echelons of the artisan class are barely distinguishable from those small masters who comprised such an important segment of capital. Both the objective mobility between these groups (with some skilled workers becoming small masters during prosperous times and returning to employed status at others) and the vertical bonding which took place by skilled workers adopting the outlook, values and aspirations of those immediately above them, acted to obscure, the delineation of capital and labour. Similarly, the state may be identified as a diverse institution with, for example, the judiciary often acting against the spirit, if not the letter, of legislation emerging from Parliament. Indeed, in their defence of individual rights, the courts more consistently acted in sympathy with the interests of employers than did the legislature. Such assessments are complicated, however, by their being contingent on the time scale adopted and the importance of distinguishing between the short- and long-term interests of the various groups.

THE POLITICS OF INDUSTRIALISATION AND WAGE LABOUR

The 19th century for Britain was *the* century of industrialisation, impacting on the work experiences and opportunities of increasingly large proportions of the labouring population, and also impacting on the political alliances ruling the country. With regard to the latter, the century opened with landed interests dominant within the Parliament but, outside of it, still tied through the Bank of England and the National Debt to finance capital. But even this alliance was not yet adequate to finance the state's expenditures, accelerating sharply as a result of the Napoleonic Wars and the growing numbers of Britons on poor relief. There was also the not inconsiderable problem of how to administer and control the growing concentrations of labouring and poor people in urban areas, especially given the revolutionary fervour of many of their French counterparts. Expedience and changed circumstances prompted Parliament to pay ever greater attention to the industrial manufacturers as a source of wealth, economic dynamism, job opportunities and social discipline. But the interests of the different parties were sufficiently at odds for the years between 1790 and 1846 to be marked by intense political debate as to economic and domestic policies. The older-established landed interests, reflecting their feudal ancestry, preferred protectionism in trade and patriarchy (with a heavy sanctioning hand) in domestic affairs. It was from such prefer-ences that sprang the Corn Laws, which guaranteed the price of grain in Britain by limiting its importation; the Combination Acts (1799 and 1800) which prohibited trade unions; and the first of the Factory Acts (1802), which were an exercise in socially protective legislation intended to curb the worst of the exploitative excesses of the industrial employers in the provinces. The industrialists had no great aversion to state efforts to curb trade unions, nor to state direction of pauper and orphan labour into compulsory employment at cheap rates and without rights. But they were averse to the socially protective legislation, especially since it appeared to be directed solely at manufacturing employ-ments. They retaliated with strident and theoretically rational-ised demands for free trade both domestically and abroad. Perhaps the most dramatic of their successes was, 14 years after their political enfranchisement in the 1832 Reform Act, the repeal of the Corn Laws, with dire consequences for the sub-sequent fortunes and status of the landed sector. But of equal, arguably greater, significance as far as British workers were concerned, was the cultivation by the free traders of Adam Smith's rationale. Ruling elites in Britain had long been sensitive to trade as a source of wealth. Where labour costs had comprised the largest single element in production costs, it had made sense to keep wages low in order to improve price competitiveness.

But the application of machinery to production innovated in the 18th century, backed by the arguments of Smith, had demonstrated that technology could improve productivity, which in turn meant either lower prices and expanded markets, or wage rises with no impact on product price. Higher wages could then be turned to incentives to work, to placation of workers through greater consumer power, and to the fuelling of a demand-pull economic dynamo. Such arguments had strong appeal to a Parliament which was short of cash and was worried by the various factors making for popular disorder and protest. Thus, although the early 1800s were marked by state efforts to intervene in industry (for example, in the Arbitration Act, 1800, for the weaving industry; the Select Committee on Artisans and Machinery, 1824; the Arbitration Act of 1824, amended 1837 and 1845; the first of the Truck Acts in 1831; and the various Factory Acts), those years also saw the introduction of legislation which was now beginning to acknowledge the individual worker's freedom to contract (by the 1814 repeal of the Apprenticeship clauses) and to associate (by the 1825 repeal of the Combination Acts).

Such freedoms, although consistent with free trade arguments, were a mixed blessing for workers: either they constituted a tardy legal recognition of a *de facto* situation, or they were negated in many instances by the use of other punitive legal measures against workers, or they merely exacerbated the exposure of workers to the full force of a capitalist labour market. The first was represented in the 1814 repeal of the apprenticeship clauses, the substitution of semi-skilled machine minders for skilled workers being already very well advanced. The seven year pattern of apprenticeship had been enshrined in the 1563 Statute of Artificers which gave Justices of the Peace power to enforce apprenticeship regulations. By the early 19th century, however, the need for apprenticeship was becoming undermined by the technological transition to semi-skilled labour. The Luddites, for example, although now remembered only for their machine-breaking activities, campaigned vigorously in support of the 1563 Statute 'which alone afforded any hope of legal defence against the full impact of wage cutting and labour dilution' (Thompson, 1968: 566–7). In London, too, a number of trade societies sought to prevent masters from employing 'illegal' men who had not 'served their time'. 'It was clearly time in Establishment eyes for the old statutes to go', comments Fox (1985: 71), 'and go they did'.

The second mixed blessing was represented in the repeal of the Combination laws. Fox (1985: 77) argues that these laws had offered a speedier route to conviction than the slower procedures available under the common law, but their impact was at all times patchy. In some aspects and areas the laws were largely ignored and combinations of skilled workers continued to form and meet. In part this was due to the onus to bring prosecution being left on employers: as also was the case in the early 1980s, many employers in the early 19th century appear to have judged the gains from successful prosecution to have been insufficient compared to the financial costs and the creation of ill-will (Webb and Webb, 1920: 74). Yet the Acts were not without impact. Thompson (1968: 552) considers, for example, that 'over the greater part of the manufacturing districts of the north, Midlands and west . . . the repression of trade unions was very much more severe'. Similarly the Webbs (1920: 81) identify artisans in the textile industries as being particularly harassed by the Combination Acts. One of the effects of the anti-combination legislation (and one of the arguments used by Place, Hume and others in support of repeal in 1824–25) was that it pushed unionism underground, engendering not only secrecy but also suspicion and antagonism towards the state. Yet even after repeal, harassment of unionism continued: the Tolpuddle Martyrs, for example, were transported a decade later for swearing secret oaths . . . although they were sentenced under an Act dealing with naval mutinies, not with worker combinations.

The third 'mixed blessing' of the new legal freedoms was that they coincided with two other phenomena to create wage-labour in its purest, that is, most depersonalised and dependent, form. These were firstly the consequences of the Corn Laws, and secondly the provisions of the Poor Law Amendment Act 1834. The Corn Laws were not repealed until the 1840s. Until then the interests of the landed sector had been secured in guaranteed high corn prices. This in turn escalated the enclosure of common land, hitherto a source of subsistence for rural workers. As Chambers (1953: 336) describes it, 'The appropriation to their own exclusive use of practically the whole of the common waste by legal owners meant that the curtain which separated the growing army of labourers from utter proletarianisation was torn down.' With the repeal of the Corn Laws, grain prices did fall as the imports came in but as the century advanced the fall in prices depressed many agricultural fortunes, again with debilitating consequences for rural labourers (and one can add, with debilitating consequences for landed interests within the British polity).

Besides the general impact of agricultural capitalism on rural labour's means of feeding itself, a more specific increase in labour's dependence on capital was embodied in the Poor Law Amendment Act 1834, which swept away the provisions of the previous century. Earlier Poor Laws had provided outdoor relief for the unemployed, the old and the infirm. In the 18th century this was gradually extended to include the granting of relief to low-paid workers. From 1795 this practice became regularised under the 'Speenhamland system' which provided relief based on the price of bread and number of dependents. [The system was devised initially by Berkshire magistrates meeting at Speenhamland near Newbury in May 1795. The scale of relief varied to some extent but the criteria of bread prices and dependents were generally adopted. Under Speenhamland the scale became operative when a gallon loaf of bread 'shall cost 1 shilling, then every poor and industrious person shall have for his support 3 shillings weekly, either procured by his own or his family's labour, *or an allowance from the poor rates* and for the support of his wife and every other of his family, 1 shilling 6 pence' (quoted in Polanyi, 1957: 78, italics in Polanyi; see also Harrison, 1984: 235)]. The system supplemented low wages as well as providing relief for those with no income. Because relief was paid only to people in their own parish this acted to tie the lowest income labour to a particular parish in a similar way that the 1662 Act of Settlement had done in previous centuries.

The Speenhamland system also acted to depress wages since 'the employer could obtain labour at almost any wages; however little he paid the subsidy from the rates brought the workers' income up to scale . . . Little by little the people of the countryside were pauperized' (Polanyi, 1957: 79–80). Yet at the same time, by establishing a poor rate also applicable to those in work (a form of 18th-century Family Income Supplement) the Speenhamland system embodied both a paternalism and a social rather than simply an economic criterion for wage determination. Thompson portrays this system of poor-rates, after the widespread loss of common rights as a result of enclosures, as 'the labourer's last "inheritance"' (1968: 247).

The sweeping away of the Speenhamland system in 1834 acted as a major step in the commodification of labour which in turn represented a key prerequisite to the full development of a market society. For by tying relief to the local parish, Speenhamland hindered the release of labour from rural parishes and into the growing industrial regions. By inhibiting rural migration, the landed classes were able to compete successfully with the higher wages in the emerging industrial villages (Block and Somers, 1984). The Poor Law Amendment Act drastically reduced the availability of outdoor relief, leaving those displaced from the land with a choice between entering the purposely harsh workhouse, or seeking industrial employment either in outwork or in the growing workshops and later factories. Underlying the 1834 Act was a concern not only for the growing cost of poor rates but also to remove all barriers to the workings of the labour market, thereby acting in accordance with the increasingly popular doctrine of *laissez-faire* (Currie, 1979). The 1834 Act 'was the announcement that henceforth the labouring poor must abandon many of their traditional attitudes and expectations and conform to new standards of social and economic rectitude' (Harrison, 1984: 234). 'This', write Block and Somers (1984: 56), 'was the full institutionalization of labour as a commodity in that workers now had only themselves to sell in order to survive. The right to live outside the wage system no longer existed as the "social net" disappeared in favour of allowing the market, not the state, to allow wages to find their proper level; industrial capital was now in its true inaugural moment'.

Brown (1982) links the creation of the wage-labour form to three factors: (1) equipment costs being beyond the capacity of the uncapitalised to purchase; (2) manufacturing processes which by their nature require large numbers of workers; and (3) the production of large numbers of standardised units of output requiring mass markets to valorise. The necessity for capitalisation (that is, major financial resources) of enterprise in industrial wage-labour developments explains the continuing significance of finance capital throughout the 19th century. Previously active in investing in the guilds and trade monopolies of the mercantilist period, these finance capitalists had shown a slightly later proclivity to invest in agriculture's shift towards the capitalist mode of production. Their class was, of course, already deeply embroiled via the National Debt in financing the war activities of the state from 1694 onwards. The parliamentary reforms of 1815 to 1830 had in part attempted to reduce and contain the significance of the City of London in Britain's political and economic affairs, with the consequence that these financiers turned their attention increasingly to foreign fields and the development of international financial transactions. Their development along these lines coincided nicely with industrial capital's free trade achievements and the simultaneous erosion of landed capital's position following the repeal of the Corn Laws. Free trade and minimal government regulation of economic matters suited the pockets of finance capitalists, and were pursued politically by them. As Britain's industrial capital moved into economic ascendancy from the 1850s, finance capital went with it . . . but with its international dimension already well developed and kept in reserve as an alternative arena of activity for the time when British industry ceased to be sufficiently profitable. Through the reliance on finance capital, however, market considerations clearly influenced the rate and direction of Britain's industrial development. The only alternative, where technological innovation was expensive, to a reliance on finance capital was a reliance on the state. In certain areas, for military reasons or to improve the country's infrastructure, the state did indeed sponsor industrial development, by funding research and development and/or by proposing itself as the primary or a major consumer. Thus were metal manufacture, armaments, the railways, shipbuilding and civil engineering stimulated in their development.

One aspect of this development was 'factoryisation'. In past accounts the pace of transition from cottage to factory-based production has tended to be overdrawn—by 1830 the majority of workers were still employed in small workshops or their own houses, rather than in factories. Nevertheless, the growth of factory organisation was an important feature of the first half of the 19th century, this and other aspects of capital intensification appearing at different times in different industries. In engineering it was the decades of the 1830s and 1840s which saw the main impetus in capital intensification. Prior to this certain skills had been at a premium and the state of technology 'did not permit the substitution of cheaper forms of more abundant labour in place of the scarcer and more expensive millwrights' (Burgess, 1975: 3). From the 1830s onwards, however, the progressive application of machine tools reduced the demand for the all-round skills of millwrights, in favour of easier-to-learn and more narrowly specialised skills, notably those of fitter and turner, who set up and supervised machines which could then be manned by semi-skilled workers. The upshot was a widening of the industry's labour market, with semi-skilled machine minders supervised by skilled workers whose apprenticeship had taken five rather than the customary seven years to complete. By the end of the 1840s the position of labour in the engineering sectors had significantly declined: unemployment and wage reductions were common in the industry, with labour increasingly vulnerable during cyclical downturns (Burgess, 1975). Further increases in productivity were also being sought through the use of piecework pay systems and systematic overtime, both anathema to the traditional engineering craftsman's ideology. In fact, these practices, together with unemployment, encouraged the founding of the Amalgamated Society of Engineers in 1850, and figured prominently in its early disputes with employers.

The pattern of development in the cotton industry reveals certain similarities to that in engineering. In cotton, however, the period of intense spending on labour-saving technology began much earlier, around 1780. Between this date and the 1840s, cotton manufacture industrialised as the putting-out system gave way to factory organisation to meet demand which to the 1870s derived from a dominance of world markets (Burgess, 1975; Joyce, 1980). Employment grew, although not as quickly as output. By 1851 half a million people, a high proportion women and juveniles, were employed in cotton textiles. As in engineering, however, this growth was predominantly in machine minding and did not provide the basis for any significant exertion of persistent labour power. Machine minding skills were relatively easy to teach (attentiveness and dexterity to mend the threads and change the bobbins being the main skills required); also the suitability of women and young people for many of the jobs ensured an adequate labour supply. The resulting low bargaining power, together with increases in labour-saving technology, was reflected in the declining share of net output allocated to wages throughout the period up to 1867, despite increases in the total numbers employed in the industry (Burgess, 1975: 232).

Even in industries where there were no major technological breakthroughs, the increase in population and the release of rural labour due to the capitalisation of agriculture, weakened labour's bargaining power in the first half of the 19th century. In coal, for example, the lack of craft occupations and skill demarcations meant that employers had access to a wide labour market to meet the increase in demand for their product. In the construction industry, part of the expansion in building activity was partly met by increased resort to the 'cheap end' of the industry with employers utilising 'inferior' workmen who had not served out their apprenticeships (Burgess, 1975: 100, 151–2).

It would be wrong to suggest that in the first half of the 19th century the interests of labour exerted no influence over capital. Remnants of paternalism continued to exist, certain skills remained in short supply and early factory legislation imposed certain restrictions on the utilisation of the cheapest sectors of the labour market. In addition, movements such as Luddism, Chartism and the Swing riots suggested a potential for revolt if the labouring poor were pushed too far. The repeal of the Combination Acts in 1824–25 was in part an acknowledgement that trade unions were continuing to meet and expand in spite of the legal prohibition. Some years later, in 1833–34, the attempt at mass unionism in the form of the Grand National Consolidated Trades Union further pointed (albeit briefly) to a potential for combined worker action.

Yet by the mid-century what did these elements add up to? Trade unionism was evident only among the more privileged workers and there was little indication of these higher grades extending bonds of fraternity to the rest of manual labour. The 1832 Reform Act, although in the long perspective of history an important step towards expanding the base of political participation, in itself brought little enfranchisement to the artisan class, let alone anyone lower in the occupational structure. In contrast, the burgeoning industrial labour force, swelling both through population growth and the movement of labour into towns, provided employers with the potential to undermine skilled workgroups attempting to exert power through controlling the supply of their labour. Technological change enabled employers to turn this potential into actuality in several industries with the dependence on skilled labour being partially offset by advances in machine development. In other industries, where craft barriers did not exist, employers enjoyed almost unfettered opportunities to use the growing labour force to establish a pattern of employment geared solely to short-term profit maximisation, with scant regard to the adequacy of the employment contract for sustaining a healthy and well-nourished workforce. The general lack of opportunity to engage in small-scale food production meant that the newly forming urban populations were all the more exposed to their lack of bargaining power. The results were clearly to be seen in the widespread distress during cyclical downturns, the scandal of child labour, the long hours and the low pay.

DOMESTIC AND FOREIGN LIMITS TO *LAISSEZ-FAIRE* GOVERNMENT

Such widespread distress set the limits to which governments of the day could happily and for long adopt a minimalist, *laissez-faire* stance. The distress was evidenced in two primary ways— in the increasingly sophisticated and vocal forms of popular organisation and protest, and in the revelations of the factory inspectors. Twenty years of sporadic Luddite machinery-breaking, the protest movement culminating in the Swing riots of 1830, the industrial stoppages enforced by textile workers pulling the plugs from factory boilers in the 1840s, and the articulate, rational and popular appeals of the Chartists combined with the development of 'official knowledge' (that is, government compiled knowledge) to ensure that by mid-century the social condition of the British working classes had become a major parliamentary concern. In the process the free traders in manufacturing were converted to the paternalism, the moralising, and the preferences for state intervention which had long characterised the older ruling interests of landed capital and the aristocracy.

A key element in this process of change was Althorp's Act of 1833 which gave the state, via an inspectorate, the right to command information from any citizen (Choi, 1984). Popular protest, worker combinations and strikes across the first 40 years of the 19th century had persuaded manufacturing interests of the need for state help in quelling potential worker insurrection. (Oastler's Factory Movement had threatened armed insurrection, and some Chartists on arrest were found to be armed. Some connections between Irish dissidents and the English were also uncovered. These facts in themselves were enough to alarm the English authorities but the alarms were exacerbated by the propensity to damage property evidenced by the Luddites and Plug-drawers). The industrialists therefore did not oppose Althorp's proposals for the beginnings of 'official information' as the basis for subsequent government decision-making. Within Parliament the 'condition of England question' became a major issue, informed by the Mines Report, the Sanitary Report and the Factories Report, all of 1842. The political goal which emerged from this debate was primarily for an orderly population, self-disciplined by virtue of moral and religious education. In this way state intervention could be portrayed as state enablement of self-help, a portrayal not incompatible with the then powerful beliefs in the free market and sovereign individualism. (Similarly state interventions to promote conciliation in industrial conflict could be construed as facilitating self-help: legislation to this end passed through Parliament in 1824, 1837, 1845 and the 1860s.) Since, however, education up to that time was fragmented across several religious and self-help bodies, only the state was in a position to make universal provision (Paz, 1980: 126–41). But for workers to have access to education required firstly that not all their waking hours be spent in work. From Althorp's Act of 1833 to the reduction of the working day to ten hours in 1847, there waged a conflict between the desires of employers to extract maximum labour power from their employees, and the desires of politicians (sometimes the same set of people) to educate and pacify the working masses. Peel, the free-trading Tory Prime Minister, in 1846 broke his earlier alliance with the protectionist Whigs by repealing the Corn Laws. In the same year recession weakened manufacturers' economic powers and thereby also their arguments in favour of free trade. One year later the Whigs replaced the Tories in office, and the Ten Hours Act went through. As Choi (1984: 474) reports, 'the British State became an administrative state (in the sense of managing) society in the light of credible reporting of objective conditions rather than just trusting the claims of particular class interests . . . The authority of the state was enhanced by scientific social knowledge, and the manufacturers' interest was deprived of its absolute ideological status.'

State authority was enhanced in another direction, however—namely, the military one. The loss of protectionism for British agriculture opened up a strategic weakness. By 1885 65 per cent of UK grain was imported (McNeill, 1983). Between 1870 and 1900 the acreage under wheat fell 50 per cent (Ensor, 1936). At the same time free trade had meant the export of technological knowledge and industrial capacity. The 'almost accidental expansion of empire' (McNeill, 1983) resulting from British military superiority and the demise of the French Navy at Trafalgar, nonetheless contained the seeds of its own undoing in that the elites in the colonies grew richer, stronger and more experienced by their imperial contact. They began to demand and were granted political autonomy, albeit with pro-British trading links maintained. Such concessions, necessitated by the unacceptable costs and difficulties of doing otherwise, could be construed by opposition voices as a sign of the British government's failure to defend national interests. From the time of the Second and Third Reform Acts the issue of Britain's military strength became a political hot potato. From this time also the 'modern military industrial complex . . . came of age' (McNeill, 1983: 285). The two dimensions *are* related.

'In pre-industrial England the labouring poor could safely be ignored or taken for granted by the educated classes for most of the time . . . They were not directly or continuously involved in important decisions; their views were neither sought nor heeded; and popular unrest was regarded as unfortunate but transitory' (Harrison, 1984: 243). At the turn of the 19th century, however, population growth, industrialisation and the escalating costs of interstate rivalries combined to ensure that the administrative-extractive apparatus and attentions of the state would grow. By 1814 government expenditure represented 29 per cent of GNP, public expenditure having shot up from £22 million in 1792 to £123 million in 1815 (Peacock and Wiseman, 1961: 37). The bulk of this expenditure was on war. Grants made to foreign allies amounted to a further £65.8 million. Additionally, the state was a major customer and sponsor for Britain's metal-working developments; naval demand for provisions stimulated agricultural production, and many of the (male) labouring poor who might otherwise have been rebellious were absorbed into the armed forces. The 72 separate war campaigns of Victoria's reign (1837 to 1901) meant that military prowess was a major element in national identity (Bond, 1967). It was thus entirely reasonable for *The Times* at the start of the Crimean War (1854–56) to declare 'we must popularise the Army and militarise the civilian society'. The 1832 Reform Act had admitted professional financiers and provincial manufacturers to the electoral roll primarily because the state's political goals for domestic peace and international strength, as then assumed by landed interests, could not be fulfilled without their contributions to economic growth. The 1846 repeal of the Corn Laws had exposed landed interests to the forces of the international market. The Whig Party representing those interests in Parliament lost authority accordingly. But the resultant more equal balance of power within Parliament accelerated the development of the two-party system, each party looking to find new allies in its hungry search for ascendancy. Their eyes lit upon the British public. Thus the expansion of the franchise was more to do with competition within the British ruling sections than it was with popular pressure from beneath them.

This is not to say that there was no popular demand for the vote. As early as the 17th century the Levellers and Diggers had been articulating such a demand. The Chartist movement in the 19th century embraced, through the Complete Suffrage Union, a similar demand for political reforms and enfranchisement. But such demands seem more to have emanated from middle class radicals than from their working class allies, many of whom insisted that 'neither politics nor religion should be permitted to interfere with the subject of labour and wages' (Brown, 1982: 118).

The Second Reform Act of 1867 extended suffrage to a further 1.5 million people, in particular the urban male householder. The Third Reform Act, 1884, expanded the franchise yet further and in the following election two-thirds of the adult male population had the vote (Harrison, 1984: 333). Thus from this time on the electorate contained a significant (male) working class vote, its magnitude making it essential that working class interests be acknowledged by both Liberal and Tory candidates eager to win over this sizeable group within the electorate. Simultaneously, however, the new voters were exposed to the populist rhetoric and jingoism of politicians now seeking majority demotic support. 'The new suffrage altered the dynamics of politics' (McNeill, 1983: 270).

The change also stimulated considerable growth in the scale, scope and complexity of government, especially in economic affairs (Coombes and Walkland, 1980), as the world recession developing from 1873 translated into British electoral demand for jobs and material relief. For 1884 was not only the year of the Third Reform Act, it was also a year of recession, unemployment and idle shipyards. Through newspapers and music halls, the Tories played on popular fears of Britain's loss of naval supremacy and on Russian and French aggrandisement so as to undermine confidence in the Liberal government. In order to allay such fears while also re-activating the shipyards, the government agreed naval appropriations beyond what the Admiralty had asked for and generally increased its expenditure on armaments. The 'defence of the realm' was now a vote-catcher, to be mobilised by fear-inducing, jingoistic political rhetoric. The relationship between the state and arms manufacturers—never weak—grew to the point of obliterating the public/private divide. This was not only because the state was the primary customer, it was also as a consequence of the enormous costs of military innovation. In the years between 1839 and 1860, for example, the British government had subsidised the development of mail-carrying ships where these could be deemed useful in war: this was one way of getting the private sector to innovate without those costs being borne by the Royal Navy. From the 1840s onwards the Navy was becoming industrialised, a process accelerated by the Crimean War (1854–56). The patriotic fervour of Bessemer, Armstrong and Whitworth meant the application of civil engineering principles to artillery production and, following the Great Exhibition of 1851, American mass production techniques were adopted for the manufacture of small arms in the British defence industry. But although command technology became the norm (that is, the state specified its particular needs to private designers and consumed the outcome of their work), the heavy costs of such developments both prohibited the emergence of any state monopoly and prompted private manufacturers to merge and to seek international arms sales. Thus, in its defence procurements, the state could simultaneously support domestic employment levels and the nation's military strength, but it did so at the price of a deep embroilment in a global, industrialised, armaments business.

All three aspects—employment, military strength, the arms trade—became terrain on which the political parties subsequently competed for the voters' attention. By 1909 naval expenditures were so high and popular pressure for jobs and material improvement so intense as to persuade Lloyd George to introduce a form of progressive taxation and some social welfare measures. Many elite sections bitterly resented these Liberal innovations and, on the issue of Irish Home Rule, certain prominent Tory politicians incited the Army to mutiny. This act of treason was never punished, nor even widely publicised. It meant that effective political power moved away from the elected government and outside of Parliament; an event identified by Dangerfield (1970) as the 'strange death of liberal England' and by others as the beginnings of a major erosion of parliamentary democracy. This erosion began *before* universal suffrage was awarded to the British people, at a time when the Labour Party was only just entering Parliament.

LABOUR SECURES OFFICIAL STATUS

Whilst the 1867 and 1884 Reform Acts extended electoral representation to much of the adult male working class, it was not for another generation that an independent voice representing the labour vote was heard in Parliament. From 1867 into the new century it was the Liberals who benefited most from the working class vote. This was secured partly by a Liberal-Labour alliance, which involved introducing a small number of 'suitable' Labour candidates into the Liberal party machine. In the 1874 election this resulted in two Lib-Lab MPs, both from the miners' union. The number of Labour MPs increased to 11 after the 1885 general election, but several writers (including Pelling 1965; and Harrison, 1984) have recorded growing dissatisfaction with this arrangement towards the end of the 19th century. In part this was due to the greater aggressiveness of unskilled unions formed in 1889 and 1890. It was also because of the unwillingness of the Liberals to select more working class candidates and their reluctance to promote greater legal protection for union activities at a time when unions felt their legal gains of the 1870s (see below) and bargained concessions of the 1880s to be coming under increasing threat (Pelling, 1965: 199). One of the outcomes of this tension in the Lib-Lab arrangement was an electoral alliance between a number of socialist parties (the Independent Labour Party, Social Democratic Federation and Fabian Society) and parts of the trade union movement: after several years of debate within the TUC, this alliance became institutionalised by the establishment of the Labour Representation Committee in February 1900. Several larger unions, including the engineers and textile workers, did not at first take up the invitation of LRC membership. However, the eventual union defeat in the Taff Vale case (see below) persuaded many doubters within the union movement of the wisdom of joining it. This alliance went on to win 29 seats in the 1906 election, and adopted the name of the Labour Party. This was to be the beginning of a long rise in the Party's popularity which in its first half century increased its aggregate poll in every General Election save two (Pelling, 1965: 227).

To what factors can we attribute the rise of a parliamentary Labour Party in the last quarter of the 1800s? One factor already identified was the competition among elites seeking new power bases among an expanded electorate. But while that opened the door for popular (male) participation, it did not predict that the shape of its expression would be the Labour Party. If elite tactics can be construed as the 'pull' factor, the 'push' factor was the unions: more precisely, it was unions forming around workers whose technological position in the second half of the 19th century was in many industries substantially stronger. Whereas the half century before 1850 was characterised by the rapid development of labour-saving technology in many industries, the period following the mid-century has been characterised as one in which investment was directed as much towards labour-using as labour-saving machines. Burgess (1975) has noted this to be particularly true in British engineering, which dominated world markets at this time. 'The nature of investment changed as firms found that they could sell established products using existing methods to customers overseas. Investment tended to be in existing techniques rather than new ones' (Burgess, 1975: 305). Blaug (1962) indicates a similar picture prevailing in the cotton industry. From statistics on capital, output and manpower in the industry between 1834 and 1886, Blaug argues that whilst before 1860 'the course of technological change seems to conform to the labour-saving bias popularly attributed to nineteenth century development . . . the slant of technological change *after* 1860 was largely capital saving' (Blaug, 1962: 360, emphasis in original). Blaug's use of the term 'capital saving', like Burgess's 'labour-using', relates to changes which resulted in economies in the use of working capital. This was reflected in the application and increase in scale of *current* techniques rather than any major impetus towards a greater degree of automated production. These are examples of what Harris (1983) has referred to as 'extensive growth', as distinct from 'intensive' in which growth is secured via labour-saving technological innovation. The markets abroad, largely the outcome of 'accidental empire' (McNeill, 1983), appear to have encouraged a continued application of existing technology rather than a pursuit of breakthrough innovations. In itself this acted to improve the position of labour since it reduced the threat of substitution by new techniques: at the same time the demand for labour grew in response to a general prosperity and growth in product demand. Indeed, even as the 19th century wore on and foreign markets became increasingly competitive due to the inflow of goods from America and Germany, labour's position did not decline since the competitiveness of home industries such as cotton became more and more dependent on operators' efficiency to ensure that the machinery ran at full capacity.

The general prosperity of mid-Victorian Britain has an important bearing on the position of labour both economically and politically. First, higher profits facilitated rises in wage levels where these were demanded or were necessary to attract workers. The market situation of labour was further improved by less pronounced cyclical fluctuations, reflecting the importance of exports to the home industry and the tendency for downturns not to occur in all markets simultaneously. Second, the optimism created during this 'high noon' of Victorian prosperity encouraged a greater (although in many cases grudging) acceptance of 'respectable' trade unionism. With unions concentrated mainly within the labour aristocracy of skilled workers, and their leaders overwhelmingly moderate in character, unionism did not represent a fundamental threat to the existing social and economic order. Disturbances did occur among the rank and file but tended to be dampened down by union leaders who acted as 'a steadying and uplifting influence on their members' (Phelps Brown, 1983: 22). More characteristically, individual and bourgeois values permeated this early unionism and its objectives were as much concerned with maintaining a separateness from lower grades as with improving the members' own pay rates.

Unionism was at this time not a mass movement nor a militant one. In many ways, it was more akin to the earlier guild organisations and to the later professional associations, with their emphasis on occupational qualifications and standards, than to the large-scale unions which developed in the 20th century. In 1850 trade union membership was probably no more than a quarter of a million, concentrated in London and the North in craft occupations, textiles and mining. Among the skilled unions in particular, the central organising tenet was exclusiveness. Not for more than another generation were the organising abilities of the mass of semi-skilled and unskilled workers to become evident. The skilled unions presented a relatively acceptable and reassuring face to the state and to capital—both anxious to avoid giving succour to a more militant unionism by rejecting the extant version. Establishing relations with the 'new model' unions of the 1850s (although their emphasis on craft, moderation and exclusiveness was anything but new) represented a means of accommodating the articulate section of the working class, with its 'responsible' leadership, into the political and economic structure without disturbing the assumed prerogatives of land, capital and title. By doing so, employers also gained an additional source of supervision over worker behaviour and an institutionalised means of pay settlement. The aftermath of the repeal of the Combination Acts a generation earlier may have added further support to the growing acceptance of trade unions after 1850, in that it had not opened the floodgates to a tide of militant unionism as some had feared. On the contrary, removing the secrecy surrounding unionism may have dissipated militancy at a time when popular disturbances were relatively common (particularly focused by Chartism but also including other grievances such as the rural poverty at the centre of the Swing riots in 1830).

By the 1850s the beginnings of trade union bureaucratisation were present. Both the newly formed Amalgamated Society of Engineers and the Amalgamated Society of Carpenters and Joiners, for example, were developing centralised organisations staffed by full time officials (Harrison, 1984: 274). What we now understand as collective bargaining (then more commonly termed 'conciliation') also began to develop from this time. Its orientations and powers were reflected not only in its wholly economic character but also in the way employers secured agreements over pay settlement which relied heavily on selling price, sliding scales (as in coal) or similar indices. These acted not only to bolster and legitimise the prevailing patterns of income distribution, but also to penalise workers in certain industries where gains in efficiency and resulting reductions in price acted against union claims for pay increases (Burgess, 1975: 194). Indeed, during this period, increases in wages had more to do with market forces of labour supply and demand than with the presence of bargaining arrangements or trade unions (Phelps Brown, 1983: 21).

It is evident that while unions became gradually more involved in bargaining, employers accepted the legitimacy of only a limited sphere of union activity, centred on pay and other basic terms of employment. This contrasts with the traditional areas of concern of craft unions, whose organising tenets rested in important part on control over recruitment and the ensuring of customary ways of working. That many employers and the state were able to enforce this more restricted view of unionism may in practice reflect years of success in circumventing craft restrictions, particularly by technological change but also aided by a growing labour market and one increasingly mobile as a result of communications improvements.

The growing acceptability of trade unions and 'responsible' sections of the working class began to be reflected in the political as well as the economic sphere, and specifically in the areas of franchise qualification and the legal protection of trade unions. In part this period may be seen to represent the state acting out the basis of its legitimation, that is as non-partisan, protecting the equality of all before the law and promoting the *laissez-faire* ideals of justice, fairness, freedom and equality. In part also these political developments may be understood as moves to accommodate sections of the working class within the prevailing system. However, as Giddens (1982: 171) warns, the emphasis on accommodation undervalues the influence of individual and group struggles to improve their lot. It is notable that in the creation of the Labour Party, union contributors saw it (and political activity generally) only as a means to secure legal conditions more favourable to union performance. This can be interpreted either as myopia or, as we prefer, an explicit rejection of accommodation in favour of autonomy.

In the years immediately following the Second Reform Act (1867), the issue of the status both of trade unions and of employees came to the fore. A Royal Commission established in the same year concluded that trade unions were useful components of the social and economic structure (Phelps Brown, 1983: 25), and recommended legal protection to unions pursuing their 'legitimate' objectives of agreements on pay and basic terms of employment. By 1875, as a result of the 1871 Trade Union Act and the 1875 Conspiracy and Protection of Property Act, those functions of a trade union concerning the defence and advancement of members' terms and conditions of employment were not to be treated as criminal offences as long as these actions were taken 'in contemplation or furtherance of a trade dispute'. The atmosphere of reform is also caught by the title of another Act at this time concerning breach of contract. The Employers and Workmen Act 1875 represented, says Pelling (1971), 'a significant change in title' from the previous Master and Servant nomenclature; the significance being a legal acknowledgement that employees should be construed and treated as free agents within the employment relation rather than as servile subordinates. Notwithstanding the continued objective subordination of workers to the owners of the means of production, this legal ratification of capitalist principles did mean that a contract of employment could begin to develop in English law.

The development of union rights did not maintain a steady upward progression, however. In the period towards the end of the 19th century unions were attacked both in the courts and at the workplace by employers pursuing new work methods and asserting their prerogative over technological change. It became evident that union protection established in the 1870s was far from comprehensive. Under the 1870s legislation unions enjoyed immunities, that is, if they were engaged in normal industrial disputes they could not be held liable for prosecution under criminal law. However, in certain circumstances, individuals within the union could be sued for damages under civil law. Moreover, in 1900 during a strike by the members of the

Amalgamated Society of Railway Servants, the Taff Vale Railway Company in South Wales won an injunction against the Society's officers. The injunction was reversed by a Court of Appeal which favoured the union argument for immunity but the House of Lords upheld the initial judgement against the Society. This opened the way for the company to sue the union for damages for conspiring to induce workers to break their contracts and prevent the movement of goods. This Taff Vale judgement of 1901 thus revealed unions to be more vulnerable still, since it established that unions had a corporate legal identity and so could themselves be sued for damages. The judgement 'was at once recognised as momentous by alert trade unionists' (Phelps Brown, 1983: 32), representing as it did a fundamental threat to their financial security and ability to engage in industrial action. Indeed, this was not the first (nor the last) sign of a legal challenge to union security following the 1870s legislation. Two years earlier in the case of *Lyons v. Wilkins*, the legality of peaceful picketing had been brought into question (Pelling, 1965: 200). In the month following the Lords' ruling on Taff Vale, the case of *Quinn v. Leatham* brought another ruling against the union involved, this time for boycotting an employer (ibid.: 213–14). These cases revealed the continued vulnerability of trade unions to a civil law which gave primacy to the rights and freedoms of the individual over the collective and which was manifestly willing to treat the employer (irrespective of the actual pattern of ownership) as an individual property-owner dealing with a collective trade union. The cases also appear to reflect a judiciary acting somewhat out of step with sentiments expressed by government which, as we have seen, had been tending to support trade union security and the legitimacy of union activities within the economic system.

By the early 1900s the trade union movement in Britain was much altered in size and character from its 1870s counterpart. Membership had grown from around three quarters of a million in 1888 to over two million by 1900, much of the increase stemming from the organisation of unskilled and semi-skilled workgroups, particularly during 1889–90. Yet in other respects unions were not a particular source of concern for politicians. Strike levels were generally falling in the last years of the century and the major lock-out in the engineering industry in 1897–88 had resulted in an employer victory over working hours and the introduction and manning of new machinery (Burgess, 1975). Moreover, union demands were not becoming more overtly political in character (other than a growing, although not vociferous, demand for an independent political voice in Parliament). As a result the favourable disposition towards union security evident in the 1870s was still present among many politicians early in the next century. Hence in the years after the Taff Vale judgement responses to trade union campaigns for greater immunity resulted in a number of Liberal opposition attempts to create protective legislation, as well as the establishment of a Royal Commission on Trade Disputes and Trade Combinations in 1903.

SYSTEM UNDER STRESS: THE 20TH CENTURY TO THE FIRST WORLD WAR

It was the 1906 general election and the pledges made by Liberal candidates to attract the working class vote that finally led to legislation in the form of the Trade Disputes Act, introduced by the newly elected Liberal government in 1906. This Act placed strike action outside the scope of civil conspiracy in a way that its 1870s equivalent had done with respect to criminal conspiracy. The Act also reasserted the legality of peaceful picketing, as long as the action was taken 'in contemplation or furtherance of a trade dispute'.

Hence after a decade or more of union setbacks in the courts, 1906 represented a major achievement for trade unions and heralded a period of growing presence and power. This growth in power was manifested in various ways, not least the growth in membership. In the year before the 1906 Act total membership stood at under two million and had been stagnant for the previous five years (in fact it had fallen slightly). Between 1906 and 1914, however, the number of union members doubled. The immunities granted under the 1906 Act were also reflected in the greater number and larger scale of subsequent industrial disputes. In the five years preceding the Act there were an average of 397 stoppages per annum with an average of 2 522 000 days lost (figures calculated from Pelling, 1971). In the next five years (1907–11) the annual averages rose to 558 stoppages and 7 132 000 days lost, whilst in the years 1912–16, these annual averages reached 894 stoppages and 13 194 000 days lost. Nor was this simply a quantitative increase in strike activity. Industrial disorder took on a more militant character with troops and police clashing with striking miners and transport workers, leading to three deaths in the South Wales valleys and two more in Liverpool (Geary, 1985: 47). This time of violent picketing, repressive policing and military involvement has in retrospect been identified as a 'pivotal period in the evolution of social control' (ibid.: 47). It also reflected a stronger and more organised 20th-century trade union movement, less willing to accept the rates being offered at a time when steady increases in the cost of living gave further impetus to claims for a reasonable wage (Clegg, 1985). More generally the period is characterised by other foci of social unrest, including the Irish Home Rule issue and the demands of the Suffragettes, whilst in the trade union movement (particularly in mining) the doctrine of syndicalism and the achievement of workers' control through direct action was at its height (ibid.: see also Pelling, 1971: 139–41; Dangerfield, 1970).

Bearing in mind the judgement that it was not 'industrialisation and economic growth that led to the expanded and complex role of government in contemporary Britain but the consequences of war and economic decline' (Coombes and Walkland, 1980: 6); bearing in mind also the failing powers of the Liberal Party in the late 19th/early 20th century, we can understand government policies of the day as in the economic and civil spheres 'an uncoordinated, pragmatic search for consensus' (ibid.: 12). This is partly reflected in the persistence of long-established government efforts to encourage conciliation and arbitration in employment relations, and partly by its newer efforts to intervene in industrial disputes and—through a reorganised Board of Trade—to set up joint negotiating bodies wherever possible. But as the 20th century dawned trading conditions deteriorated, putting pressure on profit margins and wages alike. Employers increasingly looked to the United States' examples and experiments in scientific management and in the legal control of labour for solutions; meanwhile workers were increasingly dissatisfied with their trade union and parliamentary leaders, and increasingly strident and organised at the rank and file level; in short, both sides of industry were more radical, less conciliatory. The Liberals hung on to power by an alliance with the labour vote and the trade union leadership. But if the Tories had not broken them on Home Rule and if the First World War had not suddenly solidified the masses around the national interest, the indications are that British capital and labour would have dispensed with parliamentary democracy and fought out their differences at the factory gate (Dangerfield, 1970).

In any event, though the First World War did much to integrate further the British state with the domestic economy and civil society, it is apparent that as the people were granted ever greater access to Parliament, its powers were being eroded— by the greater bureaucratisation of parliamentary business, by the cynical manipulation of popular opinion and by the preparedness of some elite sections to act clandestinely, even treasonably, against the elected government. That the different constituent parts of the state apparatus were by no means united under the will of the elected political representatives was to become increasingly apparent as the 20th century advanced.

5 The Impact of the Two World Wars

The First World War seems to have come as a shock to the government of Britain. In spite of the increasingly large public expenditures of the previous three decades on the Royal Navy, and in spite of the emergence of its own military-industrial complex, Britain entered the First World War almost wholly unprepared for it. This sprang largely from the inability of Britain's military advisers to consider anything but past glories, glories, moreover, of the 18th century rather than the 19th. As French's (1986) investigations reveal, Liberal military policies in 1914 reiterated those of the 18th century in giving primacy to the role of the Navy to keep the seas open, and to financial and banking support of continental allies whose armies would do the main land-fighting. Britain went into the war with a Navy confident of a short, sharp and successful engagement with the German fleet, and a small professional army not expecting to be called out but grooming their horses just in case. In the event, the German fleet proved equal to the British, the Army had to be massively expanded via conscription and Britain's ability to fund and manage the finances of its allies collapsed only marginally less quickly than did theirs. Without substantial loans from America there might well not have been an eventual allied victory.

The nostalgia of the generals and admirals might have been challenged but for the compatibility of their strategy with classical orthodox economics—the type then (and largely still) espoused by the Bank of England, the Treasury, finance and industrial capital. The various strands of this theory can be seen to have developed over time and with experience. By the 16th century British rulers were well aware of the significance of international trade to the country's strength, and therefore of the significance of wages as a cost of production. By the 19th century that understanding had been turned by Adam Smith and the experience of industrialisation to a concern for productivity and economic growth. By the 20th century, following industrial recession and trading difficulties in the late 19th, concerns about wage levels returned to accompany those about growth and productivity. Roughly speaking, classical orthodox economics argues that the nation's political strength is a function of its standing in the international economy. The best measure or reflection of this standing is the nation's international credit status: if a country can borrow abroad, it is because other parties see it as a good risk. Maintaining such confidence, so the argument goes, means never borrowing beyond the scale of National Savings. But National Savings are large and secure— in an economy geared predominantly to international trade— only so long as there is minimal price inflation. Curbing price inflation in turn means ensuring that domestic demand does not exceed supply, and (related) that wages do not rise beyond productivity increases. Thus not only does classical orthodox economics argue for incomes policy and against non-profit-returning public expenditures, it also argues against mass conscription. For when workers are pulled into the Armed Forces and out of the economy the result is inflationary—both in the economic sense of pushing up wages through labour shortages, and in the political sense of raising popular expectations via participation in the war effort.

It is for these reasons, enhanced by the unpopularity of conscription, that Britain has preferred a small professional army to a mass conscript one. But these preferences (expressed repeatedly throughout the 19th century, at the outset of the First World War, in the interwar period to 1939, and again since the 1950s) stand in contrast to those of Britain's continental neighbours. Unprotected by the seas, they have had to anticipate land-based warfare. Perhaps as a result their state structures have developed along more dominant, interventionist lines. Domestic stability for them has been bought at a cost of absorbing the masses more thoroughly into, or under, different sections of the state apparatus. The army is one such section, especially well-designed to inculcate obedience and especially rational given the land-based threat of neighbouring states. Since the late 18th century the majority of continental European powers have maintained mass armies, and in 1914 it was just such an army— one million strong—which marched out of Germany and into France and Belgium. The British state had no immediate response. Kitchener's call for volunteers was, fortunately perhaps, uniquely successful at calling into battle the ordinary

British man, but even then conscription proved necessary to replace the thousands slaughtered on the Somme, at Ypres, in Flanders and elsewhere. By the end of the war almost three million men of the British Armed Forces were dead or wounded.

The economic consequences of warfare do not just concern the labour factor, of course; neither were they entirely as predicted by orthodox economics. With the exception of artillery and small arms manufacture, and shipbuilding, few of Britain's arms industries were prepared to move speedily into war production. While patriotic fervour was—certainly in the opening stages of the war—generally strong, free enterprise was totally unclear about what to produce and, more to the point, whether the laying in of extra capacity and/or the diversion of production from civil to military outputs was commercially justified. The prevailing anticipation of a short, sharp war supported their caution. In overcoming these problems, the peculiarities of the English shine through yet again. McNeill (1983: 315) reports that the length of the war compelled, within each of the adversary nations, the bringing together under single political rule of all previously independent, market-driven, organisations . . . 'a national firm for waging war.' Only in Britain, he adds, was it 'business as usual'.

Although, through the newly created (1915) Ministry of Munitions, Lloyd George set out to convert the entire economy to the war effort, he did so by mixing voluntarism in the economic sphere with compulsion in the military: the two being held together by a vastly increased state bureaucracy which recorded, communicated among, oversaw and thus co-ordinated the efforts of Britain's various parts. One consequence of war was thus greatly to expand the mechanisms of state administrative power while—for reasons of security, speed and control—centralising its exercise in the Cabinet rather than Parliament. In that sense, the British state was propelled by war into forms and powers which more nearly resembled those of the states with which it fought. Nonetheless, voluntarism in the economic sphere remained a political necessity. The Liberal Party then in power owed its existence to the near equal balance of powers between landed and industrial interests in the 19th century. In its constitutional underwriting of sectional autonomy moderated by compromise it had represented that balance. By the end of the 19th century the erosion of landed capital's powers plus those Liberal traditions of seeking compromise propelled the Party into an alliance with the emergent labour voice. But that alliance, expressed through the mechanisms of parliamentary democracy, was yet impotent in the face of the primary owners of wealth-generating property—industrial and finance capital. Inflated naval expenditures kept government policies tied to the City of London via the institutions of the National Debt and the Bank of England. Simultaneously, the Conservative and Unionist vote in the Commons was sufficiently strong, and their policies sufficiently in tune with those of the Army, the Treasury, the Bank and the City, for the elected government of the day to be dissuaded from any thoughts of compelling enterprise.

Compulsion is one thing, direction is another. State direction of enterprise by the awarding of contracts, and by the management and direction of labour, meant that by the last stages of the war Britain 'succeeded with a directed economy at home combined . . . with old-fashioned market mobilisation abroad, financed by American bank loans' (McNeill, 1983: 328). (The latter did, of course, give the United States a vested interest in an Allied victory.) One consequence of these state demands on the economy was to stimulate the spread of mass production techniques from arms to cars, trucks, aircraft and combustion engines. The state as customer, and often too as investor, underwrote technological change in industries the products of which, with the exception of aircraft, could then—being mass-produced and therefore cheaper—seek and find domestic markets. Thus did state rivalries contribute to the birth of the Second Industrial Revolution, based as it was on vehicles, engines, petrol, electricity and synthetics. This contribution was made inadvertently rather than consciously, the reason being that orthodox economics obscured the point (subsequently made by John Maynard Keynes) that massive state expenditures can, under certain conditions, stimulate real economic growth rather than inflation. This point is not a small one given that Britain's recovery from the Depression following the First World War had everything to do with the ability of these new industries to exert an upward multiplier on the home economy. Be that as it may, in the preceding years businessmen and many political leaders were united in viewing the state's economic interventions as an evil necessitated by war and to be carefully contained by voluntary co-operation. There was in any event a general agreement between business and political decision-makers that the crucial factor and problem was manpower.

LABOUR AND THE FIRST WORLD WAR

In Britain the workforce was never conscripted, only the soldiers. But in the first phases of war the popular response of Britain's men to Kitchener's call for volunteers was so great as to leave arms production (amongst other areas) severely undermanned— with awful consequences for British soldiers in France. This and similar experiences ensured that the efficient allocation of labour became central to the state's efforts. Because of the pre-war entrenchment of the unions government officials found it useful to involve union leaders in these allocations, and the unions were exhorted to suspend traditional restrictive practices and industrial actions for the duration. Although not all British workers were ready to concede, the appeal to duty did work. By 1918, as a result of voluntary applications of additional effort, British agricultural workers had raised wheat and potato production by 40 per cent above pre-war averages, and food imports had been brought down by one-third.

In chapter 1 we asserted, following Sumner (1979), that the three basic tactics of a ruling elite are ideology, bribery and coercion. The ideological effort in Britain pertinent to mass mobilisation had been developing over at least three decades, the fears of lost naval supremacy and of Russian and German aggrandisement having been deliberately stimulated for party political reasons as well as more genuine concerns for national security. By the outbreak of war there was, claims McNeill (1983), a martial enthusiasm bordering on madness among the European populations. Once war broke out the emphasis moved to duty: men who failed to strain every sinew and make every sacrifice for the war effort were in Britain chastised as slackers or awarded a white feather to symbolise their imputed cowardice. But if these were the ideological sticks, the carrots came in the form of an extension of welfare measures both by employers and the state, in promises, and in the further incorporation of trade union and labour leaders into the institutions of political and economic decision-making.

The welfare measures included state provision of medical care for those who fought, and the rationing of food for the population generally. The latter in particular, since it fed those who were hitherto undernourished, contributed to a general improvement in the health of the population. In that sense there were genuine rewards to the British people for their wartime sacrifice—the beginnings of a welfare state (albeit supportive of a warfare state) which, as it developed, significantly expanded civil rights. By comparison, the promises—of a return to normal work practices once war was won, of a curb on excessive profits (that is, above 20 per cent), of 'homes fit for heroes'—were not fully honoured. The impact of war on the world economy saw to that. But they seem to have worked for its duration in that the majority of British people gave their assistance willingly enough throughout. This may reflect the successes of state responsiveness to and accommodation of labour's interests—the incorporation of labour representatives into government decision-making, and the encouragement of similar incorporation in the realm of private enterprise. In this the government was building on its pre-war experiences.

Legislation on pensions, national insurance and labour exchanges in the first decade had in part reflected a response to a growing working class electorate. Trade unionists sat on committees formed to administer this legislation 'thereby knitting them further into the structure of public recognition, office and status' (Fox, 1985: 231). Similarly, labour representation grew in the Labour Department of the Board of Trade which, before the creation of a separate Ministry of Labour, was the main source of the state's industrial relations policy (Middlemas, 1979: 59). In line with the 1896 Conciliation Act and the earlier Royal Commission report on labour in 1894, the Labour Department headed by George Askwith continued to advocate the development of conciliation boards and the growth of trade union organisation, employers' associations and joint machinery to regularise relations between employers and workpeople. This encouragement of conciliation was reflected in the number of conciliation and arbitration boards in operation. In 1894 there had been 64 such boards; by 1905 this had risen to 162 and by 1913 had almost doubled again to 325 (Macdonald, 1976: 79–80). Similarly, protective legislation was extended to those working in low paid and poorly organised industries, by the establishment of minimum wage machinery under the Trade

Board Act of 1909 and by the House of Commons' resolution of the same year which required those under contract to the state to pay 'fair wages'. From 1893 the government—although not invariably with success—was more frequently intervening with employers on behalf of labour. Thus, in 1893 the government successfully brought a stoppage in the mining industry to an end by persuading employers to withdraw a threatened wage reduction. Such interventions occurred with greater frequency after 1906; for example, in 1907 and 1911 in the railway industry and in 1912 in a mining dispute. Government reasons were rational enough: the growth of union membership and the unions' greater national organisation had created a situation where not only could the activities of a single employer be disrupted but also those of the whole country. This potential for disputes in certain industries to dislocate the entire economy 'brought the Government in with a powerful concern to secure a settlement' (Phelps Brown, 1983: 73).

But the concerns of government were not narrowly economic: organised labour also now had the power, or so it then seemed, to disrupt the political order of the country. In the immediate pre-war period there were numerous domestic indicators of increasing labour militancy, and there was also evidence from the continent and especially from Tsarist Russia of the growing appeal and powers of communist and socialist ideologies. Strike levels in Britain, which had averaged under 2.75 million working days lost per annum for the years 1900 to 1908, rose to 10 million in 1910 and peaked at almost 41 million days lost in 1912. In parts of the mining, railway and engineering industry this militancy was clearly orchestrated by supporters of syndicalism, guild socialism and other forms of workers' control (Cole, 1923). These advocates of radical industrial democracy, although small in number (when compared to those in France where syndicalism gained much wider support) asserted their threat to industrial and political order on a scale which far outweighed their numerical strength, appealing to those sections of labour (such as in the South Wales coalfield) 'soured by long awareness of injustice unrelieved' (Charles, 1973: 24). In at least four of the major stoppages in the strike wave of 1911–14 groups of syndicalists played 'a significant part' (Clegg, 1985: 73). With their aim of industrial unionism and decentralised workers' control, to be achieved through direct action culminating in a general strike, the syndicalists posed a threat not only to employers but also to the state and trade union leaders. This threat took on tangible form not only in outbreaks of militancy but also in the growth of unofficial shop steward organisations in engineering and shipbuilding, which acted to decentralise union power further towards the shopfloor (Cole, 1923; Coates and Topham, 1986).

Political sympathies among influential sections of the labour movement were not the only reason for increased militancy. Clegg (1985) has shown that the 14 major strikes between 1911 and 1914 were overwhelmingly industrial rather than political in nature—mainly disputes over wage claims and union recognition, fuelled by increases in the cost of living, rises in the demand for labour, certain skill shortages, employer resistance to unionism (particularly evident in the railway industry) and frustration at the lack of impact of the Labour Party (see also Macdonald, 1976). The vigour of the strike wave was further stimulated by a number of notable successes for the strikers, such as the 1911 Seamen's strike which gave impetus to unrest in the dockworking industry (ibid.: 75). But while in themselves not explicitly political, the magnitude of the strike wave and its periodic violent outbursts (see Geary, 1985) gave the strikes a political importance; particularly so in the light of events taking place simultaneously both within the industrial sphere (such as the formation of the Triple Alliance of unions organising miners, transport workers and railwaymen) and beyond (notably the Suffragette protest and the conflict surrounding the Irish Home Rule Bill: see Dangerfield, 1970, for detailed discussion). Together these contributed to a general atmosphere of unrest which forced the government among its other actions to establish a more clearly defined policy towards labour issues than it had hitherto.

It was thus not by chance that the overtures of the state and employers towards organised labour took place against a background of growing labour electoral power, industrial unrest and demands from a vocal minority for the overthrow of traditional forms of capitalist control. Ramsay (1977, 1978) has drawn a direct link between the two—the growth of joint representative machinery being explained as a direct response to labour pressures and a desire to accommodate potential conflict and thereby head off any rank and file shift towards 'direct action'. The link holds good for political as well as economic spheres of activity. As early as 1870 'democracy' had become a major element in the rhetoric of politicians courting the electorate, whereas hitherto earlier generations of politicians had feared and spoken against it (Miliband, 1982: 27). By the early 20th century the power of organised labour within and beyond Parliament was strong enough, and its contributions to economic strength and the war efforts crucial enough, to ensure that labour's demands would be taken seriously. The nature of those demands, however, as expressed through the official structures of trade unions and the Labour Party, was far from revolutionary. Rather it was merely to get a better deal for the unions and workers within the established hierarchy (Fox, 1977: 142). Thus it was with official labour advice that the pre-war Liberal government commissioned labour exchanges, health and unemployment insurance provisions, and welfare measures. Similarly, in the preparatory period of the First World War, it was by an agreement with union leaders that the government was able to secure a temporary dilution of skilled labour and subsequently a Treasury Agreement (later incorporated into the 1915 Munitions of War Act), under which unions accepted arbitration in disputes and the relaxation of customary practices so as to maximise output. In return for such co-operation the government agreed to ensure restoration of customary practices after the war and, under union pressure, also to pay dilutees at skilled rates. A number of union-originated MPs were also given office in Herbert Asquith's and particularly in Lloyd George's coalition governments. In Lloyd George's case this indicated not simply a general dependence on labour but also a more immediate dependence on the Labour Members to bolster his vulnerable position at the head of a coalition government. As Phelps-Brown (1983: 75) comments, the government 'recognised that the power lay with the unions and dealt with them realistically'.

The onset of war heightened the necessity for peaceful and predictable industrial relations ... to ward off any internal insurrectionary threat, to maintain economic performance generally and to ensure that the labour factor could be directed and controlled to best advantage in the war effort. Reflecting 'the patent truth that victory depended on the workers continuing to work and the soldiers continuing to fight' (Bentley, 1974: 44), labour representation at all levels increased yet further within both government and enterprise. Regarding the former, the war brought an increased scale of involvement of Labour MPs and trade union leaders (together with employers) in government administration and in government discussions on improving munitions output and army recruitment. Indeed, such was the union presence on government-established committees that critics within the movement accused those holding government posts of being 'agents of the state' although, as Clegg (1985: 175) observes, this exaggerates their lack of opposition to government policy (for example, over conscription). Regarding the latter, the fostering of plant-level consultative relations and state-sponsored conciliatory schemes (resting squarely on notions of 'unity' and 'national interest') did not eliminate strikes entirely. In 1917 over 5.5 million working days were lost due to stoppages. But there was a significant reduction, the average number of working days lost in 1915–18 being less than half that of 1911, 1913 and 1914 and only just over one-tenth the number lost in 1912 (Clegg, 1985: 578). By 1917 national bargaining systems were becoming increasingly common, and operated in industries accounting for at least a third of the employed labour force and over half the total trade union membership (ibid.: 168). In many instances these national bargaining systems were industry-wide.

With some notable exceptions (such as the railway industry), employers were coming to terms with trade unionism, having found it less difficult than first imagined to reconcile union demands over wages and conditions with the goal of profitable growth. Trade unionism, which had grown only slowly in the first decade of the 20th century (2.02 million in 1900, 2.57 million in 1910; Pelling, 1971: 280), accelerated in subsequent years to stand at a little over 4 million by the outbreak of war. It increased rapidly thereafter to reach a peak of over 8 million in 1920 (a union density of 48 per cent) although this was not sustained in the interwar years of depression (Bain and Price, 1980). Already, by the outbreak of war, semi- or unskilled workers were numerically dominant in the union movement. Only three of the largest ten unions in this period were truly craft unions (Clegg, 1985), although the craft union traditions of 'moderation' and 'responsibility' had a broader influence on the wider union movement than this proportion might suggest. Additionally, shop steward organisation, which had been developing in the years leading up to the war, became established in a wider range of industries and, as Cole has pointed out, was able to secure power due to the great shortage of skilled workers and the near impossibility of replacement during wartime (Cole, 1923: 45). Labour power as a whole increased as the effect of war stimulated growth and profitability and gave rise to labour shortages, especially among skilled trades in engineering and shipbuilding. The rise in the cost of living (up 23 per cent in 1915) and the continuation of high profits, despite government attempts to curb them, led workers in a number of industries to flex this industrial muscle in pursuit of higher wage settlements.

Such experiences were augmented by suspicions among the rank and file, some of whom as we have already noted were ready to accuse their leaders of becoming 'agents of the state'. A wave of strikes in May 1917 led both to a Commission of Inquiry on Industrial Unrest and indirectly to the Whitley Committee on the Relations between Employers and Employed. This latter committee was a sub-group of the government's Reconstruction Committee, chaired by the deputy speaker of the Commons, J. H. Whitley, and charged with seeking a structure of industrial relations which would avert conflict and quell any post-war demands for worker's control. The Committee, which included trade union and employer representatives, issued five reports in all during 1917–18 (although the First Interim Report is by far the most important). The conclusions emphasised the importance of 'adequate organisation' of both employers and workpeople, and recommended industry-wide collective machinery centred on Joint Standing Industrial Councils (JICs) supported by District Councils and Works Committees. These joint committees were perceived as more than wage fixing bodies, however. Building on the wartime experience of consultation and 'obviously influenced by the current propaganda for industrial democracy' (Milne Bailey, 1934: 292), the Reports expressed support for more participative relations which would result in:

the better utilisation of the practical knowledge and experience of the workpeople . . . means for securing to the workpeople a greater share in and responsibility for the determination and observance of the conditions under which their work is carried on . . . the improvement of processes, machinery and organization . . . with special reference to cooperation in

carrying new ideas into effect and full consideration of the
workpeople's point of view in relation to them
(para 16 Interim Report, quoted in Charles, 1973: 104–5)

The overall effect of these various developments (namely, state
and employer willingness to recognise and bargain with unions;
their emphasis on conciliation; the sense of national unity
produced by war conditions) was to support an ideological vision
across the country of a unitary society, in which the co-operation,
loyalty and dedication of all was both generally assumed and
forthcoming. Such beliefs were to remain prominent in the
debates and initiatives attending workers' participation over the
next half century.

But there were limits to the process, and they became
increasingly evident as the war progressed. It is too simple to
characterise the wartime period unidimensionally as one in which
labour representation advanced due to the importance attached
by the state and employers to co-operation. On the contrary, in
the first half of the war any gains made by labour leaders in
being party to state decision-making were more than matched
by a marked reduction in the liberties of workpeople in both
work and civil contexts. At the workplace (or at least those
plants engaged in wartime production), the Munitions of War
Act 1915, precipitated partly by ammunition shortages in France,
sought a relaxation of the Factory Acts and the removal both
of restrictive practices and the right to strike, with disputes being
settled by compulsory arbitration. In the event, parts of the
Act (notably the clause banning strikes) proved unenforceable
although workers' liberty was restricted by the clause which
introduced a 'leaving certificate' restricting the movement of
labour out of munitions work. More significant in terms of
customary rights, however, was the part of the Act dealing with
skill dilution whereby skilled jobs were to be made available to
unskilled or semi-skilled men and women for the duration of the
war. Despite some opposition to dilution (for example among
the Clyde Workers' Committee), this provision of the Act took
effect quickly, not least because so many union activists were
away at war.

Outside the workplace a more fundamental challenge to
worker liberty came with the introduction of conscription in
1916, the voluntary systems of recruitment (including recruit-

ment drives by the Trades Union Congress itself) having failed to supply adequate numbers. At first only single men were conscripted but after March 1916 married men were also called-up. The labour movement was unsuccessful in resisting conscription despite a TUC decision to oppose it in favour of voluntary schemes, a Labour Party vote of more than 2:1 against it and a 'vast majority of trade unionists (who) were horrified at the prospect' (Clegg, 1985: 153).

There were, in short, as a result of war and alongside the greater accommodation of labour demands, major restrictions on labour's liberty, both as citizens (for example, compulsory conscription) and as workers (the suspension of traditional restrictive practices, for instance).

THE INTERWAR AND WARTIME PERIODS

As Hepple (1986) notes, the First World War did see the unions move into tripartite national economic government. But that incorporation split the labour movement between reformism and revolution, the official trade union and labour leadership strongly favouring the former—as indeed they were expected to do. As Bonar Law told the Cabinet in 1919, 'trade union organisation . . . is the only thing between us and anarchy' (Bagwell, 1971: 106). Even during the minority Labour governments of 1924 and 1929–31, the unions preferred industrial to parliamentary action. The weaknesses of these governments perhaps reflects the failures of the official leadership to live up to the more radical, potentially revolutionary, demands of informal labour leaders at grass roots level. Certainly Britain's coalition government of 1921 felt this revolutionary possibility probable enough to use its new Defence of the Realm Act to imprison the General Secretary of the Communist Party of Great Britain, and to arrest four years later (under the Incitement to Mutiny Act of 1797) 12 leading members of the same party (Miliband, 1982: 115). Predicated on the same fears, the Emergency Powers Act of 1920 (expanded in 1964 and exercisable without reference to Parliament) ensured that troops used to replace strikers would remain under military discipline all the while (Lewis, 1986). In other words, this legislation ensured that any part of the economy dubbed 'vital' by the state could be brought under martial law, a political fact of considerable significance even though the troops are often incapable of properly substituting for skilled and specialised workers.

In the same year (1920) the government secured a temporary settlement of a miners' dispute, whose effects the Triple Alliance between miners, railway and transport workers threatened to broaden. A similar intervention occurred five years later when the threat of a general strike brought a temporary government subsidy to avoid the imposition of wage cuts in the mining industry. The government in 1925 felt confronted 'by a great alliance of trade unions who had the power and the will to inflict enormous and irreparable damage on their country' (Phelps-Brown, 1983: 82, quoting Parliamentary Debates 1924–25, Vol. 187). By the 1920s the spectre of general strikes, and strikes affecting essential services, spurred political fears not previously encountered in an industrial relations system whose focus had become almost wholly economic in orientation.

When at the end of April 1926 the miners' wage subsidy was ended and the employers reimposed demands for wage cuts, the ensuing stoppage of work revealed a trade union movement much altered from its 19th-century counterpart. Where previously the unions had acted sectionally, now the Trades Union Congress was committed to calling for solidarity across the country in support of the miners. Accordingly workers in many industries (including transport, printing, building, chemicals, power, iron and steel) were called out. The General Strike had begun. One week later engineering and shipbuilding workers joined it (Pelling, 1971: 174). The strike underlined the ability of the unions to organise a widespread stoppage and halt production across many essential industries. But, in that it did not bring about an immediate resolution, it also highlighted the continuing and inherent weaknesses of labour's position. The difficulties facing the Trades Union Congress in maintaining unity, exacerbated by the opportunities for employers to hire non-union labour and, if necessary, call upon direct state labour in the form of the military, helped to ensure that when the strike was called off after nine days no significant concessions had been won by the strikers.

The same pressures which prompted the General Strike also revealed weaknesses in Whitleyism, in that the primary consultative role which Whitleyism envisaged for unions at workplace level failed to reflect the developing functions and authority of shop stewards (particularly in the engineering industry where they were increasingly involved in the negotiation of piecework rates: Clegg, 1985: 83–4). Although between 1918 and 1921 some 74 Joint Industrial Councils had been established (covering 3.5 million workers), the unitary style of Whitleyism did not take hold to the extent that some had hoped. It has been said that some of these hopes were less for genuine employer-employee unity, and more for diverting attention from the revolutionary example of Bolshevism. Many employers viewed warily the implication that unions would be much more involved in the running of business, and/or they were reluctant to alter their extant industrial relations machinery. At the same time the more militant among trades unionists viewed Whitley as a way to incorporate labour and to suppress the voices calling for root and branch changes in the way industry was run. The recommendations also suffered from a vagueness which made them easier to ignore. Management and unions could read very different things into aims such as providing workpeople with 'a greater share in and responsiblity for the determination and observance of the conditions under which their work is carried on' or 'securing to the workpeople a share in the increased prosperity of the industry'. This level of generality was maintained throughout and no specific rights for worker involvement were extended in the Reports. Similarly the precise role and interrelations of the three tiers of national, regional and local representation were unclear, there being little attempt to formulate precise constitutions. The role and operations of local works committees were particularly vague and their development much more patchy than the national Joint Industrial Councils. So much so that Cole concluded in 1923 (119) that 'the proposals for joint workshop organization have been almost completely abortive', the major exception being local committees in the government's own industries (Flanders, 1954). Cole attributes the lack of development in other sectors to the opposition of both employers and shop stewards to the more formalised system of relations which Whitleyism would involve. Additionally, the lack of a clear role, compounded by the different interpretations and aspirations of employers and trade unions, led to a number of committees—particularly in smaller industries—falling into decay. Nonetheless many of the largest survived the 1930s depression and by 1939 there were still around two million workers covered by them (Charles, 1973: 125). However, in the present argument what remains important about Whitley is its reflection of the state's ambition to foster orderly relations which avoided crises and which emphasised the unitary concepts of co-operation and consensus. Besides Whitleyism there were also other initiatives such as the short lived National Industrial Conference (1919–21), a tripartite attempt to promote a view of industrial relations not as conflicting interests striking temporary bargains but as interests capable of more lasting reconciliation through consultation and co-operative agreements (Charles 1973: 27; Clegg, 1985: 280–2). This desire for co-operation continued after the First World War as post-war expectations mixed with a release of commodity demand to create a sharp rise in prices. This in turn stimulated wage demands and contributed to a return to near 1912 levels of strike action (35 million days lost through stoppages in 1919).

These initiatives and the rhetoric of 'shared control' diminished as the 1920s wore on (although they periodically resurfaced, as in the Mond-Turner talks; see Charles, 1973). Following Ramsay's argument that participation and industrial democracy develop in waves corresponding to periods when management power (and we would add state power) is 'felt to be under siege' (1977: 382), the 1920s and 1930s can be identified as periods of decline in labour's influence—a decline principally caused by the weakened position of workers in the labour market.

The reason for this weakened position was, of course, that fundamental, war-induced, dislocation of the world economy known as the Depression. The devastation of Europe's economies meant that these nations had nothing to sell and could not afford to buy. America had cash and commodities but no customers. The paralysing hand of illiquidity gripped the international economy. Within Britain, where by 1920 union membership had reached a new height of 8 million, the numbers in unions began to decline and were not to recover until late in the 1930s, stagnating around 4.5 million for 16 years. In June 1929 just over a million British workers were unemployed, or 10 per cent of the total labour force. In July 1930 the figure was 2 million, in July 1931 it was 2.8 million. Never throughout the 1930s did the proportion fall below 10 per cent. Yet, although weakened, the British trade unions survived this period more or less intact, unlike their counterparts in continental Europe where, from the late 1920s, they were 'being crushed under the heel of dictatorship' (Pelling, 1971: 207). Perhaps the British bourgeois separation of political from economic spheres, and the preferences for voluntarism in the latter, afforded the unions here a protection from interference not enjoyed elsewhere. Alternatively it may be that the weaknesses in labour leadership and solidarity were sufficient to dispel any serious belief in their threat to the British political order. Whatever is the case, in Britain the unions were able to recover their position quite rapidly once the economy picked up, membership moving above six million in 1938. Part of this growth can be accounted for by the expansion of union membership in newly developing industries such as motor vehicle manufacture; in addition, as the Second World War approached, rearmament activity together with import tariffs stimulated both domestic employment growth and economic revival. As war threatened and hostilities began, the strategic position of labour ought to have begun improving markedly. Any improvement was however significantly delayed and dampened by the greater powers and the thinking of the Treasury, the City and industrial capital.

LABOUR IN THE PERIOD TO REARMAMENT

In 1928, although there were still elements of plural voting to be found, all adults over the age of 21 in Britain were given the vote. In June 1929 a Labour government was elected with 287 seats, under the premiership of Ramsey MacDonald. This Labour government was sensitive to its constituents' needs for employment, income, and so on, but it was not able speedily to reinvigorate Britain's trading activities nor to find some other basis for economic recovery. It therefore wished to expend public revenues in greater proportion on the public's needs for food, shelter and clothing. The Bank of England, the Treasury and the National Confederation of Employers' Organisations were uniformly hostile to the idea. Within Parliament the Tory-dominated May Committee vociferously and publicly articulated these hostilities. For them orthodox economics indicated that to move greater amounts of the National Income into consumption meant less for National Savings, which in turn meant loss of international credit status and confidence in the currency. The situation for the Labour government was exacerbated when, by 1930, the German and Austrian currencies collapsed under the pressure of hyper-inflation. This prompted a crisis in the international finance markets and thence a run on sterling. The Labour government sought to curb this loss of confidence by seeking loans abroad but the terms insisted upon by the lenders were those indicated by orthodox economics, namely, cut back on public expenditures such as unemployment and social security benefits, and cut wages in the public sector. Philip Snowdon, as Labour's Chancellor, attempted a budget compromise which succeeded only in splitting the Labour Party. He then turned, with Ramsey MacDonald, to the Tories and the Liberals so as to form a National government. This three-party alliance made some of the budget cuts and secured the loans, but was unable to stop the run on sterling. Britain was subsequently driven off the gold standard. This failure prompted a new election, in October 1931, for a National government dedicated to 'saving the nation'. The outcome was 472 seats for the Tories, 46 for Labour and 38 for Liberals and others. George V, knowing the unpopularity of the budget measures, felt it better that they be implemented by what was perceived to be a Labour government. To that end he persuaded Ramsey MacDonald to remain Prime Minister. Labour thus remained notionally in government but it was emasculated, and further cuts were made in social provisioning and wages. But while in some towns unemployment remained unrelieved at around 80 per cent throughout the 1930s, the business sections were in general highly content. Not only had their political representatives secured a victory over the Labour Party, not only had their prescriptions for national strength been borne into government policy but, in addition, they could see growth. These were new forms of growth concentrated around London and the south east—the Second Industrial Revolution of cars, engines, electricity, synthetics, even houses. The sun may have set over some sections of industrial capital but it was rising over others. Finance capital, ever mobile, moved its attentions to the lusty newcomers. Thus did growth in the domestic market rather than the recovery of international trade contribute to Britain's recovery from the interwar Depression.

But if the uncommercial demands of British labour had been quelled, another threat was developing to which the British ruling elites had no immediate response. Indeed, quite how to respond divided them acrimoniously and put the nation in jeopardy. This threat was the resurgent German nation, headed by Hitler, influenced by fascism and seeking retribution. Immediately following the First World War the British government had adopted the Ten-Year Rule, that is, all defence budgets were to be calculated on the assumption that Britain would not be involved in major warfare for at least ten years. (We are indebted to R. Shay, 1977, for these points.) Thus could public expenditures be turned instead to the more immediately pressing problems of unruly labour. Military advisers, of course, regarded the policy as lunacy, but it was not until the changed conditions of 1932 that they could get the policy revoked. This was a decision of the first National government. A second National government was elected in 1935, Labour securing some recovery with 154 seats but nonetheless still outnumbered more than two to one. At this election (the last until after the Second World War), the parties fought over the rearmament issue. Both Labour and Tories argued for rearmament but Labour stressed the need for international action through the League of Nations, an aspect the Tories ignored. But this non-pacific policy further divided the Labour Party, causing George Lansbury to stand down as leader in favour of Clement Attlee. With Labour divided and in a minority, the task of rearmament fell to the Tories under the leadership of Baldwin and Chamberlain. But their party more than any other represented the interests of free enterprise which, whether industrial or financial, preferred to pursue low risk, high return commercial strategies. A nation at war was to the contrary a high risk and, although returns might be good, they might also be short-lived. These commercial concerns were conveyed into government policies via the City of London connecting up with the Bank of England, in turn connecting up with the Treasury. They meant that British rearmament was both delayed and very seriously underfunded.

When in 1937 the government tried to float a National Defence Loan, it was seriously undersubscribed because the financial markets judged it far too great a sum at far too low a rate of return—a judgement warned in advance by the Bank and the Treasury trying to forestall the government endeavour. An immediate consequence was to re-emphasise taxation as a form of revenue. One government proposal was for a National Defence

Contribution, that is, a percentage (tiny) on all profits inflated by production for the rearmament or war efforts. Industrial heads, with Tory back-bench support, resolutely resisted this proposal—not because they disliked taxation but because under the terms set for the NDC by the Treasury, they would not be able to pass it on to the customer. Such a constraint, they felt, was undue government interference in the workings of the market. Accordingly, the Treasury rewrote the tax so that it could be passed on, and industry then accepted it. The burden of taxation thus passed exclusively to the consumers. But industry remained recalcitrant in other ways. The government needed productive capacity to be given over to the manufacture of field transports, aircraft and machine tools. Field transports meant the new automobile industry. This, because of its strengths in the domestic market, resulted in meetings, company by company, with government officials to negotiate the terms of contract. By comparison the machine tools and aircraft industries were intransigent. The latter—for reasons of its higher investment costs and shakier market position—operated as a cartel, refusing to supply the government except where the government made massive investments and gave commitments to purchase in a way that secured the industry a constant high rate of return. Labour representatives, of course, continually charged the industry with profiteering—the only communist Member of Parliament, Willie Gallacher, declaring in 1937: 'It has been very clearly demonstrated to the House and to the country that when profits are at issue, patriotism fades away'. Shay (1977) indeed attributes the whole policy of appeasement to the failure of capital to support in practical terms the British state's, or rather the British government's, efforts at rearmament.

This was because one section of the state, namely the Treasury, by and large operated from the same rationale as industrial and finance capital. The rationale informed Treasury attitudes even towards military strategy. A modern, equipped, mass army was unnecessary, argued the Treasury: the main battle-fighting would be done by the Air Force with the Navy in support. Chamberlain agreed: the continental allies would fight the land-battles because these would be confined to continental Europe. Britian had only to defend itself by air and sea. Thus it was that in December 1936 the British Army had no motorised field transports (the amount spent on hay exceeding that spent on petrol—see Liddell Hart, 1965: 261–76), no tanks and very few anti-tank and Bren guns. The idea of conscription was ruled out—on political grounds because of labour's antipathy to it, and on economic grounds because of fears of inflation. Indeed, although from 1932 the government was consulting with heads of the business communities about rearmament, it chose to ignore labour completely until 1938. In some part the aloofness of government and business leaders to labour reflected the antipathy publicly voiced by labour for rearmament. But the threat which fascism posed to the European labour movement prompted a change of heart, and by 1936 the Trades Union Congress, Ernest Bevin, Lord Citrine and Hugh Dalton had pledged union and labour assistance. The practice of consulting labour thus commenced some two years later than labour's declared willingness to co-operate. This policy of ignoring organised labour was stringently followed in spite of acute shortages of skilled labour because, as Cabinet papers reveal (Shay, 1977: 125), official thinking was that 'Wages in the armaments industries must not be such as would attract labour from ordinary civil and export industries in such numbers as to impair their productive capacity; nor must wages in the industries be forced up in sympathy with wages in the armaments industries, to a point that would destroy their competitive power in the world market'.

LABOUR IN THE SECOND WORLD WAR

While resolutely ducking the issue of consulting with labour until the last minute, government leaders nonetheless were painfully aware of their dependency for uninterrupted output and steady price levels on good labour relations. 'Nothing could be done', Baldwin told the House of Commons in 1936 'which would menace organised labour or trade union standards' (quoted in Middlemas, 1979: 249). The sensitive subjects which the government were wary of raising for fear of antagonising the unions included skill dilution, new training schemes and transfer of labour.

As war approached labour shortages exacerbated the short-comings of the state's defence preparations. By mid-1938 the TUC had been granted some involvement in the state's industrial policy, although its General Council continued to complain of inadequate consultation, particularly on key issues such as the schedule of reserved occupations (Middlemas, 1979: 261, 263). Postponement of emergency legislation and conscription has also been seen by Middlemas as a sign of the government's recognition of the strength and strategic importance of the organised working class (ibid.: 264).

In the summer of 1940 Chamberlain invited Attlee, as leader of the Labour Party, to join in a coalition government. Attlee agreed on condition that Churchill, not Chamberlain, led it. Attlee, Herbert Morrison and Ernest Bevin, as Labour MPs, entered the War Cabinet, in which all three demonstrated considerable skills. Bevin in particular faced directly the task of managing what war had made 'the ultimate resource' (Middlemas, 1979: 270), namely, labour power. It was largely Bevin's doing that war legislation prohibiting strikes and incitement to strike was little used, that voluntarism rather than compulsion ruled in wage restraint, that dilution did not proceed without consultation, that employers recognised unions and that no employer secured a state contract without first offering satisfactory working conditions and welfare arrangements to its employees. It was also at Bevin's initiative that a Joint Consultative Committee was created at national level to be a more efficient replacement of the National Joint Advisory Council.

The JCC pulled top union leaders directly into government decision-making, and enabled workable agreements to be obtained on crucial issues such as strikes and lockouts, and skill dilution. These measures, augmented by a fair rationing system, by improvements in social welfare provisioning, by the freezing of rents, and by full employment, secured both social peace and diligence (Brown, 1982: 286–7).

As well as direct labour involvement in the state apparatus, the Second World War saw a burgeoning of collective bargaining and participative machinery on a scale larger than had occurred in the First World War. As before, however, these arrangements reflected not only labour's strength but also the state and employers' keenness to institutionalise and contain that strength. Forty-six new Whitley Councils were established during the war whilst, in late 1940 at local level, consultation in the form of factory-wide Joint Production Committees was introduced with official government approval (Ramsay, 1977: 388). By mid-

1943 there were over 4000 such committees operating in the engineering industry, covering 2.5 million workers and dealing with a range of issues from complex technical matters to the application of dilution agreements and the level of absenteeism (Currie, 1979: 156; Clegg and Chester, 1954: 338). Similar committees were established in shipbuilding, mining and construction. Again, the declared emphasis was on consultation rather than on joint decision-making. But as Blyton (1981) has demonstrated more recently, where management is seen to value the consultative process, to be willing to share information, and to wish to demonstrate the benefits of 'co-operation', such committees can establish a greater degree of *de facto* power-sharing than is formally acknowledged.

The experiences of the Second World War have been described as bringing the British people as close to socialism as is ever likely (Calder, 1969). The state's penetration of civil society and the economy accelerated not simply because of the need to maintain the Armed Forces in battle, but also as a result of the changed nature of that battle. Whereas in the First World War the burden of sacrifice had been carried almost exclusively by the fighting men, in the Second World War technological developments in armaments systems and in energy sources ensured that the burden was now more evenly distributed across the entire population: Table 5.1 below demonstrates the difference:

TABLE 5.1   *British dead and injured as a result of war*

	Armed forces	All civilians	Women	Children (under 16)
First World War*	2,998,583	5,611	1,621	1,067
Second World War**	771,939	146,777	63,221	15,358

SOURCES   * War Office: *Statistics of the Military Effort of the British Empire during the Great War, 1914–1920*, HMSO, London 1922: 674.
    ** W. Franklin Mellor (ed.), *History of the Second World War: Casualties and Medical Statistics*, HMSO, 1972: 836.

The 'egalitarianism' of this wartime experience, augmented by rationing and the taxation of common items such as tea,

united the population in a sense of common identity as strongly
as any antipathy to the Nazis. When in 1945 war ended and
parliamentary democracy resumed a Labour government was
overwhelmingly returned committed to the comprehensive development of a welfare state, full employment, and the nationalisation of major industries. The strength of labour's position is
perhaps even better reflected in the Conservative's *Industrial
Charter* of 1947 which 'accepted as irreversible the nationalisation
of coal, the railways and the Bank of England' (Miliband,
1982: 34), and which committed the Conservatives to a programme of state intervention in pursuit of full employment and
expanded social services. Much of this change in the Conservative
position is attributable to the activities of the Tory Reform
Group, constituted in 1945 and led by Quintin Hogg (later Lord
Hailsham). Hogg argued that the role of the Conservatives in
revolutionary times was 'to lead and dominate revolution by
superior statesmanship, instead of to oppose it; to by-pass the
progressives by stepping in front of current controversy instead
of engaging in it . . .' (Calder, 1969: 532). Nonetheless, for the
party of free enterprise and minimal government to make such
public commitments indicates how widely it seemed that labour's
day had truly arrived.

But appearances can be deceptive. Obscured by the institutions
of parliamentary democracy was the reality of new economic
and interstate dependencies, forged under battle conditions. A
decisive improvement in the Allies' fortunes had been brought
about by the entry of the United States into the war, late again
but with its enormous resources making all the difference.
Churchill, as Britain's *generalissimo* for the duration, courted a
new political alliance with these brash, friendly, wealthy people.
He did so for three primary reasons: (1) technological developments in weapons systems meant that they were now largely
beyond the British pocket, and national security was thus in
jeopardy; (2) unless the Americans made major loans to Europe,
another Depression could be expected to follow the close of
hostilities: and (3) the Soviet Union, formerly an ally, under
Stalin had demonstrated a cold-blooded nationalism and had
become so strong as now to be felt a threat. For these reasons
Churchill brought the Iron Curtain down across Europe. In this
way he secured for the western European nations the vast loans
of US Marshall Aid by which post-war reconstruction was largely

funded, and Europe's shelter via NATO under the US nuclear umbrella. He also added new weight and authority to the processes whereby any ambitions, however articulated, for workers' rights and control could be tarnished by association with Stalinism. Where previously British workers had been exhorted to produce 'guns for Uncle Joe' (Calder, 1969), now they were warned against the dangers of anything resembling communism. In the ensuing decades of the 20th century, in part at the initiative of the Labour Party and union leaders, this message was both thoroughly orchestrated and thoroughly absorbed.

6 Labour as an Arm of the State?

British political history from the 1940s to the late 1970s is very much that of ascendant labour. In harnessing a labour-consuming economy more or less in its entirety to a labour-consuming war effort, Britain's fight against fascism had ensured the incorporation of its labour representatives at the highest levels of government decision-making. It was a 'People's War', says Calder (1969), and in the votes they cast in 1945 the people seemed to show a decided preference for perpetuating this people's society. The first Labour government with a workable majority was elected, a 12 per cent swing in its favour resulting in 393 Labour seats, 213 Conservative and 12 Liberal. In the next six years, Labour ruled over full employment, the initiation of the welfare state, and the relocation of 20 per cent of the national economy into public ownership. It repealed, in 1945, the 1927 Trades Dispute Act, thus enabling Bevin to continue the wartime concordat with the unions such that, by 1948–49, the Trades Union Congress had representatives on 60 government committees (as against 12 in 1939). The figure was to rise yet further in subsequent years (180 by 1977 according to the *Observer*, 7 September 1977). These achievements were secured in spite of the abrupt ending of US lend-lease monies and swift disinvestment from the country of £400 000 million; the reduction on pre-war levels in shipping by 30 per cent and in visible exports by 60 per cent; the severe run-down and destruction of capacity in civilian industries; and the needs to maintain rationing and conscription. All these difficulties were carefully adumbrated for the new Cabinet in 1945 by J. M. Keynes, now firmly ensconced at the Treasury (Calder, 1969: 586).

But the responsibilities and constraints of government put the labour movement under great strain, revealing the fractures within its various constituencies and the frailty of its grip on the seats of power. A Labour Party in parliamentary opposition can ignore the dilemma posed for it by parliamentary democracy— that election to government means accepting responsibilities to the entire electorate rather than solely or primarily to party members. But, in or out of government, the same Labour Party depends on those party members and affiliates for its organisation, campaigning and funds. In return the members, given the democratic ethos of the party, increasingly have wanted its MPs mandated by and accountable to them. Balancing these twin, often conflicting, claims while also trying to secure union co-operation in the economic management of the nation has proved to be one of Labour's two Achilles heels. The other heel is constituted by private capital and militarism, that is, by the internationalisation of capital, on the one hand (part way driven out by Labour's successes in nationalisation), and on the other, the (shifting and costly) military-political alliances of the post-war world (of which more below).

The inadequacies of objective, as distinct from nominal, powers of Labour government are well-reflected in two facts: (1) that the bulk of Labour's most popular and noteworthy measures in the 1945–51 period were initiated and prepared prior to the 1945 election by its Coalition predecessors; and (2) that subsequent Labour governments have failed to eradicate or even stem the trend to increasing social inequality. By 1951 the country was still short of between one to two million homes; the rich could still buy privileged health services; equality of opportunity in education in practice meant increased access for the children of the middle classes but not the lower; and—as late as 1960—one-seventh of the adult population were calculated to be existing below the minimum standard of living indicated by National Assistance rates. These facts would seem strongly to imply that labour representatives were brought into government only for the purpose of the better management of labour and that, once there, they were kept carefully hamstrung by the greater economic and political powers concentrated outside Parliament.

Thus it is possible to interpret the actions of the Coalition government of the Second World War in bringing Labour MPs and trade union leaders into its structures—because without them it could not manage that most crucial factor of production, labour. Part of this management exercise entailed responding to popular demands with a view to improving the people's morale and commitment. As Sir William Beveridge expressed it, 'the purpose of victory is to live in a better world than the old world

... each individual citizen is more likely to concentrate upon his war effort if he feels that his Government will be ready in time with plans for that better world' (Beveridge, Cmnd 6404, 1942: 167–71).

Prompted by a TUC delegation to the Ministry of Health in 1941 to protest against the inadequacies and discrepancies of extant insurance and health provision, the coalition Cabinet had passed to a civil servant, Sir William Beveridge, the task of exploring and recommending improvements. His recommendations, although widely popular across all parties, classes and the electorate, were shelved by Churchill until the war should end. Churchill feared that to debate and act upon them before that time would be a dangerous distraction from the war effort but he earned himself widespread criticism by this. The consensual rationale behind the popular support for the Beveridge recommendations seems to have been the general acceptance that the state *should* intervene in the economy and the operations of private capital so as to make both more efficient and more humane. The Tory Reformers indeed enunciated the principle of society's duty to ascertain and meet the basic human need of its members. The moment is a remarkable one in British political history—feudal notions of *noblesse oblige*, liberal traditions of seeking compromise and consensus, and labourist ideals of socialism coming together in a remarkable harmony.

But in itself Beveridge's rationale was less than socialist. It was not to be a *social* security on offer so much as an individually-based one, that is, the individual was insured only if the individual contributed to the insurance scheme. Moreover, the contribution was to be a flat rate and thereby retrogressive. Thus wrote Beveridge:

> Social insurance fully developed may provide income security: it is an attack upon Want. But Want is one only of five giants on the road to reconstruction ... the others are Disease, Ignorance, Squalor and Idleness ... The State in organising security should not stifle incentive, opportunity, responsibility; in establishing a national minimum it should leave room and encouragement for voluntary action by each individual to provide more than that minimum for himself and his family. (Beveridge, Cmnd. 6404: 6–7, 1942)

As Calder says (1969: 528), Beveridge 'married the doctrines of

Liberal individualism to the revolutionary sentiments of the People's War.'

The insurance recommendations were built by Beveridge on the assumptions of the provision of a national health service, and of the absence of mass unemployment. Both these assumptions enjoyed the same wide popularity as did the insurance recommendations, to the extent that Churchill felt compelled to broadcast in March 1943 his own Four-Year Plan for cradle to grave national insurance, for a national health service, for equal opportunity in education, housing for all, and the expansion of public enterprise and ownership. Thus 1944 saw Butler's Education Act (notionally) guaranteeing equal educational opportunity; a White Paper outlining a new National Health Service, and another on employment policy. The latter (Cmnd. 6527) marked the acceptance of Keynesianism, that is, state intervention in the economy so as to maintain high employment in ways which would extend the wartime state controls over industry into the peace. These various attitudes and commitments—revolutionary by British standards—were forged during the coalition government of the war years, but it fell to the new post-war Labour government to execute them.

Labour's electoral victory has been attributed to disquiet about the idea of Churchill as a peacetime leader (particularly given his delay of the Beveridge recommendations), to commitments to the idea of a 'new world', and to the public's anticipation of disingenuity in the Conservative's professed acceptance of state planning and ownership. Labour's argument for nationalisation so as to improve efficiency (that is, not for other, more political, reasons) by comparison was widely palatable to an electorate revealed by Gallup Polls (June 1945) to be primarily concerned with housing, social security and full employment.

Unhappily, Labour's interventions to secure these goals— against a backdrop of wartime destruction, the lack of reserves and earning powers, and the opening of the Cold War (on which more below)—were accompanied by substantial wage and price inflations. By 1949 the government was obliged to devalue sterling, and it sought from the unions a voluntary wage freeze. Economic crises were repeated, however, and by 1951 the TUC was declining further wage restraint and demanding an end to the wartime ban on strike activity. It was also 1951 which saw the Conservative's return to power. Notwithstanding that Labour polled its highest ever popular vote, some 20 000 *more* than did the Conservatives, the Conservatives took office on what they declared was an anti-socialist mandate.

Middlemas's (1979) authoritative studies of the post-war period conclude that Britain was now a corporate state, with the unions being an arm of the state apparatus. This conclusion needs moderating in that the unions (and also socialist radicals within and beyond the Labour Party) persisted in defending the principle of free collective bargaining, and private capital persisted in defending the principle of free enterprise. Yet Keynesian policies and the electoral commitment of governments (of whichever party) to intervention in national economic planning and management inevitably entailed incomes policy, and thus intense political attention to the structures and outcomes of pay bargaining. This issue alone was to prove the weakest point, indeed the flashpoint, in union-government relations over subsequent decades.

It was not, however, the only problem to plague the Labour Party. The ideological divisions, always present in the British labour movement, between the pursuit of socialist change and the reform of the free enterprise system, recurred and intensified around the issues of nationalisation, nuclear arms and foreign affairs. Almost without exception, Labour's parliamentary leaders upheld the reformist position. This they did on the basis of three principal beliefs; (1) that it was preferable to the condition of state omnipotence which they ascribed to socialism; (2) that it was all that could be achieved in the circumstances; and (3) that it was all the electorate demanded or would accept of them. No doubt these beliefs had a sound basis but one additional factor needs to be explored, relating to the balances of power emerging and developing in the world in the wake of the Second World War.

BRITISH LABOUR AND THE INTERNATIONAL DIMENSION

Military—Political Alliances

In the 20 years, roughly speaking, from 1945 the world was dominated by two great powers which between them had carved up Europe into rival zones of political, military and economic alliance. Their rivalry expressed itself in many ways but included concerted efforts to influence popular political attitudes within the nation states of Europe, most especially in Britain. Most especially in Britain because, ideologically, the rivalry was about free enterprise capitalism versus workers' control, and the British labour movement was the only one in Europe to have escaped unscathed from the ravages of fascism and Stalinism. British labour was thus at the head of what remained of Europe's socialist movement.

Stalin's Comintern was as interested in influencing British labour as was America's Information Agency and the CIA; but it was America, because of alliances forged at state level, which held the trump cards. The Marshall Plan, under which vast sums of US money were loaned to western European states for their post-war reconstruction, proceeded not merely for humanitarian or even for commercial reasons but so as to influence world public opinion in favour of United States' objectives (Bogart, 1976). Thus, American foreign aid was, not unexpectedly, an element of US foreign policy. The Marshall Plan was augmented by the 1948 Smith-Mundt Act which authorised the first peacetime propaganda programme in United States' history, to present a 'full and fair picture' of the United States to the world. The US Information Agency was the primary public vehicle for this programme and there is nothing sinister about its operations (although its Voice of America radio broadcasting did antagonise many eastern European leaders!). But additionally there were clandestine operations to channel large sums more discreetly into the development and orchestration of people and attitudes favouring American ideals and interests. As was revealed in the US journal *Ramparts*, and in the *New York Times* in 1967 (Hirsch and Fletcher, 1977), the CIA was the primary funder of the explicitly anti-communist Congress for Cultural Freedom. This was launched by the Americans in Berlin in 1950. British participants included Anthony Crosland, Denis Healey and Hugh Gaitskell of the Labour Party. From America came Daniel Bell, author of *The End of Ideology* (1960) in which he argued that growing affluence and the bourgeoisification of workers entailed an end to working class politics and the class struggle. These themes were similarly articulated in Anthony Crosland's *The Future of Socialism* (1956) and in *Socialist*

Commentary, an influential labourist journal which Crosland ran
in concert with Allan Flanders, the respected industrial relations
academic who subsequently joined the Labour government's
(1964–70) Prices and Incomes Board. In the same period (from
late 1940s to early 1960s) Denis Healey, an MP from 1952,
worked as the London correspondent to Daniel Bell's anti-
communist American magazine, *New Leader*. Healey was also
active within the European Movement, whose key theme was
Atlantic unity against the Soviets, and which constituted the
collaboration of top European business and political leaders with
some US generals and the US Secretary of State George
Marshall. Before becoming Minister of Defence in Labour's 1964
government, Denis Healey wrote some 80 articles favouring
European-Atlantic unity. As with the Congress for Cultural
Freedom, the European Movement was subsequently revealed
before the US Congress to have been funded illegally—initially
by misappropriations of Marshall Aid repayment monies and
subsequently by the CIA. There is, of course, no suggestion that
any of the participants to the Congress for Cultural Freedom,
or the European Movement, knew who was funding their
conventions, conferences and literary activities. And it must
remain a moot point whether, albeit less well resourced, the
same political outcomes would not have been forthcoming.
Moreover, although with considerably less ease of access, Warsaw
Pact support for alternative political opinions was also active:
Britain's only communist newspaper, *The Daily Worker*, for
example, being financially aided by its sales in eastern Europe.
Nonetheless, this 'propaganda war' does demonstrate how intima-
tely were national politics now linked to international forces and
how, within that war, the US had the advantage at least where
Britain was concerned.

In terms of domestic policies, Crosland was accepted as the
chief theoretician of the then Labour leadership. This, by 1959,
embraced not only Crosland, Gaitskell and Healey but Douglas
Jay, Roy Jenkins, Will Rodgers and Patrick Gordon-Walker.
The 1959 defeat of Labour was interpreted by them to reflect
electoral antipathy to class-based politics and consequently they
campaigned to remove Clause IV from Labour's constitution.
Clause IV was that element which committed the Labour Party
to pursue 'common ownership of the means of production,
distribution and exchange.' With its abandonment the British

Labour Party also abandoned any pretence of being a party of socialism. But it should be remembered that the precedent for such a position was already set in the Labour manifesto of 1945, the nationalisation programme of which had been justified on the grounds of efficiency rather than the redistribution of wealth and power. Thus, well before Crosland and his colleagues articulated it, the dominant ideology of the post-war Labour leadership embraced a belief in the instrumental, politically neutral, management of economic affairs. In this regard at least the efforts of US political agents were probably redundant.

What remains less clear is the extent and significance of American involvement in the Campaign for Democratic Socialism, which the anti-Clause IV group subsequently formed so as to promote Labour's return to NATO and a nuclear defence strategy. A nuclear military capability had long been a sensitive issue in the Labour Party. In 1947, following America's decision not to share its nuclear knowledge with Britain, Clem Attlee (then Labour Prime Minister) had decided to develop and build a British version of the A-bomb. He did this without consulting his full Cabinet, Parliament or the people, and the matter thus remained without public debate. By 1960, however, the Labour Party Annual Conference was won to a non-nuclear position. Gaitskell, the new Labour leader, refused to accept this decision and he, within the Campaign for Democratic Socialism, initiated a massive effort to win the movement back to the Atlantic fold and the US nuclear umbrella. The campaign ran on seemingly unlimited funds, supporting significant numbers of full-time workers, conferences and free publications, and causing some observers (for example, Hirsch and Fletcher, 1977) to speculate on CIA involvement. Whatever the source of its funds, the campaign was successful and in 1961 the Labour Conference reaffirmed its commitments to NATO and nuclear weapons.

Thereafter the Campaign for Democratic Socialism group split on the issue of entry to the Common Market: Gaitskell and Crosland opposing, Rodgers and Jenkins favouring (at a later stage, these last two were to break away from the Labour Party to form the Social Democratic Party). The split on the Common Market enabled Harold Wilson to capture the Party leadership on Gaitskell's death but Labour's policies in the 1960s remained those enunciated by Crosland. In Wilson's 1964 government, Crosland became the Minister of Economic Affairs with Rodgers as his Parliamentary Under-Secretary; Patrick Gordon-Walker became Secretary of State for Foreign Affairs, and Healey became Defence Minister. Their parliamentary and Cabinet careers remained illustrious until the demise of the Labour government in 1970. Two years before this, in a *Socialist Commentary* supplement entitled 'Socialists in a Dangerous World', Crosland had written,

> . . . a continuous political activism by the great bulk of the population would . . . pose a real threat to the stability of our democracy.

No doubt the 1970 results confirmed him in this opinion.

Economic Factors

The social democrats dominating the Labour Party in the 1960s may well have been correct in perceiving the limits of electoral demands to be set by material rather than socialist concerns. But the vision of successive Labour governments unable to deliver their manifesto promises, unable to reverse Britain's recurrent economic crises, and repeatedly stymied by extra-parliamentary forces, must also have been a major electoral consideration. Fingers of accusation pointed in particular at the strength of the unions, and the Labour Party's incestuous relationship with them. This we consider further below.

The problem with such a focus is that it occludes attention to failures elsewhere—for example, in management (see Nichols, 1986, for a detailed argument of the contribution of management failures to Britain's economic problems) and in the levels and direction of domestic investment. Improved labour productivity, without which Britain loses its competitiveness in world markets and fails to relieve its dependencies on imports, necessitates technological modernisation. But without investment there is no modernisation. In attempting to explain the reluctance of capital to invest many writers (for instance, Price, 1986) highlight entrenched union powers and a consequent mix of profit-destroying high wage levels and resistance to technological change. Others, however, identify nationalisation as a key problem—not merely in withdrawing certain industries from the market for private investment, but also in that their cost structures and efficiencies have been impaired by political interventions. Recurrent balance of payments problems during the 1950s and 1960s prompted governments of the day to adopt 'stop-go' policies. Faced with inflation, they would effect deflationary measures over the economy by, among other things, making cuts in public sector expenditures: subsequently, just in advance of the next election, they would allow a respite so as to attract votes to their party. The nationalised industries and public sector generally did not benefit from being the combined tools of national economic management and vote-catching. Neither was there any benefit from being a political football— as was the case for the steel industry—as successive Labour and Conservative governments nationalised, denationalised and renationalised with seeming gay abandon. In any event, with the exception of steel, nationalisation was of industries in which private capital had little interest for reasons of their overall low profitability. Far from moving the commanding heights of the economy into public ownership, Labour governments tended to use public monies either to make infrastructural investments or for the provisioning of public goods, or to bail out industries where low competitiveness put jobs at risk. The emergent and money-spinning jet engine industry which was in 1945 proposed for nationalisation by the inventor, Frank Whittle, Labour declined to adopt. Thus, although doubtless of great social utility, British nationalisation overall delivered far fewer political and economic rewards than had been intended by the original proponents of the common ownership of the means of production, distribution and exchange. The mixed economy crafted by post-war Labour governments thus met neither socialist demands for public ownership, nor capitalist demands for low-risk, high-return investment opportunities.

But it would be inadequate to attribute capital's failure to invest in Britain simply to union strength and Labour government policies (or even to Conservative 'stop-go' tactics and management failures). An additional, arguably greater, influence on capital's decision-making was (and remains) the presence within the British economy of the City of London as an international money and securities market. The longstanding and incestuous relations between the City, the Bank of England and the Treasury around the management of the National Debt and the value of sterling, has meant that these finance capitalists have operated with very little state regulation. The lack of regulation has extended to the export of investment capital abroad, with only occasional government efforts to impede that outflow. Deterred from investing in Britain by recurrent inflationary crises and 'stop-go' government policies, much British capital has gone abroad or into speculative gambles in the international money markets. Chalmers (1985) calculates that from 1946 to 1959 between one-quarter and one-third of domestic net investment went abroad. This relative deprivation of the domestic economy has been exacerbated by developments among the strongest sections of manufacturing and service capital towards conglomerate and multinational status; British capital's representation among the world's multinational corporations being remarkably high given the frailties of the home economy; indeed, 'second only to America's' according to Fox (1985: 377). The effect is not merely economically felt but also politically in that the international footing and interests of British capital, and its greater strengths *vis-à-vis* home-based interests, render it a force which British governments have been unable or loathe to resist. Smith (1980: 238–9), for example, argues that 'the weakness of the domestic economy is counterpointed and to some extent caused by the strength of British capital abroad'. This is because government measures to protect the home economy cannot be taken without provoking international retaliation harmful to British capital abroad, whose personnel thus prevail on governments not so to act. The irony here, of course, is that without domestic recovery, the British state's ability to protect these internationally-based interests is impaired. Successive governments have found themselves stymied by the vicious circle of decline at home, flight of capital abroad, further decline, further flight.

This is not simply a question of being unable to pay Peter without depriving Paul. It is also that Paul has in any event superior powers by virtue of the British government's dependence on his operations. The post-war period has been marked by the British state's needs to borrow abroad—Marshall Aid at first, subsequently recourse to the International Monetary Fund and elsewhere. The IMF has been described as 'largely a vehicle by which domestic groups including the City, the Banks and the Treasury can get extra powers behind their elbows to jog HM-elected Ministers' (Hirsch, *Guardian*, 18 January 1977, quoted in Miliband, 1982: 96). Callaghan's Labour government during the years 1976 and 1977, for example, experienced very damaging negotiations with the IMF. In his efforts to fund the 'social wage' (that is, better social provisioning) which was the reward to the unions for wage restraint, Callaghan sought IMF loans. But the IMF's co-operation was made contingent upon the government imposing public expenditure cuts and other deflationary measures. Thus, in the course of 1976–77, the Labour government finally abandoned Keynesian economic policies in favour of a diluted form of monetarism. The IMF's rationale was just as had been the Bank of England's and the Treasury's in the 1920s and 1930s—classic orthodox economics geared to supporting international confidence in sterling and the British economy. History in 1976 and 1977 was thus repeating itself: the manifesto of the Labour government of 1929–31 had been scuppered on the terms demanded by the financial institutions: Wilson's Labour government of 1964 had gone the same way. As Wilson himself commented (1971: 37–8):

> . . . not for the first time I said we had now reached the situation where a newly-elected Government with a mandate from the people was being told . . . by international speculators, that the policies on which we fought the election could not be implemented, that the Government was to be forced into the adoption of Tory policies to which it was fundamentally opposed . . . Democracy itself . . . was in danger.

Defence

It would, however, be inadequate to attribute the decline of the British domestic economy and British democracy entirely to the activities of capital and the unions. Governments of the day, pursuing political goals (often secretly) which have been too costly for and harmful to the British economy, have also been culpable. Wilson's government before 1967, for example, could have accepted the devaluation of sterling as an alternative to public expenditure cuts. It chose not to because it calculated that Britain had more to gain from protecting sterling as an international currency. The gains, however, were political rather than commercial. The British state was (and still is) quite literally 'buying' influence abroad. By offering economic aid, military support and preferential investment opportunities, Bri-

tain 'pays' foreigners to hold sterling (Chalmers, 1985). What is
reflected here is the seemingly ineradicable resistence of British
state leaders (of whichever political persuasion) to accepting a
minor or neutral role in world politics. Nowhere is this more
important than in British defence policies which, under closer
inspection (for example, Smith, 1980), seem to have little to do
with defence and more to do with securing influence. That
political goal, evident since the close of the Second World War,
has been pursued to the detriment both of the British economy
and of British democracy.

With regard to the economic implications, it is the case that
since 1945 'the United Kingdom has consistently spent more of
its National Income on the military than any of its main
allies . . . with the important exception of the US' (Chalmers,
1985: 112). By 1983 the United Kingdom's defence budget was
the second largest within NATO and fourth largest in the world.
Several studies demonstrate a relationship between high military
spending and poor general economic performance, the relationship being an accumulation of factors. Research and development
(crucial to technological advance, labour productivity, and the
creation of new products) is one such factor. Since Attlee's decision
in the late 1940s to go ahead with developing a British nuclear
capability, the United Kingdom has been heavily committed to
defence-related research and development. In 1980–81, 28 per
cent of the total UK (private and public) budget for research
and development was directed to military projects (Chalmers,
1985: 119); and in 1985–86, of the state's research and development budget of £4.5 million, some £2.3 million went to defence-
related projects (Rose, 1986). By comparison, only 4 per cent
went to health research. By further comparison, the West
German state dedicated less than 12 per cent of its 1985–86
research and development funds to defence and Japan less than
5 per cent. We are, concludes Rose (1986), 'the most militarised
of all democracies'.

One immediate consequence of high military research and
development commitments is to drain many of the best scientists,
engineers and skilled workers from non-defence sectors of production. The effect is the under-development and under-production
of goods which could otherwise secure strong civil and export
markets. The Japanese world lead in home electronics is not
fortuitous but the direct result of their research and development

priorities. This point is a large one given that, whereas in 1899 the UK took 33.2 per cent of the value of all world exports in manufacture, by 1983 the figure was down to 8 per cent (Chalmers, 1985: 126). Hoggarth and Salama (*Guardian*, 27 March 1987), disputing the Department of Trade's current choice of statistics, argue that the United Kingdom share in volume terms of world manufactured exports has not increased over the years from 1980 to 1986 in spite of a 10 per cent improvement in price competitiveness resulting from the depreciation of sterling. Indeed, they say there has been a net loss in value terms.

Moreover, the development and direction of industrial capacity to military production has entailed not only low levels of productive investment elsewhere but has also entailed the creation of capacities not readily absorbed by civilian consumption. In metals, machine tools, engineering, shipbuilding and the aerospace industries, capacities have been developed which relate to the state's concern to achieve self-sufficiency in armaments production. Such capacities are economically rational only where demand is sustained by state purchases or by arms sales abroad. Both France and Britain are aggressive arms sellers; the high cost of keeping up with and/or buying US weaponry prompting them to seek earnings from arms sales to the Third World (Sampson, 1977). The figures are suspect but, according to Freedman (1985: 73), between 1975 and 1984 116 nations spent $250 billion on armaments; one-third each from the United States and the Soviet Union, a significant remainder from France and a smaller but still significant proportion from Britain. But the peak of world arms demand seems to have been around the mid-1970s and, primarily as a function of market saturation, sales are now declining. This is very bad news for a British government already driven out of space research by America's overwhelming lead and the inordinately high costs of research and development. But the net result of a buyer's market in arms (Freedman's phrase, ibid.) is a greater reliance on continued state purchases to keep capacity (and therefore workers) working. The last point opens up for government a very particular set of political pressures in that there are concentrations of defence-related employments in geographical areas of Britain especially vulnerable to unemployment, for example, around the shipyards of Belfast, the Tyne and Barrow-in-Furness. Because civilian consumption is inadequate to keep these yards in business (as also is the case for the British aerospace industry), some trade unions are therefore as active as the arms manufacturers in the lobby to keep defence spending high. Labour governments and MPs in particular are compromised by this fact since their Party includes an atypically high proportion of people committed to the ideals of internationalism and pacificism.

Ideals of internationalism and pacifism are arguably evident in the 1987 disarmament accord between the United States and the Soviet Union on reductions in intermediate nuclear weapons. They are, however, by no means apparent in the actions of the Western European heads of state. Encouraged partly by the United States' shift of interest to the southern hemisphere, and partly by the slump in world arms markets, the Western European states (most especially Britain, France and West Germany) seem now intent on perpetuating the division of Europe into east and west by building an independent Western European military bloc. That military-political ambition and the escalating costs of armaments research, development and production have had a number of important consequences. For example, they have encouraged the western European allies to enter into joint development and production projects for conventional weapons systems or items. The Italian, West German and British consortium currently producing a multi-role combat aircraft is a case in point. Such projects require the creation of multinational bureaucracies to manage them and are in consequence harder for any individual nation to control. Delays, cost increases, bad design and other deficiencies emanating from the contributing companies or scientists escape unsanctioned by loss of contracts, or cancellation of projects (Smith, 1980). The effect is to fuel further cost inflation.

Additionally, escalating weapons costs have impacted on defence preparedness itself in the sense that the protection of equipment purchases has been secured by the under-resourcing of fighting and support personnel, and of maintenance and repairs. The shift towards capital-intensive fighting modes has accelerated since the Second World War. The mass army mobilised during the war was maintained for several years into the peace but at great cost. The Conservatives in power from 1951 cut those costs by, among other measures, phasing out conscription in favour of a smaller, professional army. The benefit was two-fold; directly, to the defence budget, and indirectly to the general economy by the release of an additional pool of workers. It also made sense given the increasingly specialised, machine-based, modes of modern warfare. The transition is reflected in the defence budget: in 1974–75 some 48.4 per cent of total UK military spending was dedicated to military personnel, while equipment purchases counted for 31 per cent. By 1984–85 the proportions were reversed . . . 34.9 per cent to personnel and 45.8 per cent to equipment (Cmnd. 9763–11, 1986). But there is a limit to which the human factor can be written out of warfare, and the more technically specialised the job the less easily replaceable and more costly the trained fighter. The Conservative government of 1979 had to allocate substantial additional funds to the raising of Service pay so as to staunch the outflow of men, but Conservative commitment to the Trident nuclear programme cannot be met without implications for the UK's conventional armed strength. To purchase Trident over the years 1985–86 to 1989–90 reduces the amount available for other equipment purchases by 32 per cent (Chalmers, 1986). In real terms, given cost inflation on conventional weapons, the reduction in what the UK can buy is even greater. The Conservatives could of course, massively increase taxation but they need a wealthy and healthy economy for that option to be meaningful. In the absence of significant economic growth, present defence policies imply, as Smith (1980: 150) argues, 'a combination of cuts in other public spending, private consumption and civil industrial investment. This in itself would require a change in the political balance of Britain and the jettisoning of many assumptions about the welfare state'.

The democratic gains secured in the course of the last war thus seem to be jeopardised by the preparations for the next. Or rather by the British state's efforts to ensure itself high status in the realignment of world powers occasioned by, among other things, America's relative economic decline. An argument could be made here that democracy within a nation is contingent upon its first securing sovereignty in the international arena. This is to confuse a necessary condition with a sufficient one. National sovereignty is a necessary but not a sufficient condition of domestic democracy: if its fruits are enjoyed by the privileged few at the cost of the greater containment and relative deprivation of the majority, then democracy is degraded.

This brings us to the question of the political implications of Britain's defence policies. Not only have these policies impinged on general economic development, not only do they now jeopardise the continued welfare provisioning of the population, they also have entailed an erosion in the public accountability of government. The example of Attlee proceeding to a British nuclear capacity in virtual secrecy has already been given. His decision led, with the same level of secrecy, to the Polaris decision in 1962 and thereafter to the Trident decision of the late 1970s. The groundwork for the latter had been laid discreetly during the course of the 1974–79 Labour government in that Labour's 1974 manifesto commitment not to purchase any new generations of strategic nuclear weapons was slowly but surely whittled away by the Labour leadership. More recently, revelations about the Zircon spy satellite (Campbell, 1987) suggest a further attempt to keep secret a major military project. Clearly there cannot be a totally free hand in the dissemination of defence-related information. But military projects are simultaneously public expenditure projects and it is the case that not only has public expenditure in Britain grown enormously over the 20th century (standing at 53 per cent of GNP in 1974, and rising: see Robinson, 1978) but also that control over its application has become increasingly centralised and unaccountable (Robinson, op. cit.: Coombes and Walkland, 1980).

Thus, taking together the economic and political implications of Britain's defence policies, we arrive uncomfortably close to McNeill's (1983: 381) gloomy prognostication, that

. . . governments and their armed forces can perhaps (now) afford to dispense with popular support and rely on force and the threat of force, exercised by specialised professionals kept systematically separate from the subjected population at large. Such a pattern of governance would conform to the norms of the past, however much at odds they may be with modern political rhetoric and democratic theory.

It is in this context of the threat, jointly mounted by state militarism and capital's internationalisation, to national economic strength, to the welfare system, public accountability and participation, that we must locate the experiences and contribution of Britain's organised labour.

BRITISH LABOUR IN THE DOMESTIC ARENA

The strategy of postwar Labour governments for securing social progress and greater equality entailed Keynesian-type government interventions into a mixed economy, with a view not only to redistributing its wealth but also to supporting its growth and international competitiveness. There are some simple logical deductions to be drawn here. Keynesian economic policies indicate political attention to the structures and outcomes of pay bargaining, while growth and competitiveness imply that such bargaining must be founded upon productivity improvements and/or profitability. Since Britain's unions have remained wedded to the principle of free collective bargaining, with pay rises being structured upon the maintenance of differentials and upon cost of living increases, the frustration of Labour government strategy was thus guaranteed from the start.

That frustration cannot have been widely anticipated, otherwise—assuming rational actors—the strategy would have been different. Doubtless the successes of voluntary participation in tripartite national economic management during the war years led to great faith in the possibility of its continuance thereafter. Thus Ernest Bevin, for the 1945–51 Labour government, sought and secured a continuation of his wartime concordat with the unions in achieving voluntary wage restraint. But severe price inflation, the devaluation of sterling, housing shortages and rationing made such restraint increasingly difficult to sustain and by 1951 the TUC announced its abandonment of the effort. Moreover, the wartime rhetoric and experience of worker involvement and consultation acted as an impetus not merely to material but also to political expectations. These expectations, taken against dissatisfaction with Labour and union leaderships' difficulties in ameliorating all material discomforts, contributed to a devolution of effective power to the shopfloor.

While most of the Joint Production Committees did not continue after the war, the more general interest in joint consultation did. It was indeed established as a statutory feature of the newly-formed nationalised industries. In the general debate over nationalisation which had taken place in the Labour Party and trade unions in the 1930s, the objective of 'workers control' had been emphasised. However, although the idea of democratic control had taken root within parts of the union movement, the realities of this (in terms, for example, of achieving adequate levels of competence) were never faced and the exact meaning of workers' control remained vague (Currie, 1979: 148–9). The lack of any comprehensive programme for achieving industrial democracy, together with the wartime experience of consultation and the overall union antipathy to having worker representatives on nationalised industry boards, resulted in a nationalised sector which continued the general model of labour representation based on free collective bargaining and joint consultation. Similarly, in the private sector, joint consultation was widely adopted by managements, seeking to continue the integrative relations achieved under the wartime conditions and to provide a restricted participatory role for the union organisation growing within the workplace.

But whereas in the late 1940s almost three-quarters of larger firms had workplace consultative arrangements in operation (NIIP, 1952), by the late 1950s-early 1960s the focus of workplace activity had shifted away from consultation towards shop steward organisation and workplace bargaining. By the 1960s shop stewards numbered around 175 000 (out of a total union membership of about ten million): their growth was identified as one factor contributing to the increase in unofficial strike action which in this period came to account for 95 per cent of stoppages and two-thirds of total man days lost (Phelps-Brown, 1983: 145). Shifts in power to the shopfloor had occurred before but the unusual aspect of this post-war experience was its longer term, more entrenched, development. This derived in part from full employment and in part 'out of the increased confidence of the worker, at a higher level of education and higher standard of living, equipped through modern media with greater information and assured by practical experience of the power of combination' (Phelps-Brown, 1983: 146). Other developments too acted to strengthen labour's hand—the growing interdependence and specialisation of production which increased the strategic power of particular work groups, the growing rate of profitability which put increased emphasis on maintaining output, and a growth in union density among white-collar workers.

Growing union powers at the workplace, as already indicated, were in large part a result of the 1950s improvement in labour's market position, generated by growing product demand and labour scarcity. Unemployment declined to just over 1 per cent by 1951 and never rose much above 2 per cent during the next decade. This new labour strength was evidenced in the close union relations with successive Conservative governments which continued the pattern established during the war and under the post-war Labour administration. Such was the strength of this relationship that a TUC spokesman was able to comment in 1960 that 'no minister refuses to hear our views or take them into account . . . our influence is powerful and continuous; not infrequently it is decisive. It is exercised on matters of principle as well as detail' (quoted in Currie, 1979: 169).

As Sid Weighall of the National Union of Railwaymen said, 'no-one could govern Britain without the acquiescence of the unions' (Hawkins, 1981: 208). However, despite or perhaps because of this power, little emphasis was placed on advancing those forms of industrial democracy which directly involved worker representatives in management decision-making. After the years of scarcity which had stubbornly attended post-war reconstruction, the main objective of workers was to share in the growing affluence through the achievement of higher earnings. According to Currie (1979: 173) unions at this time were 'eager to abandon the collectivist false gods of "workers' control" for an individualist "affluence"'. Collective bargaining did spread over a wide range of issues but the wage effort bargain remained the focus of attention for the shop stewards. It was countries where plant-level bargaining did not develop to the same extent, such as in Scandinavia, which began at this time to make much stronger headway in introducing both direct forms of worker participation and indirect, representative forms.

With only minor exceptions during the 1950s, the state in Britain pursued a voluntarist approach to industrial relations, reassured by the substantial growth in the Gross National Product (up by a half between 1951 and 1957), the absence of industry-wide stoppages and the accord reached through several years of tripartism. Indeed, the decline in large, confrontational strikes and the range, flexibility and essential voluntarism of industrial relations encouraged some commentators at this time to characterise British industrial relations as a 'mature' case, in contrast to those systems heavily reliant on centralised bargaining or legally bound industrial relationships (Kahn-Freund, 1954; Fox, 1985).

But as the economic indicators of the 1960s began to express more clearly Britain's relative decline (a decline which had begun much earlier but which had been masked by the exceptional conditions of wartime and post-war reconstruction), British industrial relations lost their aura of success and began to be depicted as a major contributor to low productivity, in turn identified as a principal cause of the decline.

In 1961 the Conservative government had created the National Economic Development Council with a view to the better tripartite planning of the economy: in fact, the government wanted union assistance in effecting an incomes policy. But by 1965, under Wilson's Labour government, an incomes policy was forged in which the TUC was afforded very little say: the policy tried to insist on productivity improvements as the basis for pay deals. It was applied until 1970 although it became increasingly inefficient because negotiators (from both sides of industry) increasingly ignored it. In 1970 there was an explosion of pay claims as people fought to re-establish differentials, to catch up with the cost of living, and so on; and at that point Labour left office. In November 1972 Heath's Conservative government mimicked Wilson's 1966 pay freeze and also established a Pay Board to impose a flat rate ceiling on all pay rises (and a Prices Commission to monitor and curb increases in prices, profits and dividends). Both the Wilson and the Heath governments also attempted to limit the right to strike and the efficacy of strike action. The 1960s was, of course, the era when social democrats such as Crosland, Healey and Rodgers were dominating the parliamentary Labour Party; and Crosland's antipathy to 'continuous political activity by the great bulk of the population' was exceeded by Wilson's public contempt for the activists organising the 1966 seamen's strike (Foot, 1968: 175).

Under conditions of full employment and inflation, the unions generated economic pressures which were intolerable to government. Governments therefore increasingly intervened directly in industrial relations. But as they did so, industrial relations became politicised. Even in peacetime conditions, the old bourgeois separation of economic from political spheres could no longer be sustained.

In July 1973 the National Union of Mineworkers broke loose from the Conservative's incomes policy, imposing an overtime ban to which the government responded by putting the entire

country onto a three-day working week. The TUC made conciliatory noises and might have succeeded but their endeavour was
pre-empted by Heath's decision to call an election on the theme
of excessive union power. This theme was by no means new.
The upsurge of unofficial strikes in the early 1960s had prompted
Wilson's government to establish, in 1965, the Donovan Royal
Commission on Trades Unions and Employers' Associations.
The sentiments informing this Commission were, firstly, that
collective *laissez-faire* (Kahn-Freund's term for free collective
bargaining) could not pass unregulated in a society whose
members were now thoroughly dependent upon the public and
private production of goods and services; and secondly, that
major sections of workers (for example, manual workers in
the private sector) remained unprotected by either collective
agreements or statutory regulations. The Commission, reporting
in 1968, saw the problem as one of the diminishing effectiveness of
industry-wide agreements and, relatedly, the growing informality
and authority of workplace bargaining. Its focus was thus on the
authority structures existing within the unions, and it was
sensitive to the democratic constraints under which official union
leaderships operated. Its major recommendations were for a
substantial expansion of the statutory floor of individual employment rights, and for the trade unions to be afforded corporate
legal status. The latter recommendation marked a major break
in the traditions of British industrial relations in which, as best
expressed in the 1906 Trades Dispute Act, unions had had only
a very limited legal identity. Corporate legal status was to
be contingent upon formal registration, without which union
members undertaking industrial action would not be immune
from breach of contract liabilities. In making these recommendations for legal intervention, Donovan was articulating a general
recognition that national economic management could not rely
upon voluntarism. But Donovan's respect for the voluntary
tradition was yet sufficient for its other recommendation—the
setting up of a Commission on Industrial Relations—to have no
legal powers but only persuasion with which to encourage long-
term institutional change in industrial relations systems. As
Hawkins (1981: 52) says, 'Politicians were looking for a short,
sharp legal antidote to unofficial strikes.' Donovan inevitably
disappointed them.

The political goal did not, could not, go away. Donovan had

sought a return to responsible unionism through a formalising of plant-level relations so as to counter wage drift and to reduce unofficial strikes. But relations in subsequent years between governments and trade unions became increasingly strained as the former sought more thoroughly to limit the latter's scope for engaging in conflict. Labour's proposals contained in their document *In Place of Strife*, published in 1969, were even more interventionist than had been Donovan's, in that they included the intention to introduce criminal sanctions against strikes. The unions were mortified: not only was the right to strike now criminalised but the voluntarist principle itself was attacked . . . and by a Labour government! Trade union leaders succeeded in persuading Ministers to drop the idea of criminal sanctions in return for greater TUC efforts to settle unofficial strikes, but this proved an arduous and difficult path to tread. The Conservative's subsequent Industrial Relations Act 1971, mindful of the weaknesses of TUC authority, gave statutory force to many of the ideas of both Donovan and *In Place of Strife*. They required that trade unions be formally registered in order to secure legal protection for their members, and that trade union officials be legally responsible for the actions of those members. Simultaneously, civil liabilities against strikers were expanded, and individual workers were granted legal means to act *against* their unions. The Industrial Relations Act also created the National Industrial Relations Court, which was the first court in English history to recognise industrial relations as a legal issue. But in the event neither side of industry acknowledged the law, both sides being reluctant to weaken the already frail authority of official union leadership. The dock strikes of 1972, for example, showed the readiness of workers to follow unofficial leaders regardless of the consequences for themselves and their officials, and Heath's government was obliged to back-pedal in its efforts to defuse the situation. With the return of Labour in 1974, the Industrial Relations Act was repealed (and with it went the National Industrial Relations Court) by the Trade Unions and Labour Relations Act. (Various aspects of this ill-fated Industrial Relations Act are contained in the Conservative's 1987 Green Paper, *Trade Unions and their Members*—see chapter 7.)

In 1973–74 the tensions between unions and government were further exacerbated by a world oil crisis which jolted the economy and pumped up the rate of inflation. By the spring of 1975 inflation had reached 25 per cent per annum and was rising, as was unemployment. March 1974, however, had seen the return of a Labour government and the TUC accepting responsibility for the creation of a workable incomes policy. There was to be a new social partnership of Labour government and trade unions— a Social Contract—a 'social wage' to be created by the Labour government in return for union control over direct wage increases. The 'social wage' was translated into food subsidies, a freeze on council house rents, increases in pensions, and other measures. The Pay Board and wage control legislation were overturned, and authority in this area passed back to the unions. But the Social Contract—although reasserted and reinforced in 1975, and again in 1976–77—did not work. According to Donoughue (1987), himself active in the Policy Unit advising the government, ministers favoured pay restraint in general but hesitated to apply it within their own departmental areas. Alternatively they hesitated to jeopardise their union sponsorship. The low paid remained low paid, and employers continued to feel the need for pay incentives to attract and secure specialised workers. It was apparent that the TUC had no effective response to members more sensitive to the rapidly rising cost of living than to the social wage. Pressures and anomalies within the unions became so acute that, from 1977, the TUC declined further involvement in the partnership.

Especially vocal in opposition to TUC collaboration in the government's incomes policy had been the public sector unions. The public sector constituted an area of employment where successive governments had attempted to create examples of good industrial relations practice, for example, Whitleyism. But they had also used the sector as a tool of national economic management and occasionally as a political football, to its detriment. Very many workers in the sector were increasingly aggrieved at their poor levels of pay when compared to counter-parts in the private sector, and they were ready to take industrial action to pursue their claims. In order to cope with these tensions, in May 1979 the government established a Standing Committee on Pay Comparability which, as Hawkins (1981: 211) comments, was yet another 'ad hoc safety valve' just like the 'special case' awards already made to the firemen, miners, nurses and police. Perhaps not surprisingly the Conservatives from 1979 have rejected any further attempt at a Social Contract and have

pursued alternative strategies to influence the unions and pay
bargaining (see chapter 7).

THE UNIONS AND FORMAL INDUSTRIAL DEMOCRACY

As a postscript to this consideration of the participation of
organised labour in the management of the political economy of
20th-century Britain, let us take a brief look at one issue which
the social partnership did put high on the political agenda—
namely, industrial democracy.

Interest in industrial democracy had been reviving for some
years; in 1966 Jack Jones (General Secretary of the Transport
and General Workers' Union) had written in favour of union
representatives on company boards and in 1967 Labour published a Report on Industrial Democracy (Currie, 1979: 219–
20). By 1974 the TUC and Labour government were both
expressing an interest in extending industrial democracy, part
of the impetus coming from developments in other EEC countries.
However, the union movement was far from united on the matter
and in government the issue was not of sufficient priority to
warrant immediate legislation. Instead a Committee of Enquiry
(the Bullock Committee) was established to investigate the
question of worker directors; its terms of reference were heavily
influenced by union concern to protect the single channel of
trade union representation. The Committee issued Majority and
Minority reports, the latter reflecting the employers' unwillingness to accept more than minority representation of worker
interest on the boards. With employer opposition to the Majority
report coupled with indifference from parts of the union
movement and the practical problems of implementing such a
far-reaching scheme, the government eventually issued a White
Paper on Industrial Democracy which presented a much diluted
version of the Majority report proposals. However, without a
clear basis for agreement between the parties and with the rest
of the relationship between the unions and government coming
under increasing strain from continued wage restraint and
growing militancy, the industrial democracy plans were shelved
(and sank without trace after the election of the 1979 Tory
government).

In theory the Bullock proposals represented a further example of the state promoting greater union involvement in industrial decisions as a means of securing union co-operation during a period of crisis. Yet at no time did the state, even when tenanted by a Labour government, lose faith in the primacy of private property as the basis for enterprise and for control. Thus did the themes of wartime emphasise 'consultation' and 'co-operation', whilst in the later debate on worker directors, the political will was not present to carry the Bullock proposals into effect. In no way then did labour's political ascendance amount to significant constitutional change in the principles of government, or the practice and powers of capital.

Whether this has been cause or effect of post-war electoral preferences will remain for some time an issue of intense political debate within the labour movement. What is not open to debate is that the labour vote has declined more or less steadily since 1951. In that year Labour secured 48.8 per cent of the vote: it did almost as well in 1966 with 47.9 per cent but thereafter the trend has been down—to 36.9 per cent in 1979, a disastrous 30 per cent in 1983, and 33 per cent in 1987. Meanwhile the Labour Party's direct membership has fallen from one million in 1951 to one-third of a million by 1983. As Ivor Crewe commented (*Guardian*, 15 June 1987), 'the Labour vote is largely working class but the working class is no longer largely Labour.' Already sensitive to the point, Neil Kinnock's speeches in the run-up to the 1987 election signalled the Labour leadership's clear intention in future years not to be bound or driven by the unions. There will, it would seem, be no more attempts at partnerships in government of Labour Party and trade unions.

7 The Emasculation of Labour

If the 1970s contained the high water mark of labour's influence, the tide has clearly turned in more recent years. Indeed, to continue for a moment this aqueous analogy, several undertowing currents were already present by the 1970s, handicapping labour's advance and indicating the means of its subsequent decline. Yet, whereas tides flow as well as ebb, there are indications that both employers and the state have erected strong sea-walls to reduce the likelihood of any future return to the levels of dependency on labour witnessed in the 1960s and early 1970s. What is remarkable is how a series of factors have coincided—not wholly fortuitously, as we shall see—to diminish the position of labour *vis-à-vis* both state and capital.

Most of the recent literature on labour's fortunes has emphasised the impact of economic recession on trade union membership levels (see for example Bright *et al.*, 1983). But the labour movement has been through recessions before and emerged stronger than ever in the next economic upturn—witness the relative position of labour in the early 1930s and 1950s: in 1933 union membership had fallen to less than 4.5 million; by 1951 it had expanded to over 9.5 million with a trade union presence well established within the State's executive and administrative machinery (see chapter 5). With regard to the present recession, a number of workplace industrial relations surveys, for example, have indicated that union organisation in the enterprise has remained broadly intact. A national survey of industrial relations in 1984 found that in many sectors levels of trade union recognition were similar to, or had even increased slightly over, the 1980 levels; the number of lay union representatives had also increased overall between 1980 and 1984 through an expansion in the non-manual and public sectors (Millward and Stevens, 1986; see also Batstone, 1984). Similarly, while the overall density of unionism in Britain has fallen by a fifth since 1979, density has fallen only half as much among those actually in work (Beaumont, 1987: 3). Rubery (1986: 63) has a valid point that 'British trade union organization has . . . been characterized

152

by its ability to adapt and evolve in response to changed conditions'. Nevertheless, some adaptations already evident (such as the adoption of a 'new realism') go little way to counteract the effects of state and employer strategies. The coincidence of various economic, political, social and technological factors suggests not simply that organised labour will find it much harder than in previous recessions to recover its position, but rather that it will continue to face challenges to its position as the search for lower labour costs continues.

Yet since the recession has been a key influence on state and employer responses to labour, it is appropriate to begin this chapter by briefly reviewing it, its immediate impact on the trade union movement, and its relation to various aspects of the state and capital's sustained attack on organised labour's functions and influence.

THE LATE 1970S AND THE IMPACT OF RECESSION ON ORGANISED LABOUR

The post-1979 world economic recession was experienced in Britain as only one part of a much broader economic malaise evident from the mid-1970s onwards. The roots of the country's recent economic problems go deep. A great welter of causal factors has been identified and debated: for example, an over-reliance on imperial markets; a failure to invest during the late 19th century and post-1945 periods; poor management; the uncommercial attitudes prevalent in Britain's public school system; the debilitating conflict caused by the retention of a strong social class system; a lack of investment in research and development; the City's general aversion to financing domestic industrial expansion; and the failure of the state to nurture an industrial base capable of competing effectively with the increasingly pervasive American, German and Japanese companies. Many of these factors were at work long before the 1970s but were obscured by shorter-term phenomena such as war, post-war reconstruction and periods of general economic growth. All the while, however, Britain's economy has been in decline relative to those of its leading competitors.

Following the 1973 oil crisis, however, the economic environment was less well equipped to obscure the reality of Britain's deteriorating situation. A major signal of this worsening economic position was the financial crisis in 1976 which lead to the IMF rescue (see also chapter 6). One of the conditions for this was that the Labour government should cut £12 500 million from its public spending. The result was the government withdrawing from its comparatively radical programme and replacing it with an imposition of public expenditure cuts and cash limits, together with a tightening of pay policy, with a 5 per cent target for wage increases in 1978–79. For both government and unions this period effectively marked the end of the social contract. It was also at this time that the leadership of the two largest unions was changing, with Moss Evans and Terry Duffy replacing Jack Jones and Hugh Scanlon respectively at the Transport and General Workers' Union and Amalgamated Union of Engineering Workers (now Amalgamated Engineering Union). Evans in particular was much less supportive of any pay policy than his predecessor, and became part of a growing union (and left-wing labour) group opposed to further pay restraint (Callaghan, 1987). The breakdown of the social contract was exemplified by the government's failure in November 1978 to achieve TUC support for a 5 per cent pay norm—a failure which by the New Year had been translated into substantial wage claims and bitter strikes by local authority workers, road haulage and oil tanker drivers, and others. Thus 'by 1978–79 the familiar pattern recurred of intensified industrial conflict breaching pay norms and an alienation between Labour and its supporters' (Price, 1986: 244). This cleavage between the unions and the Labour government was to represent a major factor in the general election defeat which followed a lost confidence vote by Callaghan in March 1979. Mrs Thatcher who, for the Conservatives, replaced Callaghan as Prime Minister, inherited runaway inflation, peaking around 1980–81 at 20 per cent per annum. Monetarism, the chosen Conservative government instrument against this inflation from 1979 onwards, was applied rigorously. This had the effect of pushing up interest rates (to a Minimum Lending Rate of 17 per cent) which had the further effect of increasing the value of sterling against other currencies. The price of British exports therefore moved up quite sharply in relation to British imports. Not only did this cause the balance of trade to deteriorate but it propelled many exporting manufacturers into redundancy, and sometimes also bankruptcy. 'Laker and Braniff went down, as did De Lorean, Chrysler, Ford, International Harvester, Turner and Newall, Woolworths; and a host of other household names were in deep trouble' (Johnson, *New Society*, 7 October 1982: 36). Thus, to the foreign technological innovation and stiffening international competition which rendered many British manufactured goods (and therefore the labour which produced them) over-priced, must be added government policies aimed at curbing inflation.

Nonetheless, much criticism was voiced in government and employer circles about British industry's failure to respond to increasing competition by raising productivity and lowering labour costs. In turn, productivity levels and labour costs were seen to reflect strong union organisation in British workplaces— manifested in the spread of shop steward organisation in the 1970s and the growing incidence of unofficial strikes—which to both management and the state represented a major obstacle to economic regeneration. As Anthony has argued industrial relations and trade union activities have acted in the past as a 'scapegoat' for all shortfalls in efficiency, productivity and profit: 'industrial relations is [used as] an explanation for what might have been and why it is not' (Anthony, 1986: 13). Anthony's more general case is that British management have used 'strategies of insulation' to avoid confronting the task of directing labour (see also Nichols, 1986). Nevertheless, state and employer *perceptions* in the 1970s were of trade unions as an obstacle to change (a perception which was loudly endorsed by the media; see Glasgow Media Group, 1976). As a result, part of government policy towards trade unions after 1979 has sought specifically to give employers the means to reduce union power at the workplace. Employers for their part have made use of this government assistance to introduce changes towards more flexible working practices, to locate in greenfield (and often non-union) sites, and to invest in newer, more versatile technologies. By these means they have attempted to reduce unit labour costs, raise productivity and improve profitability.

The recession has aided the state and employers in these endeavours. It has occurred simultaneously with significant technological change, the two factors jointly causing a substantial loss in trade union membership. Between 1969 and 1979 the number of unionists in Britain rose by almost three million (10.48 million to 13.29 million) and the density of unionism

increased from 45.3 per cent to an all time high of 55.4 per cent.
Over later years, however, union membership declined with
equal speed, down to 10.72 million by the end of 1985, and to a
union density of approximately 45 per cent. A large proportion
of this fall reflects the growth in unemployment and the tendency
for membership to lapse once workers become unemployed.
Excluding the unemployed from the calculations, the decline in
union density between 1979 and 1983 is less marked—down
from 58.1 per cent to 53.1 per cent (Beaumont, 1987: 3).
The decrease in membership numbers is more a reflection
of unemployment in what were previously heavily unionised
industries, many of which were the pillars of the industrial
revolution (iron and steel—450 000 workers in 1970 down to
100 000 workers by 1980–81; textiles—1 111 000 in 1951 down to
215 000 in 1985; shipbuilding and engineering—224 000 in 1951
down to 90 000 in 1985; coal—756 000 in 1959 down to 153 000
in 1987). The concentrated organisation of these workers geographically and by employment, plus their history as the first to
experience manufacturing capital as their employer, gave to
British industrial relations many of its notable characteristics.
For the unions themselves the absolute loss in membership
subscriptions has imposed a considerable financial restriction on
activities. Financial considerations have also accelerated the level
of merger activity between unions, to the extent that the number
of unions in Britain fell by almost a fifth from 453 in 1979 to
373 by the end of 1985 (*Employment Gazette*, February 1987).

The changes in the labour markets which underlie much of
the alteration in union fortunes are remarkable. Unemployment
in the United Kingdom in 1971 stood at 3.4 per cent of the total
available workforce; in 1986 it was calculated at 14.1 per cent.
Youth unemployment in 1960 was 2.4 per cent, in 1981 37.4 per
cent. These figures are, however, somewhat suspect in that,
between February 1981 and 1987, the Conservative government
made no fewer than 17 alterations in their mode of calculation,
all but two of the alterations having the effect of narrowing the
classification of those officially acknowledged as unemployed.
Peter Townsend of Bristol University, speaking in April 1987,
calculated on a variety of other bases an unemployment figure
for the UK of between 4.75 million and 8 million. These compare
sharply with the official government figure of 3.35 million at that
time.

Part-time employment as a proportion of the UK workforce stood in the mid-1980s at over 20 per cent, and was projected to rise to 30 per cent by mid-1990s (*Social Trends*, 17, 1987). More precisely, figures given in the *Industrial Relations Journal*, 13(3), 1982 allow the calculation that female part-timers in the service industries have increased some 69 per cent from 2 206 000 to 3 708 000 between 1971 and 1984, although in the manufacturing industries female part-timers numerically fell some 16 per cent, from 471 000 in 1971 to 395 000 in 1984. Male part-timers have tended to follow the same pattern but less dramatically. By 1984 male part-timers had been aggregated with male full-timers in the official figures but the rise in male part-timers in the service industries between 1971 and 1981 was 27 per cent, and the decline in the manufacturing industries between those same years was 3 per cent.

In 1964, 27 per cent of British men over the age of 65 were still working; by 1978 this had fallen to 7 per cent (Clark and Barker, 1981). The average length of the working day has similarly diminished over recent years and at an accelerating rate—by 0.1 per cent between 1960–70; 0.3 per cent 1970–73; 1.1 per cent 1973–76; 0.9 per cent 1976–79, and 2.9 per cent 1979–81. These reductions in hours spent in paid work managed with relative ease up until 1983 to prevent any secular updrift in technological unemployment. But any acceleration in such employment must necessarily mean that the problems of adjustment—whether via further reductions in working hours or whatever—become much greater (Sir Bruce Williams, 1983).

Union influence has been further restricted by more indirect effects of the rise in unemployment. Job security naturally becomes a more prominent issue for workers during recessionary periods (Brown *et al.*, 1983). The growth of long-term unemployment (by 1987, 40.5 per cent of those registering as unemployed had been out of work for more than a year) gives force to the importance of job retention and the potential costs of jeopardising job security. This is particularly the case in those regions worst hit in the early 1980s, such as the West Midlands and the North, which are also traditional locations of strong trade unionism; that is, the type of unionism characterised by independent trade union organisation, collective bargaining, negotiated rules and procedures for grievances, discipline and conciliation, and demarcation.

Inevitably the shrinking fortunes of such unions facilitates the pressures, premeditated or otherwise, for change in British industrial relations. And, of course, even a constancy in the overall rate of unionisation does not necessarily secure a constancy of industrial 'muscle', this latter being a function both of worker attitudes to industrial and political action, and of cash. With regard to worker attitudes, one observer has spoken of the 'quiet triumph of the new realism' (Bassett, 1986), by which he means the greater willingness of unions to enter no-strike agreements, to abandon strict demarcation criteria, and to co-operate rather than conflict with management. Co-operation, argues Bassett, means more enterprise or plant level trades unionism, which potentially acts to splinter union organisation. His principal research focus is on the Japanese firms of Nissan, Toshiba and Hitachi of the electronics industry, the primary union concerned being the electricians' union, the EETPU. That focus is important because it obscures sectoral differences between foreign-owned and British-owned firms, and between public and private, manufacturing and service, employments. Partly as a result of the general decline in demand for the products of the primary industries and partly as a result of the impact of microelectronics and automation on manufacturing processes in the secondary industries, manufacturing employment began to fall absolutely from the mid-1960s, to move more sharply down from 1973 and to plunge dramatically from 1979, by 1983 constituting just 35 per cent of total employment. Moreover, in state-controlled (and highly unionised) industries such as steel and coal, the recession became the reason given for large-scale reductions in manpower, although these reductions continued after the initial recessionary effects had declined (for example, in the coal industry, employment dropped by a third from 228 500 in 1984 to 153 000 in 1987). Thus, while until the mid-1970s growth in service sector employment was more or less able to compensate the jobs lost in manufacturing, thereafter government policies—both with regard to public industries and public services—have largely removed that element of compensation.

In addition, the Conservative government's monetarist policies post-1979 have acted together with the recession to accelerate the longer-term transformation of many industries (for example, textiles and shipbuilding) from labour-intensive to capital-intensive modes of production, and to give added impetus to the search for lower labour costs and greater manpower flexibility. In this, despite the investment uncertainty prevailing in a recessionary climate, the development of microelectronic and other forms of new technology has played an increasingly important role. Further, as unemployment has grown to become a key political issue, local and central government interest in attracting business from abroad has also grown. The recent prominence of Japanese manufacturing in Britain is one aspect of this but several other countries (notably, the United States) are heavily committed to foreign direct investment in Britain (Dunning, 1986; Buckley and Enderwick, 1985). In turn, these recently arrived multinationals have been able to exploit the economic climate and workers' fears over the lack of job security to establish 'no strike' and other agreements which represent a far cry from the levels of influence which unions were exerting on managements only one or two decades earlier (Bassett, 1986).

Escalating unemployment and the associated fears over job security have been one important factor behind the decline in strike activity during the 1980s. From an average of over 2300 strikes per year between 1975–79, the figure fell to an average of 1350 between 1980–84, and fell again to 903 in 1985. This is the lowest figure for any year since 1938. (The trend of working days lost through stoppages is less clearly defined over the recent period, primarily because of the effects of a small number of national stoppages which account for a very large proportion of the days lost. Most notably this includes the long miners' strike, which, according to the *Employment Gazette* of August 1986, in 1984 accounted for more than four-fifths of the total days lost for that year.)

It is necessary to examine some of these developments in more detail. Taken together they represent a challenge to labour far exceeding that simply of recession and the decline in union membership. Indeed, the changes which have occurred in the last decade would seem to have altered fundamentally the nature of industrial relations in Britain, and more generally the basis of dependence of both the state and capital on labour. These changed balances of dependence partly reflect and partly facilitate what may be termed state and employer strategies aimed at reducing labour's control over its own conditions of utilisation.

STATE STRATEGIES

The Conservative government since 1979 has aimed to reduce union power both at the workplace and nationally, to enhance management's 'right to manage', and to end the political compromising with the TUC which had formed an implicit part of the political process since 1945. 'Butskellism'—the term given to the consensus approach which developed in the 1950s under politicians such as R. A. Butler and Labour's Hugh Gaitskell— was judged by Margaret Thatcher to have failed to deliver, either in terms of economic growth or productivity. After 1979 the Thatcher government effectively silenced the trade union voice at national level, preventing organised labour from influencing the government's economic strategy, including its labour legislation. That the union movement was unable to resist this rescinding of a, by now, long-established arrangement was due largely to its weakened position in the labour market resulting from recession and growing unemployment. 'By 1982', writes Fox (1985: 417) 'this exclusion of the unions had become a general policy.' The traditions of compromise and consultation had been replaced by an implementation style which imposed economic plans on a weakened union movement and labour force.

The demise of the consensus-compromise model of post-war industrial politics removed from labour the means of directly influencing the formative stages of policy-making. At the same time the economic depression reduced the unions' (and particularly the TUC's) scope for developing other means of making their voice heard in the policy-making process. Yet this diminution in the TUC's role in national policy making is only one aspect of a much broader attack on the functions and power of organised labour in recent years. By several other means, the Conservative government since 1979 has acted to cheapen the price of labour, to reduce union powers and to enhance the powers of its 'law and order' apparatus.

Cheaper Labour

The government's advocacy of lower wage levels and its efforts to create conditions which bring these about have been based partly on the premise that lower wage levels contribute to lower inflation, and partly on the argument that high wages in the past have exacerbated the level of unemployment, such that should the price of labour fall, the unemployed would 'price' themselves back into jobs. There are a number of specific instances after 1979 of the government seeking to depress wages and reduce trade union influence over pay determination. The abandoning in 1983 of the Fair Wages Resolution is one example of this. This Resolution (which dates back originally to 1891) required that those firms working on government contracts must 'recognize the right of employees to be union members and to receive the appropriate industry wage' (Beaumont, 1987: 161). Thus the Resolution registered government support for voluntary collective bargaining and for accepting the pay and conditions of employment collectively agreed by unions and employers in an industry. In practice the Resolution appears to have had only limited success, partly because of the lack of state resources made available to 'police' government contracts (Bercusson, 1978). Nevertheless, as Beaumont has observed, the repeal of the Resolution has a 'symbolic' importance in terms of the government withdrawing its explicit support for fair wages and industry agreements (1987: 163).

The Conservative government has also actively considered the abolition of the Wage Council system. This establishes statutory minimum pay and conditions in industries not equipped with independent collective bargaining machinery. A number of wage councils have already been abolished and a government consultative document in 1985 reiterated the preference for abolition (Rubery, 1986: 111). While many wage councils continue to survive, their effectiveness has been diminished by a lack of the resources required to bring to heel recalcitrant employers.

Youth employment and wages are another area in which government action has acted to depress wage levels. Most clearly this has occurred through the conditions attached to the New Workers' Scheme (which replaced the Young Workers' Scheme in April 1986). Under this Scheme employers receive a subsidy (£15 per week for a year in 1987) for hiring young workers, providing that the rates paid to those workers do not exceed a relatively low limit (in 1987 £55 per week for those aged under 20 years and £65 per week for 20 year olds). More generally, the main youth training and work experience provision, the Youth

Training Scheme, pays only a relatively low allowance to 16 and 17 year old school leavers on approved schemes. This also tends to act to depress wage rates of young workers lucky enough to be in full employment.

Privatisation and deregulation—both prominent policies of the Conservative government—also have potential wage level implications. On the issue of contracting out work from local authorities to the private sector, for example, local authorities are required to accept the cheapest tender and to place no restriction on minimum terms and conditions of employment (Rubery, 1986: 79). The result is to depress wage levels, particularly among manual grades. A number of privatised services, such as contract cleaning, have notoriously poor rates of pay. In areas which are not suitable for privatisation, or where the private sector has been largely unsuccessful in winning tenders (such as in hospital catering, see Sherman, 1985), the imposition of public expenditure cash limits has acted similarly. It is true that within the public sector unionism as a proportion remains high, reflecting government preferences for centralisation. But the ending of pay comparability with private sector employments, plus the diminution of job resourcing which flows from public expenditure cuts, has propelled many public employees into industrial action and the government's employee relations into near crisis. Local government workers, for example, have been abandoning the Whitley system so as better to pressurise their local managements (Nicholson, Ursell and Blyton, 1981), and teachers have lost the Burnham system because the government could not accept the Department of Education and Science being deadlocked within it. Pay for social workers, apart from those at the very highest level, is deteriorating relative to white-collar workers elsewhere, and job tenure much less certain, again as a result of expenditure cuts and policies. The dramatic job losses in certain nationalised industries (for example, iron and steel; coal) as a result of government interventions is a case in point. The possibilities of applying the new technologies to service tasks adds to the fears of even more severe and enduring unemployment, but for the time being government policy alone is producing some of the same effects in the public sector as are apparent in private manufacturing, that is, an erosion of union powers and a reduction in their traditional scope for collective bargaining.

Reducing Trade Union Powers

Following a period in the mid-1970s when employee and trade union rights were considerably extended by legislative intervention and the Social Contract, the 1980s have witnessed a clear reversal of this trend. Union powers have been curtailed by legislation, by the withdrawal of recognition and by the reduced access of the union movement to governmental decision-making bodies. The state no longer seeks the active co-operation of trade union leaders, and the unions no longer exercise the same powers over the labour markets.

(1) *Legislation*

Legislation (principally the 1980 and 1982 Employment Acts and the 1984 Trade Union Act) has reduced employment protection coverage and diminished trade union powers and immunities. The legislation has had considerable impact on industrial relations and trade unionism, not least because of the timing of its introduction during a period when the union movement's defences were already weakened by a deteriorating labour market. This contrasts with the situation prevailing in the early 1970s when the Industrial Relations Act met with fierce, sustained and ultimately successfully resistance by trade unions (and incidentally much tacit resistance by employers).

Under the recent legislation employment protection has been reduced by extending the qualifying period of employment (from 6 to 12 months, or 24 months in small firms) required to gain rights of protection. Wedderburn (1985: 39) estimates that this has removed the rights to appeal to industrial tribunals from about one million workers. In addition the 1980 Act has removed statutory union recognition procedures. Between 1976 and 1980 the Advisory, Conciliation and Arbitration Service (ACAS) had examined over 1600 recognition cases, brought under Section 11 of the Employment Protection Act (Beaumont, 1987: 59). This removal of the statutory procedures increases the employers' scope to refuse union recognition claims.

However, it is the reduction in trade union immunities and restriction on unions' freedom of action which have been the most significant aspects of recent legislation. The aspects of unionism covered include the limiting of picketing to the worker's own place of work, the removal of immunity from those engaged in secondary action (that is, sympathy strikes), and the narrower definition of what comprises a legal 'trade dispute' as distinct from, for example, a (non-legal) 'political' strike. As Wedderburn (1985: 43) observes, the legislation has sought by various means to limit the boundaries of collective action to the worker's own place of employment. It thereby undermines the potential for cross-enterprise worker resistance and solidarity within the broader union movement. Where industrial action falls outside the new boundaries, unions can be held legally liable and run the risk of having their assets sequestered, as occurred in the 1983 Messenger Group dispute and the 1984–85 miners' strike.

Brenda Dean, General Secretary of the printers' union SOGAT, reflecting on the Wapping dispute (*New Statesman*, 13 February 1987) comments, 'my strongest impression is of the total unfairness and the loading of the present industrial relations laws against ordinary working people . . . An employer can appeal to a judge for an ex-parte injunction against workers in dispute . . . a union cannot so appeal . . . The law does not appoint bailiffs to investigate union accounts to determine the size of the fine . . . that appointment lies with the aggrieved employer . . . Mrs. Thatcher's industrial relations reforms oblige trade unions to negotiate . . . they do not oblige employers to reciprocate'.

The 1984 Trade Union Act adds further restrictions to the conduct of trade union activity in relation to the election of national officers, the maintenance of political funds and particularly the requirement for union officials contemplating strike action to hold a ballot (the conduct of which is specified by the Act). Such a ballot must achieve a majority in favour of striking for any subsequent action to achieve the status of a legal trade dispute. The new laws also seek to undermine the position of closed shops by extending a worker's ability to allege unfair dismissal if dismissed as a result of union non-membership. In addition, closed shops now require periodic ballots and a large majority (85 per cent of those voting or 80 per cent of those eligible to vote) in favour of the continuation of the closed shop.

(2) *Dismantling extant union organisation*
Just as the Conservative government has acted to limit the spread of trade unionism by the removal of statutory recognition procedures and by legally specifying the conditions for the closed

shop, so too it has removed trade union organisation from the General Communications Headquarters (GCHQ) at Cheltenham, and disbanded collective bargaining machinery in the case of the school teachers' Burnham review panel.

On the former, several instances of industrial action between 1979 and 1981, forming part of broader civil service disputes, demonstrated the potential disruption to intelligence gathering activities which stoppages at GCHQ could effect. More generally it demonstrated the government's reliance on trade union co-operation in an area not only central to the state's own security objectives but also to the maintenance of good relations with its US ally in the collection of Soviet-related material. As a result of the stoppages, together with a staff campaign against the introduction of polygraphs ('lie detectors') for staff security vetting following the conviction of Geoffrey Prime for spying at GCHQ, the government announced that from March 1984 union membership was to be prohibited at GCHQ. In taking this step, the Prime Minister argued that the possibility of further industrial action represented a threat to national security and held that there was 'an inherent conflict of loyalties between membership of a trade union and the defence of national security' (Arthurs, 1985: 29). The union appealed against the decision but was defeated; by early March 1984 over 95 per cent of GCHQ staff had agreed to resign from the union and to accept the £1000 compensation offered by the government.

GCHQ represents a clear example of the state acting to reduce its dependence on union co-operation, in this instance by removing the union. At the time, a fairly widely held view was that the union ban at GCHQ would be followed by other bans in sensitive areas such as the essential services. To date this has not occurred, although the 1983 Conservative manifesto promised limitations on strike action in essential services. Moreover, union powers have been usurped in other ways, most notably by the legislation passed in 1987 which imposed a pay settlement and new contract on school teachers and thereby negated the teaching profession's own collective bargaining machinery.

Finally, the Conservative Green Paper *Trade Unions and their Members*, published in 1987, reveals that the government is not yet satisfied that enough has been done to curb union powers. Reflecting the judicial creativity demonstrated in the 1984–85 miners' strike, the Green Paper proposes to give individual union members the legal possibility to dissent from their union policies. Thus even where a majority may have voted for strike action, the Green Paper proposes to give the individual the legal right *not* to strike. Additionally, there is proposed a special version of legal aid for members wishing to sue their unions, under the direction and funding of a State Commissioner. This compares with the absence of legal aid for dismissed workers appealing against their dismissal: indeed, the government has suggested the imposition of a £25 fee for workers taking an unfair dismissal case to an Industrial Tribunal. Moreover, having already insisted by law that there will be no closed shop agreements and no strike activity without a majority vote, the new proposals indicate that all closed shop agreements, even where 80 per cent have voted for them, will be made illegal, and that no individual can be obliged to join a union. It is anticipated that legislation along these lines will be introduced in the course of the present administration.

(3) *The role of the police*

In the decade following the 1972 miners' strike, and in particular following the failure of the police to prevent mass picketing from closing the Saltley Coke Depot, the policing of industrial disputes underwent a major transformation to create a more mobile, more organised and more resourced police presence. The system of Police Support Units (20–30 specially trained officers) was revamped to become the basis of public order policing, each unit capable of rapid deployment to counter, among other things, mass picketing. In the miners' strike of 1984–85, the use of PSU's and the overall co-ordination of policing activities was made much more effective by the reactivation (in the first week of the strike) of the central National Recording Centre (NRC) organised by the Association of Chief Police Officers and located at New Scotland Yard. This acted as a clearing house for information on which was based the movement of PSU's from one locality to another.

This increase in police organisation coincided in the early 1980s with an increased readiness to use force to break up mass picketing. Geary (1985) argues that this is partly the result of the police experience of the 1981 inner city riots, which led to a greater training component concerned specifically with riot control. He also attributes it to a lack of differentiation by the police between an inner-city riot situation and the mass picketing connected with industrial disputes—a development which can be construed as the growing 'criminalisation of political and social dissent' (Morris, 1987: 14). Hence, by the time of the Messenger Group dispute in 1983, pickets were confronted not by linked-armed policemen ready to engage in the 'pushing and shoving' which had typified most post-war mass pickets. Instead they faced mounted police, armed with batons and trained in riot control, plus unmounted ranks of police with shields and full riot gear, both ready to use a level of force unwitnessed before the 1981 inner-city troubles (Geary, 1985).

This more confrontational approach by the police was even more evident in the miners' strike of 1984–85 (and again later in the Wapping dispute). Much has been written on the policing of the mining dispute (Geary, 1985; Adeney and Lloyd, 1986; McIlroy, 1985; WCCPL/NUM, 1985) and it is not our wish here to review all aspects of the issue. Four points emerge from the police handling of the miners' strike, however, which give an indication of how trade union actions by the mid-1980s had become far more circumscribed than was typical a decade or even five years earlier.

First, the increased co-ordination via the National Recording Centre was evidenced not simply in the massing of police numbers at pickets and demonstrations. A particularly notable aspect of the miners' dispute was also the extent to which police turned back miners heading into the Nottingham coalfield, even from as far away as the Dartford Tunnel, where Kent miners heading north were turned back (Adeney and Lloyd, 1986: 100). An estimated 164 508 individuals were stopped from entering Nottinghamshire in the first six months of the strike (McIlroy, 1985: 106–7). In many cases this required not only the co-ordinated movement of PSU's by the National Recording Centre, but also the co-ordination of police activities across area boundaries and the relaying of intelligence down the line as to the routes which prospective pickets were taking. The reduction in the numbers of striking miners arriving at a picket line greatly enhanced the police's ability to control picketing activity and to prevent those on strike from halting all 'coaling'. This prevention of pickets from reaching their destination was also a feature of the printing dispute at Wapping in 1986.

Secondly, there is some indication that the mobility of police from one area to another acted to reduce police accountability, both to the local communities to which individual units were detailed and to the lay Police Committees overseeing the individual forces. Local accountability indeed had already been weakened by the increase in size of police areas and the resulting reduction in police forces from over a hundred in the early 1960s to less than fifty today. Indeed, some writers argue that the community's informal control over the police has disappeared altogether in the wake of the mutual aid systems of police support, riot tactics and 'the unmistakable "get tough" messages from central government' (Geary, 1985: 151). What this suggests is that even where organised labour gains a strong voice within local government, its powers over the activities of the police service have declined.

Thirdly, the actions of the police during the miners' strike were supported to a considerable degree by the actions of magistrates. In the first six months of the miners' strike over 6400 people were arrested, mainly for offences relating to obstruction and breach of the peace; by December 1984 the figure had risen to over 8700. Approximately one-seventh of these were not charged (McIlroy, 1985: 111). Of the rest, typical bail conditions acted to prohibit those on bail from further picketing activity before their cases were heard. In the event (and in many cases after considerable delay) a large proportion of miners arrested during the strike were acquitted, often through lack of evidence (for illustrations of this see Parker, 1986; also Adeney and Lloyd, 1986: 106). However, by the time the cases had come to court, the arrest and bail procedure had reinforced police control of the picket lines.

Fourthly, during the miners' strike (as also during the 1980 steel strike and the 1983 Messenger dispute) it is apparent that the police were encouraged by the Home Office to 'take whatever action is necessary' (the Home Secretary, quoted by Geary 1985: 144) to maintain control and keep the passage of coal/coke/working miners flowing. The Home Office appears to have kept close contact with the National Recording Centre (Morris, 1987); similarly, a number of Chief Police Officers have indicated that pressure from government ministers was experienced (Geary, 1985). Indeed, rather than being an impartial 'keeper of the peace' during the dispute between the National Coal Board and the National Union of Mineworkers, the police's role can be seen as more one of maintaining the government's policy towards industry and the trade unions. That the police were intended to be an important part of government policy is evident from the Ridley Plan, drawn up in the years following the miners' successful rejection of Conservative economic policies in the early 1970s. The Ridley Plan, leaked to *The Economist* in May 1978, considered the means by which a Conservative government could win a future confrontation with the union movement in general, and the miners in particular. The plan involved thwarting any future coal strike by the prior building up of coal stocks at power stations, by improving the opportunities for importing coal, by encouraging haulage companies to hire non-union labour to move coal when necessary, and by introducing dual coal/oil firing in power stations. Significantly, the plan also contained the proposal that 'there should be a large, mobile squad of police equipped and prepared to uphold the law against violent picketing' (*The Economist*, 27 May 1978).

To sum up this sub-section, the greater central co-ordination of the police, coupled with their increased riot-control methods following the 1981 inner-city riots, resulted by the mid-1980s in a force well capable of quashing mass union action in a way which confirmed the government's expressed intention of confronting union power and reducing its scope. Hence not only is the contemporary trade union movement confronted by a growing body of legislation which reduces its powers, it is also faced by a police force increasingly autonomous of local control, and increasingly equipped to act to ensure that pickets do not interrupt the flow of people and goods.

Other State Policies

In addition to these direct attempts to weaken and cheapen labour, the government in recent years has pursued a number of other policies indirectly affecting the power of labour. Three particularly deserve mention: (1) the encouraging of foreign multinationals to invest in Britain; (2) the lack of a strong regional policy to stimulate economic regeneration and industrial restructuring away from the south east; and (3) the diminishing dependency of the state on a large standing army.

(1) Further information on the growth of multinational corpor-

ations is given later in this chapter. With regard to state policies, as Harris (1983) has observed, the growth has been accompanied by growing competition among individual states to secure foreign direct investment in their own country so as to gain benefits such as increased employment. This competition has led to a growth in the financial inducements offered to companies. Britain is particularly in competition with other EEC partners concerning the location decisions of American and Japanese companies, and the establishment in 1985 of a Nissan car plant in the north east of England, for example, was accompanied by a very high level of government finance. Of course, the presence of multinationals is a double-edged sword for individual governments. The basing of plants in several different countries allows multinationals to create a considerable measure of independence over issues such as taxation (through, for example, manipulating the transfer prices from one plant to another so that profit is maximised in those locations where taxation is lowest). Also the government in Britain has experienced a number of occasions when corporate policies of multinationals have ridden roughshod over national policies, for example, on wage restraint. This was never more evident than in 1978 when the then Labour Prime Minister's attempt to gain support for a 5 per cent pay norm was fatally undermined by Ford management offering its workforce a 17 per cent pay rise in order to settle a major dispute. The government subsequently failed to gain Parliament's approval to take sanctions against Ford for breaching the pay guidelines (Callaghan, 1987). Yet however ambivalent this relationship of the state to individual multinationals, it is apparent that the recently enhanced courting of Japanese and American multinationals to establish and develop in Britain may in the longer term further undermine the powers of organised labour. There have been a number of well publicised cases of Japanese companies reaching 'no strike' agreements (for instance, at Toshiba, Hitachi and Nissan). By the broader spread of strike-free deals (Bassett, 1986: 3), it would seem, moreover, that the presence of the Japanese example in Britain has prompted native managements to seek to circumscribe their unions' ability to press claims through strike action. Moreover, the encouragement of US multinationals such as IBM, with its policy of not recognising trade unions [a policy which union officials have argued in Scotland has created a general resistance to unions among electronics companies (Bassett, 1986: 162)] provides further indication of the government's encouragement of multinationals against the unions.

(2) In the past 20 years almost £20 billion (at 1982 prices) has been spent by Labour and Conservative governments on measures intended to encourage the growth of industry and employment in the 'assisted areas'. During the 1970s the cost of each job created in the assisted areas was around £35 000. Many of these jobs were already in existence elsewhere but were transferred as a result of the government's financial incentives. In 1979 the system of assisted areas covered 43 per cent of the working population but as the result of Conservative policy, the percentage had been reduced to 27 per cent by 1982. In place of direct incentives, the Conservatives in 1980 introduced the idea of 'enterprise zones', in which there was intended to be vigorous private sector activity stimulated by the removal of tax burdens and of planning constraints. Government consultants calculated that, in the first 11 zones to be so designated, some 8065 jobs had been created by May 1983. The cost of these 8065 jobs was almost £133 million in rate relief, building allowances and public sector investment. Some 75 per cent of companies moving into the zones came from elsewhere in the same county, and some 85 per cent from within the same regions (*The Sunday Times*, 12 August 1984: 53). Despite all this, there has been little discernible improvement in the economic performance of the regions compared with south east England.

Of the 1.6 million employee jobs lost between June 1979 and June 1986, the greater percentage have gone from those regions beyond the southeast corner of the country (see Table 7.1 below). Across the country during this period, only one region experienced a net gain of jobs and that was East Anglia, to the sum of 23 000.

The 'north-south divide', as it is popularly known, is a particular expression of a more general restructuring of the British economy, stimulated substantially by the loss of foreign and domestic markets for the produce of the traditional, 'heavy' industries—iron and steel, coal, cotton and shipbuilding. The older industries, the 'originals' of the industrial revolution, have been concentrated in the north of the country, and have employed particular types of worker, men in traditional crafts or lower-

TABLE 7.1 *Regional distribution of job losses 1979–86*

Region	Jobs lost	Cumulative figure	Cumulative figure as percentage of total
West Midlands	301 000		18%
North West	278 000	579 000	35%
Yorks/Humberside	266 000	845 000	52%
The North	215 000	1 060 000	65%
Scotland	149 000	1 209 000	74%
Wales	130 000	1 339 000	82%
East Midlands	118 000	1 457 000	89%
South East	73 000	1 530 000	94%
Northern Ireland	64 000	1 594 000	98%
South West	39 000	1 633 000	100%

SOURCE   John Goddard, *New Statesman*, 9 January 1987.

skilled jobs, and women in lower level clerical work or, for cotton, in the mills. New manufacturers are coming into being but their produce (for example, electronics, chemicals) and their processes (electronic, chemical) are not generally labour intensive. Such labour as is required typically must contain a high proportion of those workers who possess higher technical, non-traditional or white-collar skills. These skills tend to be found more among southern than northern workers, as Professor Goddard's skills quotient demonstrates (see Table 7.2 below).

The distribution reflects not a differential geographical spread of innate abilities but a differential geographical spread of investment in new technology and in the training which must accompany it. Research by Thwaites and Gillespie (1983: 14) has demonstrated that northern business enterprises undertake fewer research and development activities, and make 'least use of the new telecommunication-based methods of information-gathering', compared to their southern counterparts. Thwaites and Gillespie (ibid.: 15) conclude that 'many of the peripherally-located executives may be disadvantaged in resources to generate or to collect and assimilate technical information and progress elsewhere'. Many enterprises indeed are now utilising the labour-saving potential of new technology to relocate their headquarters

TABLE 7.2 *Skills quotients: regional variations*

Skills quotient 1981 Grade	Berkshire	Tyne & Wear
Managerial	1.07	0.79
Higher Service	1.19	0.85
Higher Industrial	1.62	0.89
Lower Service	1.02	1.09
Craft/Foremen	0.89	1.22
Lower Industrial	0.80	1.01

NOTE The quotient comprises that proportion of the locally employed workforce with the specified skills divided by the national proportion with that skill: 1.00 defines the national average.

and their research and development units nearer to London, where they can be closer to government, to the City, to the mass media, and to routes to the continent. Proximity to such contacts constitutes a major, and for many companies the determining, factor; a human relational resource which sets the parameters for the application of new technology. Thus, despite the potential of the new technology for the geographical dispersal of business enterprise, there is still a marked human preference for congregation. This is partly a factor of inheritance of location, but more it reflects the extent to which successful economic enterprise is contingent upon successful political enterprise—being 'on the spot', 'in the know' and 'in touch with the right people'.

(3) Whereas investment decisions and employment policies affect workers differently in different parts of the country, one area of state activity which has a general impact on the demand for labour is that of defence, specifically, the political choice of the size and nature of the standing army. In chapter 5 we argued the economic implications of this and the fear, well-articulated by 20th-century British governments, that a mass army constitutes an inflationary pressure. In addition to this economic consideration, there is also the 'technification' of warfare which modern states must embrace if they wish to remain assertive and threatening in international affairs . . . as British governments certainly seem to want to do. The proportions of the defence budget going to personnel as distinct from equipment purchases have been given in chapter 6. What they imply for manpower is

a gradual diminution in the numbers taken into armed service. The Ministry of Defence's annual digests of defence statistics reveal the total serving in 1938 to have been 381 000, rising to a peak in 1945 of 4 682 300. Subsequently there has been a steady decline—from the demobilisation peak of 783 500 in 1955, to 406 500 in 1965, to 336 600 in 1976 and to 322 500 in 1986.

Since the late 1970s service pay has had to be improved quite considerably—partly to compensate for the under-resourcing which occurred in previous years; partly to acknowledge the highly skilled and specialised tasks nowadays required of service personnel; and partly to staunch the outflow of these highly skilled workers to more lucrative areas of the economy. The result of these changes has been the creation within the country of a small, professional and expensive fighting force. This, plus the escalating costs and greater dependency on military equipment, implies a shift in the state's relation to the civilian population. The state no longer needs the direct, personal participation of its citizens in the fighting force. But it does need their indirect, impersonal contribution in the form of taxation. The reformulation of the terms of state legitimation which this shift entails has already been considered in chapter 1: in brief it puts an onus on securing consensus about the 'national interest'.

We could add that it also puts an onus on the introduction of forms of taxation which are less easy to discern, that is, which are indirect rather than direct. It is indeed apparent that there has been a movement towards greater indirect taxation as against direct taxation since the late 1970s. For example, it has been calculated that, for a family of four with one wage-earner and two dependent children, the proportion of income taken in tax increased from 1979 (Table 7.3 below), and that the only section of the working or pensioned population to benefit from a reduction in direct taxation were the wealthiest 10 per cent, the burden of the extra taxation falling entirely on the 80 per cent less wealthy.

Conservative government policies in this regard exacerbated a trend already in evidence throughout the 1970s for the rich to get richer and the poor to get poorer. In large part this does seem, somewhat paradoxically, to be a consequence of government efforts to 'buy' jobs by offering a variety of incentives to the multinationals to operate in Britain. To attract the Ford Motor Company into Britain in the late 1970s the British

TABLE 7.3 *Taxation rates 1978–79 to 1986–87*

	Direct tax (per cent)	Total tax (per cent)
1978–79	20.9	35.0
1979–80	18.9	34.5
1980–81	22.5	39.0
1986–87	21.9	38.5

NOTE   Direct tax comprises income tax and National Insurance. Total tax comprises these plus VAT, duties and rates.
SOURCE J. Hills, *New Statesman*, 13 March 1987.

government paid out in subsidies and reliefs the equivalent of £40 000 for each job created (Harris, 1983: 108), funded from general taxation. Indeed, as a consequence of tax relief, many of Britain's largest companies paid no tax at all in the mid-1970s: for example, Allied Breweries; Bowater; British Leyland; British Petroleum; Courtaulds; Dunlop; Esso; Ford; Grand Metropolitan; GKN; P & O; Reed International; Rio Tinto Zinc (ibid.: 105). Others paid very little. As Kay & King (1978) explain it: 'Mainstream taxation yield on all industrial and commercial companies fell from £1.5 billion in 1969 (20% of all tax revenue) to some £101 million in 1975 (0.5% all tax revenue). Households made up the difference.' But they did so less by income tax and National Insurance contributions, and more through rates, duties and purchase tax.

EMPLOYER STRATEGIES

The various actions of the state during the 1980s to weaken a trade union movement already laid low by economic recession and unemployment have been matched by corresponding developments and strategies among employers. Three of the most important of these are: (1) the creation of a more segmented workforce based on a greater use of temporary part-time and sub-contracted work; (2) the application of new technologies which entail both short- and longer-term implications for the future level of manpower; and (3) the continuing expansion of multinationals and the greater emphasis on multiple sourcing.

Increased Segmentation

Labour market segmentation and the advancing by unions of sectional rather than general working class interests have co-existed throughout labour's history, both in the sense of fashioning labour's powers and, to some extent, reflecting the exercise of those powers. Thus, in some part, sectional union activity has contributed to the creation of primary and secondary labour markets, the latter being disproportionately staffed by younger people, coloured and female workers and those with few qualifications. However, in the past decade, and particularly over the past five years there has been considerable expansion in the variety of manning arrangements used by employers in both production and service sectors. Faced with increased competition, sluggish and uncertain product markets, changing technologies, and high exchange rates, management's watchword over recent years has been to increase efficiency. In this a central theme has been to increase 'flexibility': in products and responsiveness to changing market demands; in supplies and inventory control (notably through the computerisation of stock records and application of Just-in-Time methods, see chapter 8); in technologies and the ability to increase small batch capability to achieve diversification; *but most especially in the use of manpower.* Central objectives in the last have been to reduce unit labour costs, to reduce manning levels, to minimise long-term commitment to a permanent full-time workforce, to maximise the match between labour input and production (or service) requirements and to offset any overall reductions in hours by more effective deployment of labour (Institute of Manpower Studies, 1986; Evans and Bell, 1986: 10).

The quest to secure a flexible labour input is by no means new, nor has it been absent in previous patterns of work organisation. The wide use of different shiftwork systems, overtime arrangements and casual working, for example, reflects a diversity in work scheduling. Similarly the growing use of part-time working during the 1970s reflects the employers' practice of hiring manpower solely for periods of greatest demand (for example, during lunchtime in retail stores). During the 1980s, however, we have witnessed not only renewed interest in extending these schemes (via, for example, varying shift lengths and weekend working) but also the introduction of new schemes. As

Evans and Bell (1986: 8) point out, many of these developments in flexibility have been prefaced by a massive demanning, followed subsequently by more selective hiring of workers on temporary, part-time and other contracts, coupled with a widespread transformation of the job boundaries of many of those remaining in employment.

Although categorisations differ, at least five major areas of manpower flexibility can be identified. First, *functional* flexibility whereby certain previous occupational and skill boundaries are abandoned in favour of retraining and the broadening of job descriptions to facilitate movement from job to job, and to establish what Child and others have referred to as 'polyvalence' (literally, combining several powers) (Child, 1985; Cross, 1985). Second, achieving greater *numerical* flexibility by a reduction in management's commitment to a full-time, permanent workforce and a growing use of temporary workers (including young school-leavers on state-supported training schemes) who act as a buffer against market fluctuations in that their employment is more readily and less expensively terminated if demand falls. A similar pattern of permanent and temporary workers characterises many Japanese companies (Hanami, 1980; Kamata, 1982). Related to numerical flexibility but analytically distinct are what might be called *temporal* flexibility and *out-of-house* flexibility. The former is reflected in the growing use of part-time work schedules and the increasing variety of full-time schedules aimed at dovetailing labour input with periods of peak demand, reducing overtime payments and maximising efficiencies in terms of capital utilisation. Thus in recent years there has been a growth not only in five-crew and other shiftwork systems but also an increased emphasis on more flexible rostering, such as the system introduced for railway locomotive drivers (Ferner, 1985). At the time of writing (1987) the issue of extending normal shifts (that is, not subject to overtime payment) is also being discussed in the coal industry and among local authority manual workers (see, for example, *Financial Times*, 13 May 1987). Out-of-house flexibility reflects a growing tendency to use individuals, agencies, and other manufacturers from outside to perform tasks previously carried out by company employees in order that the company reduces its permanent workforce to service only its core activities and thereby cuts its total labour costs. These sub-contracted tasks range from catering, cleaning and construction to the highly technical maintenance of computer-based machinery, and the supply of components, tools, and so on, previously manufactured in-house. This is a type of flexibility closely associated with 'Just-in-Time' systems, which maps into a further type, namely, *financial* flexibility. Here employers have been assisted by state activities (discussed above) acting not only to reduce the influence of trade unions on pay determination, but also to hold down youth wages by selective subsidies and to encourage greater price competition in tenders for work formerly undertaken within the public sector.

How common are these different forms of flexibility and what are their implications for labour's fortunes? One study of over two thousand workplaces in 1984 found that in relation to workers on short-term contracts, temporary workers from private employment agencies, freelance and homeworkers, 45 per cent of establishments used at least one of these categories, particularly those organisations working near to full capacity and with low (or no) levels of union organisation. The survey identified more than half a million workers in the above categories, almost four-fifths of whom were located in private and public sector services, rather than in private manufacturing and nationalised industries (Millward and Stevens, 1986: 208–12). Secondly, a recent study of 72 firms in four industrial sectors (engineering, food and drink, financial services and retailing) found that more than half had introduced more sub-contracting over the past five years, more functional flexibility through a reduction in demarcation, together with a greater degree of pay flexibility (for example, by greater use of merit payments). More than a third of the companies had increased the number of workers on temporary contracts and part-time, while more than a fifth were making more use of self-employed staff (Institute of Manpower Studies, 1986).

Trade unions appear in general to have exercised only minimal influence on this growth of flexibility. Rather than being able to link greater flexibility with enhanced security, or with agreement over which work remains in-house and which activities are sub-contracted, the unions seem to be further weakened by it. Flexibility means growing proportions of part-timers and temporary workers who have typically maintained much lower levels of trade union membership than their full-time and permanent counterparts (see, for example, Millward and Stevens, 1986: 61).

Moreover, the reduction in skill demarcation and growth of multi-skilled craftsmen undermines those trade and occupational identities which have lain at the heart of trade union organisation in Britain since the 19th century. And, at a time of high levels of long-term unemployment, the growth of temporary contracts tends to heighten the salience of job security among those working temporarily; it is thus very unlikely to engender any significant increase in trade union solidarity. Similarly, an increase in the use of sub-contracting further heightens concern over job security among remaining employees. Generally speaking, flexibility acts to segment and individuate the workforce, since different individuals and groups of workers are subject to different terms of employment; a different relationship with the employer (indeed, in the case of those working for sub-contractors, different employers); different time horizons; and different levels of commitment to the present work context.

Unionism is also suffering in its ability to maintain the support of the smaller core of workers carrying out the key tasks in the organisation. For it is towards this group that a disproportionate amount of employment rewards, in terms of income, security and career development, are now targeted. The presence of a positive internal labour market with well defined promotion prospects is likely to reinforce tendencies towards individualism and away from the collectivism which trade unions represent, particularly as the core becomes increasingly comprised of technical and other white-collar staff rather than manual workers, as the use of computer-assisted design and manufacture spreads. Further, as the traditional apprenticeship system continues to decline in favour of a training system offering a combination of more company-specific skills, this provides an additional basis for the core worker to identify his/her long term interests with the company, rather than with a particular trade or skill, and with the collective body that has traditionally represented workers in that trade.

The groups in which collectivist sentiments and any union revival are likely to be manifested—the lower skilled and more peripheral full-time and part-time workers experiencing diminishing opportunities for training and progression—are precisely those groups in positions progressively made less influential by the skill gap which technological advance opens up. Those not required to fill key positions are left to perform less critical jobs (assembly work, clerical and secretarial activities, and so forth) which are more readily replaceable from the external labour market.

New Technology

Less than a decade ago new technology was being presaged by some commentators as the means to the virtual end of labour's role in the productive process. Save for small cadres of skilled maintenance technicians who would ensure the smooth running of automated equipment, factories would become workerless, producing goods 'designed by computer, built by robots' to coin an advertising slogan used by Fiat in the early 1980s. This 'collapse of work', as Jenkins and Sherman entitle their book (1979), was seen to encompass both manufacturing and service sectors and also to be a Catch 22—innovate and create widespread technological unemployment, or fail to innovate and risk greater unemployment through a loss in competitiveness. For others, technological change was the means by which managements could reduce employer dependence on worker skill and discretion in the work process. By increasing the degree of automation, labour could be de-skilled to allow the substitution of less skilled and cheaper workers, while enhancing management's control by reducing its reliance on worker knowledge, increasing its scope for using technology to monitor worker performance, and extending its ability to draw on the pool of semi-skilled workers in the external labour market (Braverman, 1974).

In the event, and with some notable exceptions, the impact of technological change on the quantity and quality of current employment has been less visible and less dramatic than the most pessimistic predictions. Daniel (1987), for example, found that in only about one in five workplaces had the introduction of advanced technical change resulted in reduced manning, and even in these cases the norm was for the displaced workers to be redeployed rather than made redundant. In part the lower-than-anticipated consequences to date reflect continued market uncertainty in many industrial sectors, and a lack of confidence that markets are sufficiently robust to justify a full programme of expenditure on high volume (and potentially rapidly obsolescent) equipment. The tardy application of robots in sectors such as domestic electrical consumer durables is a case in point. In part also, the coincidence of many technological innovations with widespread economic recession in the early 1980s has resulted in any technological displacement of labour being overshadowed by much greater manpower reductions caused by such factors as reorganisation, a lack of demand for goods or services and the imposition of cash limits (Daniel, 1987: 334–5). As Batstone and Gourlay (1986) have pointed out, technical change rarely occurs in isolation and in practice it is difficult to distinguish the effect of technology on employment levels from other changes taking place. In addition, the earlier predictions about the impact of new technology on de-skilling failed to take account of re-skilling effects and of the fact that, at least for some groups, new technology involves the acquisition of new skills (for example, typists becoming word processor users) and an increase in demand for (and dependence on) certain skilled tasks (notably specialist maintenance work). Moreover, Braverman's thesis on technology and management's control of the labour process does not take sufficient account of the consent required by management to achieve the sought-for increases in quality and productivity. Further, as Willman (1986: 183) has pointed out, increased capital investment and faster throughput of materials makes plants potentially more rather than less vulnerable to collective labour action, since any strike action will carry more cost in the short run. And, as Child (1985) has noted, reducing labour costs and skill dependency may not be management's prime aim in introducing new technology but secondary, for example, to creating a new product, reducing inventory or improving quality. If this is the case, any employment implications would not necessarily be immediately apparent.

Given all these limitations attaching to the earlier predictions of new technology's impact on the quantity and quality of jobs, can it still be argued that new technology represents a serious weakening of labour's long-term position and a means by which management can reduce its overall dependency on labour? On the basis of the existing evidence we would argue that although some of the early statements on new technology appear at least partly ill-founded, this should not be taken as proof that new technology has only limited implications for the future position of labour in its relations with capital. On the contrary, some of the points above may well turn out to be short-term exceptions which prove a longer-term rule. In particular, while the immediate job displacement effect appears to have been lower than formerly anticipated, the consequences for future *growth* in employment are more considerable. The middle years of the 1980s have already shown the ability of organisations to use technology, reorganisation and other means of work intensification to secure substantial 'jobless growth' whereby output rises without creating a need for additional employment. Given the versatility, power, compactness and relatively low price of microelectronics, we can expect it to be used to increase the efficiency of work processes for many years to come. Up to now, it has been the cost-cutting, *process* innovation, capability of new technology (not confined to the microchip) which has attracted most attention from unions since it is in this sphere, of automating tasks previously requiring human effort, that the threat to existing jobs and skills is most immediate (Willman, 1986). However, the applicability of new technology to new *product* development holds many of the longer-term implications in terms of future demands for labour. Summing up the findings from his recent survey, Daniel (1987: 289) comments that 'the critical question regarding the implications of advanced technology for employment was how far it enabled employers to avoid taking people on in circumstances where they would otherwise have done so, rather than how far it led directly to reductions in the workforce'.

And we should not lose sight of the fact that particular industries and work groups *have* experienced substantial job reduction as a result of technological change. In the car industry, for example, the introduction of such changes as spot-welding robots, automatic paint-spraying and improved design using CAD (computer-aided design) systems, has markedly reduced the labour input required to produce vehicles. The innovations on the Metro assembly line at Longbridge in the early 1980s, for example, resulted in the direct labour man-hours per car for the Metro body being only two-fifths those required for the more traditionally produced Mini bodies (Willman, 1986: 196). Beynon (1984: 354) quotes a similar case of underbody construction at Ford's Halewood plant where 48 spot welders were replaced by 7 men loading parts into automated welding machines. Outside vehicle manufacture, Batstone and Gourlay's (1986) survey of union representatives identifies job losses through technological change as much more prominent in some industries (notably chemicals and food and drink, both industries where process production is typical) than others. In the same way, 'Flexible Manufacturing Systems' automate out most of the direct labour input—a process which one FMS designer has characterised as 'wrestling manufacture away from human interference' (quoted in Child, 1985: 120).

In contemplating the progressive impact of new technology there is little indication so far of trade unions having been able to exert any significant bargaining leverage on its planning and implementation. Batstone and Gourlay (1986) observe that there has been no major dismantling of union-management machinery despite the economic and political climate being apparently so unconducive to union power, and yet there is little indication of trade unions exerting other than a minimum role in shaping the nature of technical change. The survey reported by Daniel (1987), for example, found that in less than 10 per cent of cases had either manual or white-collar unions established a negotiating role over the introduction of new technology. Unions have had only very limited success in establishing significant influence via New Technology Agreements. Similarly, individual case studies have generally pointed to the inability of unions successfully to overcome inadequate knowledge, low trust relations, an absence of power and a widespread lack of membership concern in their efforts to influence the introduction of new technology (see, for example, Davies, 1986 and Child *et al.*, 1984).

If the above argument is correct, that jobless growth is likely to characterise many of the contexts in which new technology is being introduced, the resulting lack of change in levels of unemployment would caution against any expectations of a return to union power in the short term. The greater union involvement of key direct and indirect workers would logically add to the unions' bargaining power, but these groups are increasingly enjoying more privileged employment treatment than their more peripheral counterparts. They are thus less likely to seek collective solutions to employment problems.

New technology augments, even underpins those other trends already in place, such as the reduction of employment in manufacturing, the creation of separate key and non-key workgroups, the decline of apprenticeship-based single skill working and the development of more company-specific multiple skills, the growth in sub-contracting due to the specialist nature of maintaining automated equipment, and the growth of self-employed teleworking and networking which acts to further individualise and segment the total workforce. Hence, as new technology increases employers' options over the nature of the work process, unions are left with less and less influence over the change process. A substantial reduction in the working population, rather than collective organisation, would seem now to be the only factor likely to prompt a return to labour's general strength in the marketplace.

Multinational Corporations

Since 1945 there has been a substantial growth in multinational corporations (MNCs) operating in Britain, the geographical spread bringing multiple advantages in terms of market penetration. Since Britain entered the EEC in the early 1970s this multinational presence has continued to expand. In 1973 foreign-controlled enterprises in the UK manufacturing sector accounted for 10.8 per cent of total manufacturing employment; by 1981 this had risen to 14.8 per cent, and in certain industries this proportion was much higher; for example, motor vehicles and parts (36.1 per cent), chemicals (30.8 per cent) and instrument engineering (30.8 per cent) (Buckley and Artisien, 1985: 11). More than two-thirds of this foreign ownership is American and is concentrated in more capital-intensive manufacturing. In recent years, however, the most visible multinational development in Britain has been by Japanese manufacturing companies of which there are now approaching 50, the majority located in Wales and the northeast of England. It was the latter area, for example, which was chosen by the car manufacturer, Nissan, to establish an assembly plant in 1985. As Dunning (1986) details, this is one of several major investments recently made by Japanese companies in Britain, partly reflecting the considerable grants and low cost loans available from the state to locate in regions of high unemployment.

This growth in the multinational presence holds a number of important implications for labour, many of them revolving around the strategic advantage which accrues to employers operating in several national contexts rather than a single one. Labour's potential power to disrupt production is clearly weakened if the company operates a policy of dual or multiple sourcing such that if production is halted at one location it can be offset by production elsewhere. Indeed, if the same product is produced in several locations, management has the power to threaten withdrawal of production from a 'troublesome' plant. Such threats typified labour relations at Ford during the 1970s (Beynon, 1984). Although the amount of capital invested in large-scale plant would in most cases make such threats highly unlikely, nevertheless, the development of co-ordinated and standardised production has reduced Ford management's dependence on individual workforces. This became particularly true with the development of Ford's global car, the Escort, of which over one million are produced each year in many locations around the world (ibid.: 327). General Motors and Volkswagen similarly have 'world' cars—the Cavalier and the Golf. Market penetration and economies of scale may have been the prime reasons for this development and for the increased automation which facilitates simplified and common production processes. But indirectly this standardisation of product has strengthened management's power over individual workforces, by increasing management's opportunities for deflecting threats of industrial action. Further, the multiple sourcing strategy has been accompanied at Ford by a policy of ensuring that key components are supplied from at least two countries, again to reduce their dependence on individual firms and individual work groups. This policy has led to a growth in multinational component supplies mirroring the multinational production of finished vehicles (Beynon, 1984: 329).

In addition to coping with management's strategic advantage accruing from dispersed yet co-ordinated production, a further obstacle facing the exercise of union influence in MNCs is the latter's ability to obscure the relative economic position of each subsidiary by aggregating much of the information disclosed to the level of the MNC as a whole, or its major divisions. The generally high level of intra-company trading and the various transfer-pricing procedures which this engenders can further obscure the true financial position of each subsidiary. Unrealistic transfer pricing can be used, for example, to increase the apparent profitability of some subsidiaries while reducing that of others. Such activity could therefore be employed to minimise profits accruing in subsidiaries where trade unions are strong (thus weakening one of the union's bases for wage claims) and to maximise profits where labour is less well organised and/or where levels of taxation are most advantageous. In fact, the question of transfer-pricing is part of a wider problem facing labour in MNCs—how to achieve greater influence in the decision-making structure of multinationals. Some European countries (for example, West Germany and Sweden) maintain legislation which requires MNCs, like all domestic companies, to disclose information relevant to bargaining. However, attempts at EEC level to develop standard practices on information disclosure and consultation with trade unions have so far failed, not least because of the opposition of US MNCs in Europe, which have gone so far as to threaten disinvestment should such proposals be made law (Vandamme, 1986: 168). Hence, although EEC proposals for consultation, disclosure and a disaggregation of information for each subsidiary were first introduced by Vredeling in 1980, they remain at the discussion stage. Other voluntary codes of conduct over consultation and information in MNCs introduced by such bodies as the International Labour Organisation and the United Nations, have met with little success (Hamilton, 1986). Currently, most multinationals provide consolidated financial statements which act to further obscure the situation prevailing in individual subsidiaries, and the influence of transfer-pricing activity (Gray, 1986: 57).

Union involvement is further complicated by the variation from corporation to corporation in the degree of centralisation and decentralisation of decisions. This variation is associated with such factors as the size of parent and subsidiary companies, their respective geographical locations and the performance of the subsidiary. It is evident, however, that certain decisions (for example, major investment and other financial decisions) are generally more centrally controlled than others (for example, personnel issues) (Bulcke, 1986: 223). Hence the issue of union involvement in MNC decision-making involves not only achieving greater information pertaining to subsidiaries but also greater access to centralised decision-making.

Moreover, effective labour mobilisation requires trade union coordination across national boundaries, which in the past has had only limited success. In recessionary periods such international solidarity is made all the more problematic by the general shortage of employment and the desires of individual unions to retain employment opportunities within their particular country. Yet union responses to management threats of production-switching and such like can only effectively be handled through union combinations across the different locations. Without this, managements in MNCs continue to reap the benefits of co-ordinated production but unco-ordinated labour.

Employer activity in the introduction of greater workforce flexibility, the application of new technology and the continued expansion in multinational operations do not exhaust the pressures on labour's present and future power base. There are also, for example, the trends to smaller-scale enterprises being established in greenfield sites where trade union traditions are far from well established, and for manufacturing employment to be located not in industrial cities but in small towns and rural areas. Handy (1984: 85) reports, for instance, that while manufacturing employment in Britain as a whole dropped from 8 million to 7 million between 1960 and 1978, manufacturing in small towns and rural areas rose by 16 and 38 per cent respectively. Moreover, the declining regions such as the northwest and northeast of England have been traditional heartlands of trade unionism in Britain—the manual unionism based on labour-intensive manufacturing industries. Much higher than average levels of unemployment in these regions means depressed conditions among the particular labour forces in which the traditions of unionism are long established. The effects of this are particularly evident in the decline in membership figures of unions such as the Transport and General Workers' Union (down 28 per cent in the period from 1979 to 1982). At the same time, however, a small number of unions organising in more buoyant industries and regions have managed to raise their membership; the Banking Insurance and Finance Union (BIFU), for example, raised its membership by 15 per cent between 1979 and 1982 (Coates and Topham, 1986: 10).

Clearly changes are occurring in the bases on which unions can recruit and organise. Thus, within private sector manufacturing union density measured by number of shop stewards has actually increased since 1980, but this is as a result of the loss of workers overall being greater than the loss of union representatives. Millward and Stevens (1986) report on the decline of the closed shop in this sector, and the narrowing of the scope of collective bargaining. But patterns of pay negotiation remain stable for manual workers and are increasingly being extended to the non-manual. This latter may well be a function of a more general growth in managerial forms of unionism, a particularly significant development in British unionism and industrial relations in the 1970s (Bamber, 1986). Additionally it could be the case that pay is being used by employers to buy worker acceptance of new technologies and new forms of work organisation and industrial relations. Such an interpretation would help explain the rise in real earnings (often above productivity increases) experienced by private sector manufacturing workers since 1981. Some of these factors (buying acceptance; increasing managerial and professional unionism) may be operative also in private sector services, where union membership and unionisation are growing, albeit from a low base. So also, however, is part-time working, up from 18 per cent in 1980 to 22 per cent in 1984. This is an employment practice which has traditionally worked against efficient worker organisation, so any continuing trend towards it implies a constraint on the nature of trade union development in this sector.

CONCLUSION

As was said earlier, the general character of British industrial relations can historically be shown to derive substantially from the general character of unionism and employer/employee relations in the older industries of the industrial revolution itself. The place of these industries in the hierarchy of the British political economy has now gone; their influence on industrial relations also. What is taking their place? What type of economic activities and organisation will generate the dominant employment forms of the 1990s and onwards?

In response to these questions one must again argue a two-nation theme; that is, following the north-south divide identified earlier, in Britain the life experiences of the population will split into those with full-time paid employment and those without. Some reduction in paid working hours may yet ameliorate the division but its essential shape seems irresistible. Finance capital, because of its strong international footing and because of conducive government policies in the arenas of fiscal and monetary control, grows stronger by the minute. But the types of employments it offers have not traditionally been unionised and, where they are becoming so, the nature of the unionism is coloured by professional and managerial concerns and values. Additionally many UK finance houses are following the US example and refusing to recognise independent trade union organisation, preferring to buy employee loyalty through strategically considered personnel policies. In this they closely resemble the more dynamic areas of manufacturing capital—electronics, chemicals, oil refining, cars, textiles and electrical engineering. These are the industries in terms of which British manufacturing will be/is recovering. All of them have or are in the process of introducing labour-saving technologies and economies of scale and scope. Many of them are not British-owned, although within them are to be found the residues of the traditional manufacturing unions. As already identified, these unions are demonstrating a 'new realism', compelled on the one hand by visions of unemployment and attracted on the other by 'new deals' offered by their employers. The 'new deals' seem largely inspired by the successes of the Japanese; indeed, in many areas of Britain Japanese corporations are becoming the major employers of British workers. In South Wales, for instance, Japanese companies will soon employ more people than the coal industry. Moreover, companies such as Lucas, Austin Rover, Jaguar and Vauxhall have declared their interest in 'Japanese' manufacturing methods and employment practices (Oliver and Wilkinson, 1987). In terms of manufacturing processes, Japanese methods require manpower flexibility and employment practices which dispense with status differences between workers. To achieve co-operation in this, they pursue consensus forms of industrial relations; company-based unions who can be consulted, for example, when considerable future investment plans are being made; and paternalistic personnel practices which bind the worker voluntarily to the caring 'parent' employer. In terms of developments in capital then, the type of unionism emerging rests on workers who are both more thoroughly incorporated and more privileged. Industrial relations systems here either reflect their types of unionism, or go one step further to outmanoeuvre unionism absolutely via paternalistic personnel practices. One could suggest that this echoes the *gefolgshaft* ties of the feudal epoch. Certainly it is a far remove from the impersonal, contractual, sale/purchase of labour advocated by early 20th-century 'scientific management' theories. It is also a far remove from the social partnership of government and unions which characterised the 40 years from 1938. Government for its own purposes has delivered labour, unprotected, back to the forces of capital.

8 Conclusions: Nationalism, Internationalism and Democracy

GOVERNMENT POLICIES IN THE 1980s

By the mid-1970s the state in Britain had become the largest single employer (*Social Trends*, 17, 1987), spending almost 60 per cent of national output each year (Robinson, 1978), the consequence of popular pressures in a context of particular types of economic problem, industrial technology and warfare needs. State employments by mid-20th century fell into the broad categories of Armed Forces and arms manufacture; law and order; welfare and education; other administration; and infrastructural provision (primarily transport, communications and energy). A failing economy leaves the state incapable of funding all these activities at unchanged levels, and forces politicians to make choices between them. The Conservative government in power from 1979 spelt out its choice as less government; a shrunken budget deficit; 'sound money'; incentives for the rich in the shape of lower taxes; and incentives for the poor in the shape of lower benefits and wages (Johnson, 1982). The steady redistribution of wealth towards the already wealthy has been detailed earlier. The monetarist fight against inflation so as to achieve 'sound money' has also been addressed, its destructive impact on manufacturing capital and employment levels being notable among its achievements. Inflation has indeed fallen but public spending, although officially declared to be falling as a proportion of gross domestic product, is being allowed to grow, thereby demonstrating the limits to 'less government'. Where policies of 'less government' are more nearly approached is in the form of privatisation of the whole or parts of nationalised industries and public amenities. This sale of national assets has been justified in terms of promoting firstly, the development of property-owning democracy and secondly, greater cost efficiency via intensified market competition. Success in the second goal usually means downward pressures on labour costs as intensified market

191

competition propels more workers into secondary labour market conditions or redundancy. Success in the first goal implies that those unable to afford property are disenfranchised. Both outcomes are consistent with the present Prime Minister, Mrs Thatcher's, publicly declared intention to 'turn back the tide of socialism' in Britain (quoted in Benton, 1986). But less government and a freer market do not relieve employers of the need to consult, nor the state of the need to collect taxes and rates. The administrative structures and popular goodwill for these exercises must therefore be sustained, even if not in the same form. There are indeed now signs that Conservative free market policies are losing appeal among some sections of British enterprise: the Confederation of British Industry in its 1986 forecast called on the government to provide more funds for infrastructural investment, while in their 1986 forecast the Association of British Chambers of Commerce called for more government attention to the problems of the regions. At the same time the Prince of Wales has aired his disquiet over the phenomena of inner-city decay and poor housing. Clearly there is concern among some of the country's leading figures and institutions that government policies should not proceed so far as to damage too fundamentally Britain's civil and industrial relations.

The state is itself, of course, a major employer, and has faced something of a 'crisis' in its own industrial relations since the 1970s. This 'crisis' embraces state employees in education, local government, health and some sections of the civil service. It does not embrace state employees in the areas of law, order and defence. The police force, for example, has enjoyed increases in its number (from 108 000 in 1961, to 176 000 in 1979, to 188 000 in 1986: *Economic Trends Annual Supplement*, 12, 1987), and in its remuneration (see Benyon, 1984: 102–3, for details). The National Institute of Economic and Social Research (1985) calculates, for example, that while between 1978 and 1984 all other government spending rose on average some 12 per cent, the amount spent on police services increased by 40 per cent. This growth suggests that the state feels increasingly dependent upon a police presence for the maintenance of law and order.

With regard to arms manufacture, the Ministry of Defence's attitude is clear: it commented in 1980, 'the ability to develop and produce arms is an important national asset'. In that year

British military expenditure took 20 per cent of total British electronics output, and 60 per cent of British aerospace output (Harris, 1983). Where these industries are nationalised, such expenditures are kept within the public account. But where arms manufacturers are private, the consequence is that public funds are directed into the private sector. The Trident programme expenditures, for example, constitute an economic dynamo for the United States but not for the United Kingdom. Britain's dependence on US arsenals also keeps relatively low the number of jobs which defence offers to British workers: by the late 1970s only 400 000 people were employed full-time in the manufacture of military equipment and support work (Chalmers, 1985). Moreover, relative to the level of investment, British arms industries do less well in international markets than do the French or Italians (ibid.).

Additionally there is in defence and defence-related state employments a delicate and difficult balance to be struck between the democratic rights of workers and citizens, on the one hand, and the need for secrecy in the national interest, on the other. All British defence workers are constrained by the Official Secrets Act and are thus debarred from exercising rights through appeals to the Industrial Tribunals system. The police, armed forces and now also communication workers at GCHQ (Government Communications Head Quarters) are debarred from participating in a trade union.

In similar vein, defence-relevant information is—it would seem, increasingly—kept from the public generally and from their elected representatives. Decisions about the A-bomb, Polaris, Trident and, more recently, Zircon spy satellite were taken without reference to the House of Commons or any of its specialist, multi-party, committees. These state practices have been explained as defending the realm against enemies seen to be not only foreign nationals but also British dissidents. Thus it is that the flexible and relatively demotic English common law is more and more circumscribed by statutes such as the Prevention of Terrorism Act, the Police and Criminal Evidence Act, and the Public Order Act: the general gist of these being to give the police greater legal powers to search and detain members of the public, and to delineate more narrowly the range of legally acceptable public behaviour. At the same time the forms and powers of local government administration are being reduced in favour of central government in a number of directions; for example, the central government clawback of the rate support grant to local authorities; the abolition of the metropolitan borough councils by central government fiat; the moves to a national curriculum in education determined by the Department of Education and Science, and the government encouragement of schools to break loose from local authority administration.

These developments have been interpreted as synonymous with a creeping growth of state oppression (Campbell, 1981; Ackroyd *et al.*, 1977; Aubrey *et al.*, 1983). If that interpretation is correct, we must ask, why is the state behaving in this 'illegitimate' manner? We must bear in mind that much the same course is being travelled by other states in western Europe and by the US, that is, many of the states of developed capitalism would seem to be experiencing the same pressures.

CAPITAL EXPANSION AND WORLD INEQUALITY

Many writers (for example, Harris, 1983; Wallerstein, 1974a and b) would argue that repressive developments in Britain, and the sharpening of social inequality with, for growing numbers, a decline in their standard of living and life opportunities, are to be viewed as a 'local response to external political and economic penetration' (Walton, 1984). What is happening to Britain, they say, is yet one more phase in the exploitative process of incorporation into the world economy. It does indeed seem to be the case that continued capital expansion and technological innovation are acting as a catalyst to the restructuring of world economic organisation, with consequences for extant political arrangements of and among nation states. But these states, we would contend, are not passive recipients of whatever world capital has to give, nor mere cyphers of world capitalist interests. They have interests of their own; resources which often amount to the command of significant areas of economic enterprise (not to mention their armed forces and weapons systems); and responsibilities to maintain the political integrity of the territories over which they hold domain. Since these territories are of interest in some way to capitalist enterprise—as sources of raw materials, production locations, labour power, consumers and investment opportunities—there must perforce be a conciliation of the interests of states and capital. What shape the conciliation takes, and how balanced or unbalanced the interests reflected within it, will be contingent upon the balance of power prevailing between the parties at the time.

One area in which a *nationalist* orientation is expressed by internationally operating enterprises is that of investment in technological innovation. Such innovation is most readily visible in the economically dynamic northern hemisphere countries and in Japan, where there is money to invest in the latest techniques and where also employers have strong incentives to replace their better-paid, unionised workers with something either cheaper and/or more malleable. These economic commanders, private and state, are not, however, entirely free from constraints. The northern hemisphere recessions of the 1970s and early 1980s, intensified competition from Japan and other Asian countries, and the destabilisation of political relations on the home front have pushed northern corporations and governments alike towards policies of retrenchment. This has been to the acute detriment of those in the Third World. Almost one-half of the fall in inflation in the industrialised nations between 1980 and 1984 was financed by the Third World's commodity price collapse (UNCTAD, 1986). The stockpiling of primary commodities on a massive scale, and the production of enormous agricultural surpluses (funded by taxation on domestic populations) in the United States and Europe have more or less wiped out entire sectors of Third World trade to the North in such items as sugar, coarse grains and animal feeds. In 1968, for example, Britain was using jute for some 71 per cent of its carpet-backing: this had fallen to 11 per cent by 1972 and has not subsequently recovered (Vaux, 1987). Notwithstanding the oil cartels which helped provoke the 1970s recession, oil prices by the end of 1986 had fallen to half their 1985 levels (UNCTAD, 1986). And as commodity prices have been forced down by the northern states' manoeuvring (substantially but not entirely based on new technology) for greater self-sufficiency, so also has direct foreign investment in the less developed countries (LDCs). IMF *Yearbooks* show this to have shrunk from what was already a minus figure: in 1970–71, there was a net loss of direct foreign investment from LDCs of $3900 million: by 1979–80 this was a net loss of $5000 million. The pattern of northern withdrawal from the Third

World is worse if debt repayments are included: the total debt of developing countries rose from $68 400 million in 1970 to $595 800 million in 1983 (Institute of Development Studies, 1985). In this context it is interesting to note that British investment abroad is said to have risen from £15 billion in 1979 to £50 billion in 1984 (Mrs Thatcher, *Panorama*, BBC, 9 April 1984). Clearly, policies of economic retrenchment do not mean pulling everything back into the home economy so much as keeping investments 'in the family', that is, wherever a mixture of business, political and military alliances makes it reasonable to do so. This interpretation receives some support from the fact that the core of growth in world trade since the Second World War has been that between the same industry operating in different countries. By 1967 such intra-industry trade accounted for nearly two-thirds of all OECD trade. By the mid-1980s the OECD, as also the United States and the European Economic Community, was taking protectionist measures against the producers of the wider world.

As already said, the northern withdrawal is seen as a response to the economic and political crises developing from the 1970s. Resources and control are being, as it were, gathered back in so to counteract the effects of recession and to finance the technological innovation which can lead the way out of it. In that sense the modern day behaviour of the western nations is mimicking the plunder of earlier centuries of formal and informal empire, when wealth taken from South America, the West Indies, Africa and India substantially financed the industrial and general economic expansion of Europe.

Today the impact is being felt not only on trading and investment but also in employment. A trend became apparent throughout the 1960s and 1970s for many multinational corporations to reorganise their technical division of labour along international lines. That trend seems to have reached its limits and, indeed, in places to have been reversed. The 'dispersed business enterprise' (Jacobsen, 1979) of the 1970s was able, on a basis of electronic communication and information-processing systems plus its conglomerate, multinational commercial structure, to renegotiate the division of labour so that unionised, well-paid workers (among whom men were over-represented) in the west could be displaced by non-unionised, cheaper and more tractible workers (among whom women were and remain over-represented) in the east. The industrial proletariat of the 1970s was alive, if not well, and living not in Lancashire or the Ruhr but in Taiwan, North Korea, Hong Kong, Singapore and Sri Lanka. It seemed then to entrepreneurs to make economic sense to have non-complex, labour-intensive parts of the manufacturing process performed in the Third World. People in those regions, given that chronic poverty was often the only alternative, were more prepared to work long hours for low wages. On the whole they were not and are not organised into unions. However, problems of social order in the home countries plus the recognition that the Japanese have been pursuing a different organisational strategy with greater profitability and ease of employment relations, have prompted many western multinationals towards the adoption of Japanese-style production. This entails not only the cultivation of quasi-feudal, in-house labour relations but also a partial return to localised concentrations of production processes. A primary motivation here—shared and reflected also in US enterprise developments—is to frustrate any attempts by organised labour to exploit production bottlenecks. Thus, instead of having production lines stretched across continents, 'Just-in-Time' (JIT) systems keep everything geographically together, but there is a deliberate cultivation of numerous local suppliers of parts and of sub-contractors. Competition among these means that they are unlikely to be able to stop the primary plant from operating by strike action, or by failing to supply on time. At the same time workers within the primary plant are expected to be flexible, to undertake multiple tasks rather than specialise. Micro-chip technology applied to the machinery of the primary plant facilitates its rapid reprogramming to a variety of different uses, thus enabling swift responses to changing market and/or supply factors (Hoffman and Kaplinsky, 1984). It is not possible to calculate accurately how many jobs were put into the Third World by the multinationals, nor how many they are drawing out. The situation is one of flux, with the companies enjoying a relatively free hand in deciding where and whether to employ labour. But that these companies are increasingly reluctant to export investment and jobs from their own national, or allied, territories to the Third World is clear.

For the peoples of the Third World this amounts not to a joyful loss of imperial exploitation but to a sad loss of any source of earnings. As Tony Vaux (1987) of *OXFAM* UK said:

At Bandel and Bhadreshvar there is no loose talk of imperialism. The fact is that many would be only too happy to see the wicked capitalists come back and exploit the industrial ruins. Their problem is not the spreading tentacles of corporate, monopoly capitalism but neglect, unemployment and consequent poverty.

What is reflected in this statement is the condition of dependency which ties the poorer countries to the richer, and which leaves them unable to develop the means to become independent. The condition is not fortuitous or self-induced but, following the arguments of Baran (1957) and Samir Amin (1976, 1982), the outcome of colonial exploitation. As joint endeavours undertaken by entrepreneurs and state leaders, the capitalist nations have treated the rest of the world as suppliers of raw materials and labour, and as markets for manufactured goods. They have built their fortunes on those relations but then made their capital investments and technological advances disproportionately in their home territories. The greater the rate of exploitation, the greater the rate of capital investment and technological advance in those home territories, and therefore the greater the discrepancy in the terms of competition between rich and poor nations.

The preferences shown by internationally-operating capital enterprise for its home, or allied, territories relates in part to the political features of economically dynamic centres already adumbrated in chapter 7, that is, the value of being 'in the know', 'on the spot' and 'in touch with the right people'. But another element has been the sensitivity of business and political leaders to the successes of wealth in 'buying' social order and peace. Preferential treatment, in material terms at least, of home populations helps create a stable social basis from which to operate. It supports a sense of national identity, which in turn supports and expresses the political integrity of the home area and the patriotism of its peoples. By and large, the populations of western capitalism have done quite well from imperialism, albeit not all of them equally. Indeed, the racialist sentiments often found among these western populations can be seen to flow directly from their sense of national 'specialness'. It expresses their effort to use nationality as the grounds for obstructing the awarding of employment and other material goods to other people 'not of their kind' (Phizacklea and Miles, 1987). This could be interpreted as an economically determined practice of discrimination in the sense that capital's division of labour generates competition among labourers which subsequently takes this form of expression. We feel that, while the 'spur' provided by labour market competition is a very significant factor, the recognition of its contribution should not be allowed to obscure the more general and over-riding concerns of human beings for self-survival and self-actualisation. In short, we contend that the will to compete—and therefore to discriminate—precedes rather than follows capitalism. What capitalism yields is a particular rather than an exclusive case of competitive and discriminatory practices.

CAPITAL EXPANSION AND BRITISH INEQUALITY

Is it then the case that everyone in the northern hemisphere can anticipate a happy and prosperous future, albeit structured on poverty in the south? The answer is no: because the gathering back in of resources and command which has been the response of states and conglomerate capital to crises occurs also *within* the capitalist countries. Just as there has been 'external' imperialism on a world scale, so there has been 'internal' imperialism on a national scale. Both are built upon the exploitation and nurturing of dependencies. As we have already discussed in chapter 7, there is within Britain also the appearance of a north-south divide. Overall the combined effect of recession, government economic and defence policies, and technological redundancy has been to exaggerate the inequalities of British society, and to exacerbate poverty. Across the five years 1976 to 1980, for example, it has been calculated that the richest 20 per cent in Britain improved their wealth by 3.5 per cent in real terms, while the poorest 20 per cent grew poorer by 10.5 per cent (*Economic Trends*, 1981). By 1987 the International Year of 'Shelter for the Homeless' could report that the number of people in Britain without homes had doubled since the mid-1970s to 100 000; while additionally some four million houses were declared officially to be substandard and a further million unfit to live in.

It is appropriate to ask what are the prospects for these inegalitarian forces at work in British society. Could it be that

present government policies, however painful, will actually help
release and stimulate factors making for new growth and new
wealth . . . such as investment in new technology? Technological
innovation—by facilitating the substitution of scarce factors of
production, and the expansion of production at constant or lower
prices—certainly has in itself the potential to remedy much of
the poverty and inequality. This is Tom Stonier's vision: he says:

> Britain is no longer the industrial workshop of the world. It
> does not matter if it stops making a lot of steel, cars or ships.
> It does not matter, economically speaking, if it makes none of
> these and imports them all. It matters no more than the fact
> that Britain imports all its tea and coffee. It could even afford
> to import all its computers if it is possible to train the
> appropriate technocrats and experts. There are only two major
> problems if Britain de-industrialises: the loss of jobs and the
> loss of foreign exchange. Both of these problems will evaporate
> once a strong post-industrial, information-based economy has
> developed. The function of government is to accelerate this
> process. (1983: 188) . . . Our children will live in a world of
> peace and plenty unprecedented in recorded human history.
> (ibid., 189) . . . just as the industrial economy eliminated
> slavery, famine and pestilence, so will the post-industrial
> economy eliminate authoritarianism, war and strife. (ibid.,
> 214)

It is good to have articulated such a strongly optimistic vision
of the future, if for no other reason than that it identifies the
possibilities, the potentialities, of the new technologies. It does
not, however, address the probable because it neglects the factor
of a political will which is confounded by national, sectional and
class interests.

Let us consider for one moment where the investment capital
for technological innovation is to come from. Broadly speaking,
we can identify two principal sources of investment finance—
one is the state, the other is capital. Taking the latter first, the
operations of capital in Britain are influenced both by government
policies and by international economic developments. As already
discussed, one sector of capital, namely British manufacturers,
has already been adversely affected by government policies, on
the one hand, of 'sound money' (see chapter 7) and, on the

other, of defence-related public expenditures (see chapter 6). Conservative monetarist policies since 1979 have favoured finance capital and the wealthy: they have not favoured manufacturing capital and the poor. The public rationalisation of these policies has been that they would curb inflated expectations and would help generate greater amounts of investment finance. There is at the time of writing an argument about whether or not there has been an upturn in capital investment in productive industry: the Department of Trade claims manufacturing to be recovering speedily from its nadir of 1979–82; Hoggarth and Salama (1987) dispute the figures used by the Department and the conclusions it arrives at. There is, however, intensified activity in the City (Hutton, 1986). The City was 'deregulated' in autumn 1986; and it does perhaps indicate Conservative government priorities that, at the end of 1986, the Police City Fraud Squad was given 150 officers to pursue more than £1 billion in fraud monies, while the Department of Health and Social Security was given 700 inspectors (rising to 1000 in 1987) to pursue £22 million of social security fraud. But the City itself is a changing institution. The growth area for the City is in securities dealings. This contrasts with the old (1960s–1970s) practice whereby banks loaned (foreign) deposits abroad to states and multinationals. This proved to be a very risky business in the wake of Third World defaults and the collapse of profits occasioned in some companies by recession and the oil crisis; and the banks therefore sought alternative practices. Simultaneously there was a commercial convergence between the high street operations of banks and of building societies, the effect of which was to open up links between finance capital and the savings of ordinary working people. These savings plus very sizeable Pension Fund monies were then directed by the banks into shareholdings and securities dealings. In short, the banks became the manager of major shareholdings in companies, a new development in the UK (Harris and Fine, 1985). But the activity of the banks now embraces *all* types of financial transactions, not just the management of company finances. That development, plus the deregulation of the City, opens up vast opportunities for insider dealing which—even with a vastly expanded City Fraud Squad—would be exceptionally difficult to identify and track down. Moreover, of all the banks represented in the City, some 75 per cent are now foreign-owned, the Japanese and the

Americans being particularly well represented. Their focus is inevitably international rather than primarily British. These various developments (deregulation; spread of share ownership; international linkages; computerisation) increase the vulnerability of the world's stock markets to the effects of doubt and panic-selling. The crash of share prices simultaneously in Washington, London, Paris, Tokyo, and Hong Kong, commencing on 'Black Monday' in October 1987 and prompted primarily by America's continued and massive indebtedness, is *the* case in point.

As Johnson (1982) expressed it, the economic alliances active in Britain in the 1980s seem best understood as 'finance capital plus historic capital versus the rest'. Lenin's vision of Britain as a rentier state seems similarly appropriate, but it is interesting to note that the rentiers are not predominantly British. It may be, of course, that these activities will benefit the British people in the longer term. but it seems unlikely that the nature of that benefit will lie in the recovery of productive industry and the jobs that go with it.

If there is a question mark over capital's willingness to invest in British industry, can we look to the state for such investment? There have certainly been large sums of public money expended by past and present governments in job-creating investments in the regions, and in encouraging multinationals to establish operations here (see chapter 7). But the assessment of the former was that it was an expensive way to effect little real change, while of the latter, the relative weakness of both state and labour *vis-à-vis* the incoming multinationals remains marked. Moreover, recent state policies have been increasingly directed to the encouragement of private, rather than state, enterprise. Under Conservative direction, the state is attempting to limit its growth as an employer and investor in enterprise—except where defence is concerned. Defence is clearly a top priority in terms of government investment and enterprise activity, a priority which we have argued is pursued to the detriment of the country's general economic strength and development (see chapter 6). The decision to purchase the Trident submarine missile system, with its consequences for the weakening of Britain's conventional strength in addition to its consequences for the economy, is a notable indication of a political will at work to the negation of an economic one. The Trident decision has been spurred by the breakdown of 'the old bipolar balance' of world powers, this being 'replaced by new multilateral exercises of force' (Bogart, 1976). But it represents a longer-standing state commitment to the assertion of British sovereignty in international affairs. All governments since the Second World War, of whichever party, have pursued military ambitions and plans well beyond the capacity of the British economy to support. History since then has been a series of reductions in such plans as the politicians accepted the need for financial realism. But, cut or no cut, the plans have involved enormous sums of money, with debilitating consequences for the rest of the economy and for the nature of British society. That 20th-century Britain has been so impoverished shows remarkable parallels with the Tudor reign, when monarchs similarly were prepared to sacrifice economic and social goals for the achievement of political ones (Crowson, 1973).

One of the major factors prompting the breakdown of the 'old bipolar balance' has been recession in the United States. The United States is now the world's largest debtor, world surpluses being accrued now by the Japanese and West Germans. Without major population decline, it is not expected that unemployment in the United States will fall below 10 per cent for some considerable time. The British *Department of Employment Gazette* gives the June 1987 US unemployment rate as 6.1 per cent, but Jay and Stewart (1987) calculate it to be at least 3 per cent above the official government figure. As a major political and military ally, what happens in the US is very relevant to Britain. Attempting to identify solutions to these problems, Jay and Stewart (ibid.) call for international rather than nationalistic attitudes; for greater attention to the production for export of non-military commodities; and for competitive exchange rates. Since the British government is still committed to supporting sterling as an international currency, to high levels of armaments production, and to national sovereignty, such a change in direction would surely be revolutionary. At the same time, Jay and Stewart propose that in future wages should be linked to profitability – which for British labour would also require a revolutionary change in attitudes.

LABOUR AND DEMOCRACY

Is British labour in any condition to respond to such a challenge, given the context in which it must now operate? British labour has become accustomed to the exercise of 'industrial muscle', using differentials and the standard of living as the primary bases for its wage claims. These claims succeeded so long as the needs of the state and entrepreneurs for soldiers and labourers were high, but began to fail as those needs diminished. More recently, in consequence, the unions have been agreeing productivity deals. By the logic of productivity deals, redundancy is bound to follow unless there is simultaneous economic expansion generating new jobs. Some new growth and some new jobs are visible in the economy but not (yet) on a scale sufficient to absorb all redundant and new labour. Profitability bargaining has little appeal to those in secondary labour markets or unemployed. Such people have no industrial muscle to flex.

Moreover, industrial muscle—even where the employment conditions for its exercise do persist—is yet contingent upon worker attitudes and union cash. There are problems for organised labour on both counts. The lack of cash is increasingly a problem for the British labour movement—not only because Conservative legislation has opened up and encouraged employer actions for damages and the sequestration of union assets but also because of falling membership dues. This diminution of union funds in turn afflicts the campaigning and organising abilities of the Labour Party. Transport House, the headquarters of the Labour Party, in 1986 calculated that in the general election of 1983 the Conservatives spent more than £10 million and the Labour Party £2.5 million, the 1986 income of the Conservatives being £11 million as against Labour's £4.5 million. The relative paucity of Labour's campaigning abilities must be weighed, moreover, against the propensity of the Conservative government to utilise the law, privatisation, and the mass media, as Hobsbawm put it in 1982, to 'by-pass the traditional Establishment so far as is possible, while appealing directly over its head to the masses'. A concerted Conservative rhetoric stressing the undesirabilities of union restrictive practices and the 'looniness' of the Labour Left, against the desirability of consumer sovereignty and property-owning democracy—taken against the backdrop of inflation and unemployment—has been potent enough to dislocate substantial elements of the electorate from their traditional voting allegiances. According to a National Opinion Poll for Granada TV's programme *Union World*, conducted at the end of January 1987 (and subsequently confirmed by the election results), less than half the trades unionists polled said they would vote Labour at the next election; some 26 per cent intending to vote Conservative and another 24 per cent intending to vote SDP/Liberal Alliance.

Some of the success of the Conservatives must be acknowledged as a failure of the Labour Party and the unions, which in turn has much to do with Labour's weakness in Parliament (see chapters 5 and 6) and the unions' essential economism. The success of the bourgeois social system has been precisely its ability in terms of social practices and beliefs to discriminate and keep separate the spheres of economic, political and cultural production. Labour, self-regarding, could then be ideologically contained within the economic sphere and, by the same token, excluded on the grounds of impropriety from the political and cultural. For working people the separation posed a set of choices: either they could accept it as legitimate and voluntarily work in ways which kept their self-help organisations (that is, the trades unions) distinct from political action; or they could eschew the bourgeois political system and attempt to develop an alternative and rival one on the basis of their labour power; or they could challenge the separation and instead work for incorporation via worker representation in the bourgeois parliament. All three options have their advocates within the British labour movement, now as in the past, but the fact of choice dissipates labour's political potential by creating divisions while, whatever the choice, it remains a reaction to an agenda set largely by others. In the circumstances it is not unreasonable that many unions and union activists have preferred to pursue economistic goals as the surest grounds on which to maximise membership support.

Economism, however, means adopting and exploiting all the restrictive practices indicated by market competition, namely, organising for monopsony in the labour markets. The unions have had little or nothing meaningful to offer the un- and under-employed. They have found it near impossible to organise workers caught in secondary labour market conditions. They have sometimes employed exclusionary tactics against people construed as 'not one of us'—dilutees, blacks (Gordon and Klug, 1984; Green, 1979; Miles, 1984) and women (Barker and Allen, 1976; Cockburn, 1983; Ashton, 1986). These restrictive practices have fuelled popular and (more disingenuously) bourgeois criticism of the unions even though they are necessarily a function of exacerbating and exploiting the particular dependencies of an employer on labour power.

Moreover, even at times when labour power was at its strongest, advances in industrial democracy were relatively limited. The gains to those dependent upon labour power appear to have far outweighed the concessions extended to labour itself. Although radical forms of industrial democracy have occasionally captured much publicity (such as the ideas of workers' control advocated in the 1910–14 period, and of worker directors in the 1970s), in general labour aspirations in this area have been limited. Trade union representatives have doggedly emphasised the priority of collective bargaining, supported where necessary by joint consultation, rather than seeking more radical forms of joint control. This is perhaps hardly surprising given the weight of factors hindering the development of the more radical forms of industrial democracy—not least the legal rights of property, and the problem of inculcating the necessary participatory competence among labour representatives (Pateman, 1970). Moreover, the inability or failure of labour to utilise its political gains of the 1914–79 period to secure greater economic power has meant very little possiblity of more thoroughgoing change in the representation of worker interests.

One can suggest, in contrast to present government belief, that union strength is contingent upon labour market conditions rather than vice versa. That being so, it is predictable that the unions will follow the jobs—into the 'new realism' and the quasi-feudal world of the multinationals and conglomerates. Outside of this world they will find it more difficult to operate. Even their own political party, in its pre-1987 election statements, has indicated an end to the social partnership of government and unions; while the present Conservative Chancellor has just (July 1987) declared the substantial reduction of the National Economic Development Committee and its little 'neddies'. ('Neddies', big and little, were established in the mid-1960s to secure tripartite decision-making in national and sectoral economic matters.) By this downgrading, the government is also signalling the downgrading of tripartite decision-making.

Patterns of employment are decidedly changing, towards enduring and high levels of un- and under-employment concentrated especially among the youngest, the oldest and the noncausasian. Women are appearing in greater numbers in the workplace but mainly as part-timers, casualised, lower paid. Men, unless especially well-skilled, will be less attractive to employers in the future. The unions have to find a way to respond to these changes.

Unions affiliated to the TUC have since 1979 lost some three million members, with a loss of £100 million per annum in annual subscriptions. Given the new deals now offered by employers to the more secure workers, and given the predilections of increasingly large proportions of the workforce for Conservative policies, the unions are having to offer a whole range of new services in their efforts to recruit. These services include insurance, skills training, mortgage finance, legal advice, holidays. They involve the union in much higher costs of operation and therefore become a strong pressure for increased membership fees. In that regard, British unionism is developing along lines akin to their US counterparts. But the cost pressures are also compelling union mergers, just as unemployment in the 1920s compelled mergers. Whereas in 1900 there were some 1323 trade unions with a combined membership of 2 022 000, by 1985 there were only 407 unions with a combined membership of ten million. The process is continuing and it raises the question, on what rationale will mergers be based? Will, for example, mergers reflect and exacerbate divisions between blue- and white-collar workers? Or perhaps British unions will follow the French model in having separate TUCs, distinct by virtue of their political orientation. At the moment, the bigger, general unions like the Transport and General Workers' are making a concerted effort to recruit and organise in the weaker and secondary labour markets. Whether they succeed remains to be seen, but if they do not they must develop an alternative strategy for survival.

In terms of general social development, for the highly skilled and in-demand worker, Toffler's (1980) vision of the nuclear family working from home and taking it in turns to man/woman the electronic terminal which links employer to employee may well be an outcome. For the rest, Pahl's (1982) vision seems more appropriate—the under-skilled man without adequate or any paid employment staying at home while the woman goes out as the family's sole wage-earner to her second-class existence as sweated, insecure labour on an assembly line. The man, if he has any enterprise, will move into the informal economy and/or street life; and kith and kin will become far more significant to survival and progress.

These developments are essentially reactive. Is there yet something proactive to be done in the assertion of democratic rights and the accountability of government? One can suggest that the days of mass political pressure exercised in the form of industrial muscle are largely over. There is a need to find alternative ways to convey popular feeling into political and economic practices. On the political front there could be a great deal more pressure for constitutional change towards a Bill of Rights and a separation of powers. Unlike most other liberal democracies, British citizens have never been awarded a Bill of Rights. The laws of Britain stand essentially to proscribe certain activities or to award immunities against prosecution. They do not indicate positive rights, although Conservative developments in employment legislation are moving in this direction. Without a consitutional assertion of the formal rights of citizenship, there is no basis upon which individuals and collectivities can defend their actions against the state (although 'public law' does stand to limit the abuse of power by local and central authorities: Denning, 1983). This significantly circumscribes the ability of, for example, journalists to publish details of state activities, without which disclosure there can be no adequate accountability of government. This inadequacy is compounded by the absence of formal legal mechanisms for the investigation and exposure of official malpractice. Unlike the constitutional arrangements of parliamentary-type democracies such as the United States, France and West Germany, the British legislature and executives are so tightly intertwined as to conceal rather than reveal. As Lustgarten (1987) says:

> Britain relies entirely on non-statutory and often informal arrangements of accountability to Parliament, centring upon the convention of individual ministerial responsibility. Yet ours is a parliamentary system of party government in which . . . it is an essential function of Parliament to sustain the Government. Hence the paradox that for scrutiny and accountability of government we rely on members elected primarily to maintain their party in office.

One can suggest that this state of affairs is the inheritance of the *laissez-faire* philosophy of the early 19th century. The 20th century saw this philosophy take a back seat in favour of the collectivist ideologies necessary to the waging of mass warfare and supported by the work experience of mass, industrialised production (both of which were 'mass' in the sense of aggregating together large numbers of ordinary people in a common task). The movement away from mass, industrialised production and from mass warfare has allowed the reassertion of the individualism and property-oriented values of liberal philosophy. These values are those utilised by the Conservatives in their form of government, and they are thus vulnerable to popular judgements of whether the values are being properly honoured in government policies and practices. With the unions and labour movement contributing more weakly to political developments, the debate becomes one less coloured by the ideologies of socialism and more by those of liberalism. Freedom of assembly, of speech, of affiliation, of contract, and so on, should be the 'natural' claims of those encouraged to regard themselves as sovereign individuals.

The vulnerability of government to these claims could be partly reduced by the erosion of universal franchise. This move would, however, thoroughly disturb the political integrity of the whole, put greater onus on the police and judiciary for the securing of social order, and involve a fundamental change in the whole character of British society. Nonetheless, given that the government is seemingly intent on delivering working people unprotected to free enterprise, while simultaneously pursuing defence policies which are, at very least, of doubtful value to the British nation understood as the people who live here, perhaps that is indeed the road we are now travelling.

To reiterate a Marxist point, people have the potential to be self-determining but the conditions in which they act are not often of their own making. This point has frequently been construed as a deterministic one. Further, the primary source of determination has been seen as a mode of production in which the means to survival are held in one set of hands to the partial exclusion and detriment of others. We accept that determination for some springs from the superior command of essential resources which others exercise, but we would stress that these relations should be seen as political rather than economic. 'Economic logic', the 'logic of the market' is a rationale mobilised so as to direct and legitimise courses of human action in preference to alternative courses. To accept the logic of the market as irreducible is to be convinced by the terms of practice and legitimation supportive of a particular social order. Such a conviction facilitates attitudes of moral irresponsibility and encourages dull and fatalistic acceptance. It obscures the possibility of alternative courses of action.

Classic Marxist accounts have treated the state as a derivative function of capital. Thus they have construed the international political relations of the modern world as being structured upon the world economy of capitalism. Indeed, we can *pro tem* concur with Wallerstein (1974a) that 'the high cost of political imperium' in the modern world has prompted the emergence of such alliances as the European Economic Community. But if Wallerstein's emphasis is on 'costs', economically understood, then we must disagree. The financial equations of military capacity, economic strength and domestic stability within individual nation states *are* out of balance, and new political solutions *are* being forged. But the effort of the parties is not to restore overall equilibrium so much as to find new ways to service their particular national or sectional interests. It is less the high cost of political imperium and more the *fact* of political imperium which explains present world developments.

Rather than treat the state as a derivative function of capital, we would firstly challenge the separation of economic and political spheres as being anything other than culturally specific and inessential. Secondly, we would argue that capitalism (understood as a particular means to generate and regenerate wealth) has been prompted and in large part fashioned by political competition among extant elites. But, because within its own systems of organisation, it has entailed relations of dependency and subordination—that is, power—its relationship to other extant political systems has always been that of a potential rival. The other political systems have had either to defer to it (for example, the US with no historical endowment of a strong political order); to subordinate it (for example, the Soviet Union and China, both countries with long traditions of dynastic rule), or to establish working relations with it (for example, Britain, a country whose wealth has depended largely on trading and foraging abroad). In none of these instances are the arrangements made at any one time immutable: they can change according to recalculations of political interest and the balances of power.

In these recalculations, economic costs and capacities will certainly figure but they will not be the motivating or determining force unless the people doing the recalculation make it so. The driving force remains the pursuit of self-advancement and determination, a pursuit sometimes expressed as rivalry and sometimes as co-operation with others. The 'selfs', for our purposes, are the extant political systems of the nation states. The inter-state rivalries of western Europe in medieval times prompted an intense focus on and specialisation in ways of generating the cash and weapons to fight wars more effectively. The warring states did not merely harness a pre-existing capital to their purposes; they acted as mid-wife to its birth, stimulated its growth and directed its development. Thus finance capital initially was geared to the funding of war efforts; major sections of industrial capital were either solely or partly dependent on state military investment and custom; and agricultural capital was given a state boost so that public order and loyalty could be fed. Simultaneously the state has extracted taxes from wherever the political balance allowed, and penetrated ever more thoroughly both civil society and the economy. Even the most ardent of *laissez-faire* governments did not/does not shrink from the Keynesian effects of its defence-related expenditures, nor from the totalitarian drift of its defence-related policies.

What has to date marked out capitalist enterprise as a particular political system different from others has been firstly, its disavowal of its essentially political nature, and secondly (related to that) its non-appropriation of the mechanisms usually associated with political rule—namely, military capacities; law and order; and the symbols and rituals of political legitimation. Explicitly political competition between groups involves more or less elaborated structures of integration, participation and mobilisation of bias within the group. It stimulates and has been largely contingent upon the construction of a common identity between the rulers of the group and the ruled. The common identity necessitates some kind of preferential treatment for members relative to that which is, publicly at least, accorded to non-members. The structuring of common identity rests on the ability to distinguish 'us' from 'them'. Historically, political integrity of groups has been vested in the ability to defend a defined geographical territory by and for the people therein. Historically, as a measure of armed and economic strength, that territory has become the nation state, extended at its height to a national empire. A sense of nationality and the ability to promote and protect the nation have thus figured very strongly in the terms delimiting and legitimating the state.

By the same token, avowedly non-political capital has no such commitments, develops no such capacities and affords no such political integrity. If capitalists have desired such integrity, they have been dependent on a successful state for its delivery. But that they might be extremely reluctant to support in material terms the state's nationalistic endeavours is evidenced in, for example, the rearmament period in Britain. Modern Britain also offers an illustration (by no means the only one available) of the extent and manner in which the state's military efforts can cause malformation and damage to economic activity.

Even though some sections of capital are able to lessen the state's various impacts by moving onto an international footing, generally speaking most capitalists prefer political integrity and stability. If the nation states no longer offer that integrity and stability, then perforce the capitalists must develop their own— by appropriating the mechanisms of law and order, the symbols and rituals of common identity and perhaps also by developing a military function. In that connection, we have endeavoured to demonstrate the 'new' (that is, imitating Japanese-style) forms of personnel management, to which can be added 'older' (that is, western) practices of building corporate identities among their employees and publics. We have suggested that these can be viewed as quasi-feudal structures, moderating the commodification of labour by awarding some degree of political status— albeit paternalistically translated—to full-time employees.

But the securing of such status is increasingly contingent upon an individuated relation to the employer; the individual worker is by various means dissuaded from identifying and organising independently of the employer with his/her fellow workers. What is offered instead is the identity and organisation of the employer. The lines of social bonding are thus vertical rather than horizontal and, given that power disproportionately resides with the employer, the social structure approaches that of a mass society.

This stands in contrast to the British experience of the 1940s to 1970s, of a social structure more nearly approaching a class society in the sense of an independent, self-regarding and assertive organisation of working people, able to participate in the highest levels of state and enterprise decision-making. This historical highpoint for labour, we have argued, sprang from the coincidence of mass manufacturing and production techniques with mass or industrialised warfare, the dependency of the state and entrepreneurs on labour constituting a leverage which labouring people could and did use to their advantage. Subsequently the independent organisations for working class promotion in particular, and for independent public debate more generally, have been and continue to be undermined by state and employer policies. In very large part, the success of this erosion has sprung from the elites' superior command of technology and its development, and from their related ability to reorganise production so as better to exploit other and weaker sections of labour, or to render labour technologically redundant. The 'internationalisation of capital' apparent in these moves should not, however, obscure the fact that, while pure economic logic may accept no national boundaries, elites do. The elites are not a homogeneous political group. Across the world they are numerous and competitive, and they use their national identities, their armed might and their economic powers vigorously in this rivalry, with consequences for all of us.

Bibliography

ABERCROMBIE, N., HILL, S. and TURNER, B. S. (1886) *Sovereign Individuals of Capitalism* (London: Allen & Unwin).

ACKROYD, C. *et al.* (1977) *The Technology of Political Control* (Harmondsworth: Penguin).

ADENEY, M. and LLOYD, J. (1986) *The Miners' Strike 1984–5: Loss Without Limit* (London: Routledge & Keegan Paul).

AMIN, S. (1976) *Unequal Development: An Essay on the Social Formations of Peripheral Capitalism* (Hassocks: Harvester Press).

AMIN, S. *et al.* (1982) *Dynamics of Global Crisis* (London: Macmillan).

ANDERSON, P. (1974) *Lineages of the Absolute State* (London: New Left Books).

ANDERSON, P. (1980) *Arguments within English Marxism* (London: Verso).

ANDREWSKI, S. (1954) *Military Organisation and Society* (London: Routledge & Keegan Paul).

ANNETTE, J. (1979) 'Bentham's Fears of Hobgoblins' in B. Fine *et al.* (eds) *Capitalism and the Rule of Law* (London: Hutchinson).

ANTHONY, P. D. (1986) *The Foundation of Management* (London: Tavistock).

ARTHURS, A. (1985) 'Industrial Relations in the Civil Service: Beyond GCHQ', in *Industrial Relations Journal*, vol. 16, pp. 26–33.

ASHTON, D. (1986) *Unemployment under Capitalism* (Brighton: Wheatsheaf).

AUBREY, C. *et al.* (1983) *Nineteen Eighty Four in 1984: Autonomy, Control & Communication* (London: Comedia).

BAGWELL, P. (1971) 'The Triple Alliance 1913–22' in A. Briggs and J. Saville (eds) *Essays in Labour History 1886–1923* (London: Macmillan) pp. 96–128.

BAIN, G. S. and PRICE, R. (1980) *Profiles of Union Growth: Comparative statistical portrait of 8 countries* (Oxford: Blackwell).

BAMBER, G. (1986) *Militant Managers? Managerial Unionism & Industrial Relations* (Aldershot: Gower).

BARAN, P. (1957) *The Political Economy of Growth* (New York: Monthly Review Press).

BARKER, D. and ALLEN, S. (eds) *Dependence & Exploitation in Work & Marriage* (London: Longman).

BASSETT, P. (1986) *Strike Free: A New Industrial Relations in Britain* (London: Macmillan).

BATSTONE, E. (1984) *Working Order* (Oxford: Basil Blackwell).

BATSTONE, E. and GOURLAY, S. (1986) *Unions, Unemployment and Innovation* (Oxford: Basil Blackwell).

BEAUMONT, P. B. (1987) *The Decline of Trade Union Organisation* (London: Croom Helm).

BECKETT, J. V. (1986) *The Aristocracy in England 1680–1914* (Oxford: Blackwell).

BELL, D. (1960) *The End of Ideology: On the Exhaustion of Political Ideas in the 50's* (Glencoe: Free Press).

BENTHAM, J. (1938–43) *Works*, ed. J. Bowring, 11 vols. See especially

'Panopticon' and 'An Introduction to the Principles of Morals & Legislation' (London: Willis).

BENTLEY, E. (1974) in K. D. Brown (ed.), *Essays in Anti-Union History: responses to the rise of Labour in Britain* (London: Macmillan).

BENTON, S. (1986) 'Thatcherism gets the Heave-ho from Business' (*New Statesman*, 5 September) pp. 5–8.

BENYON, J. (ed.) (1984) *Scarman & After: Essays Reflecting on Lord Scarman's Report, The Riots & Their Aftermath* (Oxford: Pergamon Press).

BERCUSSON, B. (1978) *Fair Wages Resolution* (London: Mansell).

BEVERIDGE, Sir William (1942) *Social Insurance and Allied Services* Cmnd 6404 (London: HMSO).

BEYNON, H. (1984) *Working for Ford* (2nd ed.) (Harmondsworth: Penguin).

BLACKSTONE, Sir W. (1765) *Commentaries on the Laws of England* (Oxford: Clarendon Press).

BLAUG, M. (1962) *Economic Theory in Retrospect* (Homewood: R. D. Irwin).

BLAUNER, R. (1964) *Alienation and Freedom* (University of Chicago Press).

BLOCK, F. and SOMERS, M. R. (1984) 'Beyond the Economistic Fallacy: The Holistic Social Science of Karl Polanyi' in T. Skocpol (ed.) *Vision and Method in Historical Sociology* (Cambridge University Press).

BLYTON, P. (1981) 'Re-examining Joint Consultation: Attitudes and Perceptions of White Collar Union Members and Shop Stewards', in *Personnel Review*, vol. 10, pp. 36–9.

BOGART, L. (1976) *Premises for Propaganda: the U.S. Information Agency's Operating Assumptions in the Cold War* (New York: Free Press).

BOISSEVAIN, J. (1974) *Friends of Friends: networks, manipulators and coalitions* (Oxford: Blackwell).

BOND, B. (ed.) (1967) *Victorian Military Campaigns* (London: Hutchinson).

BORNSTEIN, S., HELD, D. and KVIEGER, J. (eds) (1984) *The State in Capitalist Europe* (London: Allen & Unwin).

BOSWORTH, D. and DAWKINS, P. (1982) 'Woman and part-time work' *Industrial Relations Journal* Vol. 13, No. 3, pp. 32–9.

BRAVERMAN, H. (1974) *Labor and Monopoly Capital* (New York: Monthly Review Press).

BRIDBURY, A. R. (1986) 'Dr. Rigby's Comment: A Reply', *Economic History Review* XXXIX, pp. 417–22.

BRIGHT, D., SAWBRIDGE, D. and REES, B. (1983) 'Industrial Relations of Recession', *Industrial Relations Journal*, XIV, No. 3, 24–33.

BROWN, K. D. (1982) *The English Labour Movement 1700–1951* (Dublin: Gill & Macmillan).

BROWN, R., CURRAN, M. and COUSINS, J. (1983) *Changing Attitudes to Employment*, Research Paper 40 (London: Department of Employment).

BUCKLEY, P. J. and ARTISIEN, P. F. R. (1985) *Multinationals and Employment* (Chichester: Wiley).

BUCKLEY, P. J. and ENDERWICK, P. (1985) *The Industrial Relations Practices of Foreign-Owned Firms in Britain* (London: Macmillan).

BULCKE, Van den, D. (1986) 'Autonomy of Decision-Making by Subsidiaries of Multinational Enterprises' in J. Vandamme (ed.) *Employee Consultation and Information in Multinational Corporations* (London: Croom Helm).

BURAWOY, M. (1979) *Manufacturing Consent: changes in the Labor Process under Monopoly Capitalism* (University of Chicago Press).

BURGESS, K. (1975) *The Origins of British Industrial Relations: The Nineteenth Century Experience* (London: Croom Helm).

BYTHELL, D. (1969) *The Handloom Weavers* (Cambridge University Press).

CAIN, P. J. and HOPKINS, A. G. (1986) 'Gentlemanly Capitalism & British Overseas Expansion: Part One: The Old Colonial System 1688–1850' *Economic History Review*, Vol. 39(4), pp. 501–25.

CAIRNS, H. A. C. (1965) *Prelude to Imperialism: British Reactions to Central African Society 1840–1890* (London: Routledge & Kegan Paul).

CALDER, A. (1969) *The People's War* (London: Cape).

CALLAGHAN, J. (1987) *Time and Chance* (London: Collins).

CAMPBELL, D. (1981) *Big Brother is Listening: Phonetappers & The Security State*, Report No. 2 (London: New Statesman).

CAMPBELL, D. (1987) 'Spy in the Sky' *New Statesman*, 23 January, Vol. 113, No. 2913.

CAMPBELL, D. (1987) 'The Knock on the Door' *New Statesman*, 6 February, Vol. 113, No. 2915.

CHALMERS, M. (1985) *Paying for Defence* (London: Pluto).

CHALMERS, M. (1986) *Trends in U.K. Defence Spending in the 1980s* (University of Bradford: Peace Studies).

CHAMBERS, J. D. (1953) 'Enclosure and Labour Supply in the Industrial Revolution', *Economic History Review*, Vol. V, pp. 319–43.

CHARLES, R. (1973) *The Development of Industrial Relations in Britain 1911–1939: Studies in the evolution of collective bargaining at national and industry level* (London: Hutchinson).

CHILD, J., LOVERIDGE, R., HARVEY, J. and SPENCER, A. (1984) 'Microelectronics and the Quality of Employment in Services' in P. Marstrand (ed.), *New Technology and the Future of Work* (London: F. Pinter).

CHILD, J. (1985) 'Managerial Strategies, New Technology and the Labour Process' in D. Knights, H. Willmott and D. Collinson (eds), *Job Redesign: Critical Perspectives on the Labour Process* (Aldershot: Gower).

CHOI, Jungwoon (1984) 'The English Ten Hours Act: Official Knowledge and the Collective Interest of the Ruling Class', *Politics and Society*, Vol. 13(4), pp. 455–78.

CHURCHILL, W. (1956) *A History of the English Speaking Peoples*, vol. 1: *The Birth of Britain* (London: Cassell).

CIPOLLA, C. M. (1972) *Economic History of Europe Vol. 1: The Middle Ages* (London: Fontana).

CLARK, R. and BARKER, D. (1981) *Reversing the Trend Toward Early Retirement* (Washington: American Enterprise Institute for Public Policy Research).

CLEGG, H. A. and CHESTER, T. E. (1954) 'Joint Consultation' in Flanders, A. and Clegg, H. A. (eds), *The System of Industrial Relations in Great Britain* (Oxford: Blackwell).

CLEGG, H. A. (1985) *A History of British Trade Unions* Vol. 2: 1911–33 (Oxford University Press).

CMND 6404 (1942) *Social Insurance and Allied Services* (a.k.a. The Beveridge Report) (London: HMSO).

CMND 6527 (1944) *Employment Policy* (London: HMSO).

CMND 9763–11 (1986) *Statement on Defence Estimates 1986* (Defence Statistics, Vol. 2) (London: HMSO).

COATES, K. and TOPHAM, T. (1986) *Trade Unions and Politics* (Oxford: Blackwell).

COCKBURN, C. (1983) *Brothers: Male Dominance & Technological Change* (London: Pluto).

COLE, G. D. H. (1923) *Workshop Organisation* (Oxford: Clarendon Press).

COOMBES, D. and WALKLAND, S. A. (1980) *Parliaments and Economic Affairs in Britain, France, Italy and the Netherlands* (London: Heinemann).

CRANSTON, M. (1985) *John Locke: a biography* (Oxford: Oxford University Press).

CROSLAND, A. (1956) *The Future of Socialism* (London: Jonathan Cape).

CROSS, M. (1985) 'Flexibility and Integration at the Workplace' in *Employee Relations*, Vol. 7, No. 1, pp. 3–7.

CROUCH, C. (ed.) (1979) *State and Economy in Contemporary Capitalism* (London: Croom Helm).

CROUCH, C. and PIZZORNO, A. (1978) *The Resurgence of Class Conflict in Western Europe since 1968* (London: Macmillan).

CROWSON, P. D. (1973) *Tudor Foreign Policy* (London: Adams & Charles Black).

CURRIE, R. (1979) *Industrial Politics* (Oxford: Clarendon Press).

DACHLER, P. and WILPERT, B. (1978) 'Conceptual dimensions and boundaries of participation in organisations: a critical evaluation', in *Administrative Science Quarterly*, No. 23 (March), pp. 1–39.

DANGERFIELD, G. (1970) *The Strange Death of Liberal England 1910–1914* (St. Albans: Granada Publishing).

DANIEL, W. W. (1987) *Workplace Industrial Relations and Technical Change* (London: Pinter).

DAVIES, A. (1986) *Industrial Relations and New Technology* (London: Croom Helm).

DEFOE, D. (1728) *A Plan of the English Commerce* (London: Charles Rivington).

DELDERFIELD, E. R. (1970) *Kings & Queens of England & Great Britain* (2nd ed.) (London: David & Charles).

DENMAN, D. (1978) *The Place of Property: new recognition of the funciton and form of property rights in land* (Berkhamstead: Geographical Publications).

DENNING, A. Lord (1983) *The Closing Chapter* (London: Butterworths).

DEPARTMENT OF EMPLOYMENT (1985) *Employment: the Challenge for the Nation*, Manpower Papers (March) (London: HMSO).

DEVINE, J. A. (1985) 'State and State Expenditure', *American Sociological Review*, Vol. 50 (April), pp. 150–65.

DJILAS, M. (1957) *The New Class: An Analysis of the Communist System* (London: Thames & Hudson).

DOBSON, C. R. (1980) *Masters & Journeyman: A Prehistory of Industrial Relations, 1717–1800* (London: Croom Helm).

DOBSON, R. B. (ed.) (1983) *The Peasants' Revolt of 1381* (2nd ed.) (London: Macmillan).

DONOUGHUE, B. (1987) *Prime Minister: The Conduct of Policy Under Harold Wilson and James Callaghan* (London: Cape).

DUBY, G. (1974) *The Early Growth of the European Economy: Warriors & Peasantry* (London: Weidenfeld & Nicholson).

DUNKLEY, P. (1979) 'Paternalism, The Magistracy & Poor Relief in England, 1795–1834', in the *International Review of Social History*, Vol. 24(3), pp. 371–97.

DUNNING, J. H. (1986) *Japanese Participation in British Industry* (London: Croom Helm).

EDWARDS, R. (1979) *Contested Terrain: The Transformation of the Workplace in the Twentieth Century* (London: Heinemann).

ENSOR, R. C. K. (1936) *England, 1870–1914* (Oxford: Clarendon Press).

ESPING-ANDERSON G. *et al.* (1976) 'Modes of Class Struggle and the Capitalist State', *Kapitalistate*, pp. 4–5, 186–220.

EVANS, A. and BELL, J. (1986) 'Emerging Themes in Flexible Work Patterns' in C. Curson (ed.) *Flexible Patterns of Work* (London: Institute of Personnel Management).

FERNER, A. (1985) 'Political Constraints and Management Strategies: The case of Working Practices in British Rail', *British Journal of Industrial Relations*, XXIII, pp. 47–70.

FINE, B. (1985) *Democracy and the Rule of Law* (London: Pluto Press).

FLANDERS, A. (1954) 'Collective Bargaining' in A. Flanders and H. Clegg (eds), *The System of Industrial Relations in Great Britain* (Oxford: Blackwell).

FOX, A. (1977) 'The Myth of Pluralism & A Radical Alternative' in T. Clarke and L. Clements (eds), *Trade Unions Under Capitalism* (London: Fontana).

FOX, A. (1985) *History and Heritage: The Social Origins of the British Industrial Relations System* (London: Allen & Unwin).

FOOT, P. (1968) *The Politics of Harold Wilson* (Harmondsworth: Penguin).

FOUCAULT, M. (1977) *Madness and Civilisation* (London: Tavistock).

FRANKLIN, M. N. (1985) *The Decline of Class Voting in Britain: Changes in the Basis of Electoral Choice 1964–83* (Oxford University Press).

FREEDMAN, L. (1985) *Atlas of Global Strategy: war and peace in the nuclear age* (London: Macmillan).

FRENCH, D. (1986) *British Strategy and War Aims 1914–16* (London: Allen & Unwin).

GALLIE, D. (1978) *In Search of the New Working Class* (Cambridge University Press).

GEARY, R. (1985) *Policing Industrial Disputes 1893–1985* (Cambridge University Press).

GEORGE, D. (1953) *England in Transition* (2nd ed.) (Harmondsworth: Penguin).

GIDDENS, A. and STANWORTH, P. (1974) *Elites and Power in British Society* (London: Cambridge University Press).

GIDDENS, A. (1979) 'An Anatomy of the British Ruling Class', *New Society*, 4 October, pp. 8–10.

GIDDENS, A. (1982) *Profiles and Critiques in Social Theory* (London: Macmillan).

GLASGOW MEDIA GROUP (1976) *Bad News* (London: Routledge & Kegan Paul).

GODDARD, J. (1987) 'North and South' (*New Statesman*, 9 January) p. 18.

GORDON, P. and KLUG, F. (1984) *Racism and Discrimination in Britain, 1970–83* (London: Runnymede Trust).

GOULDNER, A. (1976) *The Dialectic of Ideology and Technology* (London: Macmillan).

GOWLER, D. and LEGGE, K. (1978) 'Participation in context: towards a synthesis of the theory and practice of organisational change', in *Journal of Management Studies*, vol. 15, pp. 149–75.

GRAY, S. (1986) 'The Main Systems for Informing External Parties in Financial and Commercial Legislation' in J. Vandamme (ed.), *Employee Consultation and Information in Multinational Corporations* (London: Croom Helm).

GREEN, A. D. (1979) 'On the Political Economy of Black Labour, and the Racial Structuring of the Working Class in England', *Occasional Paper*, Birmingham University Centre for Contemporary Cultural Studies.

HAIN, P. (1986) *Proportional Misrepresentation* (London: Wildwood House).

HAMILTON, G. (1986) 'Initiatives Undertaken by International Organisations in the Field of Employee Information and Consultation in Multinational Undertakings' in J. Vandamme (ed.), *Employee Consultation and Information in Multinational Corporations* (London: Croom Helm).

HANAMI, T. (1980) *Labor Relations in Japan Today* (London: John Martin).

HANDY, C. (1984) *The Future of Work* (Oxford: Blackwell).

HARRIS, L. and FINE, B. (1985) *The Peculiarities of the British Economy* (London: Lawrence & Wilson).

HARRIS, N. (1983) *Of Bread and Guns: The World Economy in Crisis* (Harmondsworth: Penguin).

HARRISON, J. F. C. (1984) *The Common People: A History from the Norman Conquest to the Present* (London: Croom Helm).

HAWKINS, K. (1981) *Trade Unions* (London: Hutchinson).

HAYTER, T. (1981) *The Creation of World Poverty* (London: Pluto Press).

HEPPLE, B. (ed.) (1986) *The Making of Labour Law in Europe: A Comparative Study of Nine Countries up to 1945* (London: Mansell).

HILL, S. (1981) *Competition and Control at Work* (London: Heinemann).

HILLS, J. (1987) 'Look Out: Its High Tax Nigel' (*New Statesman* 13 March 1987) p. 13.

HILTON, R. H. (1978) *The Transition from Feudalism to Capitalism* (London: New Left Books).

HINDESS, B. (1983) *Parliamentary Democracy and Socialist Politics* (London: Routledge & Kegan Paul).

HIRSCH, F. and FLETCHER, R. (1977) *CIA and the Labour Movement* (Nottingham: Spokesman).

HOBSBAWM, E. J. (1982) 'Looking towards 2000: the politics of decline?' (*New Society*, 7 October) pp. 8–10.

HOFFMAN, K. and KAPLINSKY, R. (1984) *Changing Patterns of Industrial Location and International Competition: The Role of TNC's and the Impact of Microelectronics* (New York: UN Centre for TNCs).

HOGGARTH, G. and SALAMA, E. (1987) 'Winning back lost export empires—a somewhat selective use of statistics' *Guardian*, 27 March).

HOPKINS, E. (1979) *A Social History of the English Working Classes 1815–1945* (London: Edward Arnold).

HUTTON, W. (1986) 'In 1986 Monetarists Ran up the White Flag' (*New Statesman*, 19 December) p. 11.

HUXLEY, P. *et al.* (1886) in Lipset, S. M. (ed.), *Unions in Transition: entering the second century* (San Francisco: Institute for Contemporary Studies Press).

INSTITUTE OF DEVELOPMENT STUDIES (1985) 'Slowdown or Crisis? Restructuring in the 1980's', *Bulletin*, Vol. 16(1).

INSTITUTE OF MANPOWER STUDIES (1986) *Changing Work Patterns: How Companies Achieve Flexibility to Meet New Needs* (London: National Economic Development Office).

JACOBSEN, R. (1979) 'Satellite Business Systems' in *Media, Culture & Society*, Vol. 1, pp. 235–53.

JAY, P. and STEWART, M. (1987) *Apocalypse 2000; economic breakdown and the suicide of democracy 1989–2000* (London: Sidgwick & Jackson).

JENKINS, C. and SHERMAN, B. (1979) *The Collapse of Work* (London: Eyre Methuen).

JOHNSON, R. (1982) 'The Pursuit of Sound Money' (*New Society*, 7 October) pp. 35–6.

JOHNSTON, L. (1986) *Marxism, Class Analysis and Socialist Pluralism* (London: Allen & Unwin).

JOYCE, P. (1980) *Work, Society and Politics: The Culture of the Factory in late Victorian England* (Brighton: Harvester).

KAHN-FREUND, O. (1954) 'Legal Framework', in Flanders, A. and Clegg, H. A. (eds), *The System of Industrial Relations in Great Britain* (Oxford: Blackwell).

KAHN-FREUND, O. (1977) 'Blackstone's Neglected Child: The Contract of Employment', in *Law Quarterly Review*, Vol. 93, pp. 508–28.

KAMATA, Satoshi (1982) *Japan in the Passing Lane: an insider's account of life in a Japanese auto factory* (New York: Pantheon).

KAY, J. A. and KING, M. A. (1978) *The British Tax System* (Oxford University Press).

KING, G. (1953) His 1688 statistics reproduced in George, D. *England in Transition* (Harmondsworth: Penguin).

KNAPPEN, M. M. (1965) *Tudor Puritanism: A Chapter in the History of Idealism* (Chicago University Press, reprint).

KUMAR, K. (1978) *Prophecy and Progress: the sociology of industrial and post-industrial society* (London: Allen Lane).

LENIN, V. I. (1966) *Imperialism: the highest stage of capitalism* (Moscow: Progress).

LEVINSON, C. (1978) *Vodka-Cola* (New York: Gordon & Cremonsi).

LEWIS, R. (1986) *Labour Law in Britain* (Oxford: Blackwell).

LIDDEL-HART, B. (1965) *Memoirs of a Captain*, Vol. 1, pp. 261–76 (London: Cassell).

LIPSETT, S. M. (ed.) (1986) *Unions in Transition: entering the second century* (San Francisco: Institute for Contemporary Studies Press).

LITTLE, L. K. (1978) *Religious Poverty and the Profit Economy in Medieval Europe* (London: ELEK).

LOCKE, J. (1696) *Several Papers relating to Money, Interest and Trade* (London: A. & J. Churchill).

LOCKE, J. (1964) in *John Locke, 1632–1704* with introduction by Garforth, F. W. (ed.) (London: Heinemann).

LOCKE, J. (1975) *Two Treatises of Government* (London: Dent).

LUSTGARTEN, L. (1987) 'U.S. Exposes, Britain never Discloses' (*Guardian* 23 January).

MacDONALD, D. F. (1976) *The State and Trade Unions* (London: Macmillan).

MacFARLANE, A. (1979) *Origins of English Individualism: Family, Property and Social Transition* (Oxford: Blackwell).

McILROY, J. (1985) 'Police and Pickets: The Law Against the Miners', in H. Beynon (ed.) *Digging Deeper: Issues in the Miners' Strike* (London: Verso).

MacKENZIE, D. and WAJCMAN, J. (eds) (1985) *The Social Shaping of Technology* (Open University Press).

McNEILL, W. H. (1983) *The Pursuit of Power* (Oxford: Blackwell).

MANDEL, E. (1968) *Marxist Economic Theory* (London: Merlin Press).

MANN, M. (1986) *The Sources of Social Power; Vol. 1 a history of power from the beginning to AD 1760* (Cambridge University Press).

MARWICK, A. (1981) *The Nature of History* (London: Macmillan).

MARX, K. (1976) *Capital, Vol. 1* (Harmondsworth: Penguin).

MATHIAS, P. (1969) *The First Industrial Nation: an economic history of Britain* (London: Methuen).

MELLOR, W. F. (ed.) (1972) *History of the Second World War: Casualties and medical statistics* (London: HMSO).

MELOSSI, D. and PAVARINI, M. (1981) *The Prison and the Factory: origins of the penitentiary system* (London: Macmillan).

MICHELS, R. (1966) *Political Parties: a sociological study of the oligarchical tendencies of modern democracy* (New York: Free Press).

MIDDLEMAS, K. (1979) *Politics in Industrial Society: the experience of the British System since 1911* (London: André Deutsch).

MILES, R. (1984) *White Man's Country: racism in British politics* (London: Pluto Press).

MILIBAND, R. (1982) *Capitalist Democracy in Britain* (Oxford University Press).

MILLWARD, N. and STEVENS, M. (1986) *British Workplace Industrial Relations 1980–1984* (Aldershot: Gower).

MILNE BAILEY, W. (1934) *Trade Unions and the State* (London: Allen & Unwin).

MITCHELL, A. (1987) 'New Rights Diary' (*New Statesman*, 13 February) p. 4.

MORRIS, T. (1987) 'Police Force' (*New Society*, 20 March) Vol. 79, No. 1264, pp. 12–14.

MOSS, R. (1975) *The Collapse of Democracy* (London: Temple Smith).

NATIONAL ECONOMIC DEVELOPMENT COUNCIL (1986) *Changing Work Patterns: How companies achieve flexibility to meet new needs* (London: NEDO).

NATIONAL INSTITUTE OF ECONOMIC & SOCIAL RESEARCH (1985) *Spending on Law and Order* Joyce, M. A. S., 2 Dean Trench Street, London SW1T 3HE.

NATIONAL INSTITUTE OF INDUSTRIAL PSYCHOLOGY (NIIP) (1951) *The Foreman: A study of supervision in British Industry* (London: Staples).

NICHOLS, T. (1986) *The British Worker Question: A New Look at Workers and Productivity in Manufacturing* (London: Routledge & Kegan Paul).

NICHOLSON, N., URSELL, G. and BLYTON, P. (1981) *The Dynamics of White Collar Unionism* (London: Academic Press).

O'DAY, R. and HEAL, F. (eds) (1981) *Princes and Paupers in the English Church 1500–1800* (Leicester University Press).

OFFE, C. (1984) *Contradictions of the Welfare State* (London: Hutchinson).

OLIVER, N. and WILKINSON, B. (1987) Address to Conference on the Japanisation of British Industry (Cardiff: University of Wales, September) pp. 17–18.

OLSON, M. (1965) *The Logic of Collective Action: public goods and the theory of groups* (Cambridge, Mass.: Harvard University Press).

PAHL, R. (1982) 'The Pockmarked Road to a Private Life' (*New Society* 7 October) pp. 12–14.

PARKER, A. (1986) *Red Hill: a mining community* (London: Heinemann).

PATEMAN, C. (1970) *Participation and Democratic Theory* (Cambridge University Press).

PAZ, D. G. (1980) *The Politics of Working Class Education in Britain 1830–1850* (Manchester University Press).

PEACOCK, A. T. and WISEMAN, J. (1961) *The Growth of Public Expenditure in the United Kingdom* (New Jersey: Princeton University Press).

PELLING, H. (1965) *The Origins of the British Labour Party, 1880–1900* (Oxford: Clarendon Press).

PELLING, H. (1971) *A History of British Trade Unionism* (2nd ed.) Harmondsworth: Penguin).

PHELPS-BROWN, E. H. (1983) *The Origins of Trade Union Power* (Oxford: Blackwell).

PHIZACKLEA, A. and MILES, R. (1987) 'The British Trade Union Movement and Racism', in Lee, G. and Loveridge, R. (eds) *The Manufacture of Disadvantage: stigma and social closure* (Open University Press).

PIERSON, C. (1984) 'New Theories of State and Civil Society: Recent developments in post-Marxist analysis of the State', in *Sociology*, Vol. 18(4), November, pp. 563–71.

POGGI, G. (1978) *The Development of the Modern State* (London: Hutchinson).

POLANYI, K. (1957) *The Great Transformation: The Political and Economic Origins of Our Time* (Boston: Beacon).

POSTAN, M. (1972) *The Medieval Economy and Society: An Economic History of Britain in The Middle Ages* (London: Weidenfeld & Nicholson).

POULANTZAS, N. (1975) *Classes in Contemporary Capitalism* (London: New Left Books).

POULANTZAS, N. (1978) *State, Power and Socialism* (London: New Left Books).

PRICE, R. (1986) *Labour in British Society: An Interpretative History* (London: Croom Helm).

RAMSAY, H. (1977) Cycles of Control—Worker Participation in Sociological and Historical Perspective, in *Sociology*, Vol. 11(3), pp. 481–506.

RIFKIN, B. and RIFKIN, S. (1979) *American Labor Sourcebook* (New York: McGraw-Hill).

ROBINSON, A. (1978) *Parliament and Public Spending: The Expenditure Committee of the House of Commons 1970–76* (London: Heinemann).

ROBINSON, R. J. (1987) 'The Civilising Process: A Critique' in *Sociology*, Vol. 21(1), pp. 1–17.

ROSE, S. (1986) 'Spend, spend, spend—on the military only' (*New Statesman*, 3 January) pp. 11–12.

RUBERY, J. (1986) 'Trade Unions in the 1980s: The Case of the United Kingdom' in R. Edwards, P. Garonna and F. Todtling (eds), *Unions in Crisis and Beyond: Perspectives from six countries* (Dover, Mass.: Auburn House).

RUESCHEMEYER, D. (1986) *Power and the Division of Labour* (Cambridge: Polity Press).

RULE, J. (1981) *The Experience of Labour in Eighteenth Century Industry* (London: Croom Helm).

SABEL, C. (1985) *Work and Politics; the Division of Labour in Industry* (Cambridge University Press).

SALAMAN, G. and THOMPSON, J. (eds) (1980) *Control and Ideology in Organizations* (Open University Press).

SAMPSON, A. (1977) *The Arms Bazaar* (London: Book Club Associates).

SCHUMPETER, J. (1934) *The Theory of Economic Development* (Oxford University Press).

SCHUMPETER, J. (1961) *Capitalism, Socialism and Democracy* (London: Allen & Unwin).

SHAY, R. P. (Jnr) (1977) *British Rearmament in the 30s: Politics and Profits* (New Jersey: Princeton University Press).

SHERMAN, J. (1985) 'Waiting for the Big Bite', in *Health and Social Service Journal*, 27 June.

SKOCPOL, T. (1979) *States and Social Revolution: a comparative analysis of France, Russia and China* (Cambridge University Press).

SMITH, A. (1976) *An Inquiry into the Nature and Causes of the Wealth of Nations 1776* (Oxford University Press).

SMITH, D. (1980) *The Defence of the Realm in the 1980s* (London: Croom Helm).

SNOW, C. P. (1964) *Corridors of Power* (London: Macmillan).

STARKEY, D. (1986) *This Land of England* (London: Channel 4 Productions).

STONIER, T. (1983) *The Wealth of Information* (London: Thames Methuen).

STRAKA, G. M. (1973) *The Revolution of 1688 and the Birth of the English Political Nation* (Boston: Heath).

STRINATI, D. (1982) *Capitalism, the State and Industrial Relations* (London: Croom Helm).

SUMNER, C. (1979) *Reading Ideologies* (London: Academic Press).

SWEEZY, P. (1954) *The Transition from Feudalism to Capitalism: a symposium* (London: Fore Publications).

THOMPSON, E. P. (1968) *The Making of The English Working Class* (Harmondsworth: Penguin).

THWAITES, A. and GILLESPIE, A. (1983) 'Technology, Information and Regional Economic Development', in *S.S.R.C. Newsletter*, No. 49, June.

TOFFLER, A. (1980) *The Third Wave* (Reading: Cox & Wyman).

TOURAINE, A. (1974) *The Post-Industrial Society* (London: Wildwood House).

TROTSKY, L. (1972) *Terrorism and Communism* (University of Michigan Press).

UNCTAD (1986) *Trade and Development Report* (New York: UNCTAD).

URRY, J. (1981) *The Anatomy of Capitalist Societies: the economy, civil society and the state* (London: Macmillan).

VANDAMME, F. (1986) 'The proposal for a directive on procedures for informing and consulting the employees of undertakings with complex structures, in particular transnational undertakings', in J. Vandamme (ed.), *Employee Consultation and Information in Multinational Corporations* (London: Croom Helm).

VAUX, T. (1987) 'Cast off Colonies', *New Internationalist,* January, pp. 21ff.

VEBLEN, T. (1906) 'The Place of Science in Modern Civilization', in *American Journal of Sociology,* Vol. 2, pp. 585–609.

VEBLEN, T. (1964) *Vested Interests and the Common Man: The Modern Point of View and the New Order* (New York: Kelley).

VEBLEN, T. (1970) *The Theory of the Leisure Class: An Economic Study of Institutions* (London: Unwin).

WALLERSTEIN, I. (1974a) *The Modern World System,* Vols 1 and 2 (New York: Academic Press).

WALLERSTEIN, I. (1974b) 'The Rise and Future Demise of the World Capitalist System', in *Comparative Studies in Sociology and History,* Vol. 16, September.

WALLERSTEIN, I. (1983) *Labour in the World Social Structure* (London: Sage Publications).

WALTON, J. (1984) *Reluctant Rebels: Comparative studies of revolution and under-development* (Columbia University Press).

WAR OFFICE (1922) *Statistics of the Military Effort of the British Empire during the Great War, 1914–1920* (London: HMSO).

WCCPL/NUM (1985) *Striking Back,* Welsh Campaign for Civil and Political Liberties and National Union of Mineworkers, South Wales Area (Cardiff: WCCPL & NUM).

WEBB, S. and WEBB, B. (1920) *The History of Trade Unionism* (new ed.) (London: Longmans, Green).

WEBER, M. (1927) *General Economic History* (Glenco, Illinois: Free Press).

WEBER, M. (1964) *Theory of Social and Economic Organisation* (Glencoe, Illinois: Free Press).

WEDDERBURN, Lord (1985) 'The New Policies in Industrial Relations Law', in P. Fosh and C. Littler (eds), *Industrial Relations and the Law in the 1980s: Issues and Future Trends* (Aldershot: Gower).

WILLIAMS, B. SIR (1983) 'Microprocesses & Employment', in *S.S.R.C. Newsletter,* No. 49, June.

WILLMAN, P. (1986) *Technological Change, Collective Bargaining and Industrial Efficiency* (Oxford: Clarendon).

WILSON, H. (1971) *The Labour Government 1964–70: A Personal Record* (London: Weidenfeld & Nicholson).

WINSTON, B. (1986) *Misunderstanding Media* (London: Routledge & Keegan Paul).

WOODWARD, J. (1970) *Industrial Organisation, Behaviour and Control* (Oxford University Press).

YOUNG, P., Brigadier (1981) *The Fighting Man* (London: Orbis).

ADDITIONAL SOURCES

The British government is a major user of data drawn on a variety of social and economic indices. These data can be accessed through such publications as:

The Department of Employment *Gazette,* a monthly journal giving principal employment statistics.

Economic Trends, a monthly giving main quarterly economic indicators.
Monthly Digest of Statistics, a monthly publication giving statistical profiles on
  principal social patterns such as demography, housing and family structure.
Social Trends, a yearly compilation of statistics on principal social patterns. All
  the above are available from the Central Statistical Office, HMSO, London.

Index

AUTHOR INDEX

SUBJECT INDEX